KEEPING THE COMPOUND REPUBLIC

Essays on American Federalism

MARTHA DERTHICK

BROOKINGS INSTITUTION PRESS
Washington, D.C.

ABOUT BROOKINGS

The Brookings Institution is a private nonprofit organization devoted to research, education, and publication on important issues of domestic and foreign policy. Its principal purpose is to bring knowledge to bear on current and emerging policy problems. The Institution maintains a position of neutrality on issues of public policy. Interpretations or conclusions in Brookings publications should be understood to be solely those of the authors.

Copyright © 2001
THE BROOKINGS INSTITUTION
1775 Massachusetts Avenue, N.W., Washington, D.C. 20036
www.brookings.edu

Library of Congress Cataloging-in-Publication data

Derthick, Martha.
  Keeping the compound republic : essays on federalism / Martha Derthick.
    p. cm.
  Includes bibliographical references and index.
    ISBN 0-8157-0202-7 (cloth : alk. paper)—ISBN 0-8157-0203-5 (pbk. : alk. paper)
    1. Federal government—United States. I. Title.
  JK325 .D47 2001
  320.473'049—dc21   2001004202

9 8 7 6 5 4 3 2 1

The paper used in this publication meets minimum requirements of the American National Standard for Information Sciences—Permanence of Paper for Printed Library Materials: ANSI Z39.48-1992.

Typeset in Minion

Composition by Cynthia Stock
Silver Spring, Maryland

Printed by R. R. Donnelley and Sons
Harrisonburg, Virginia

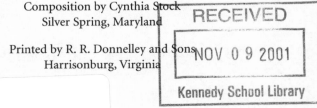

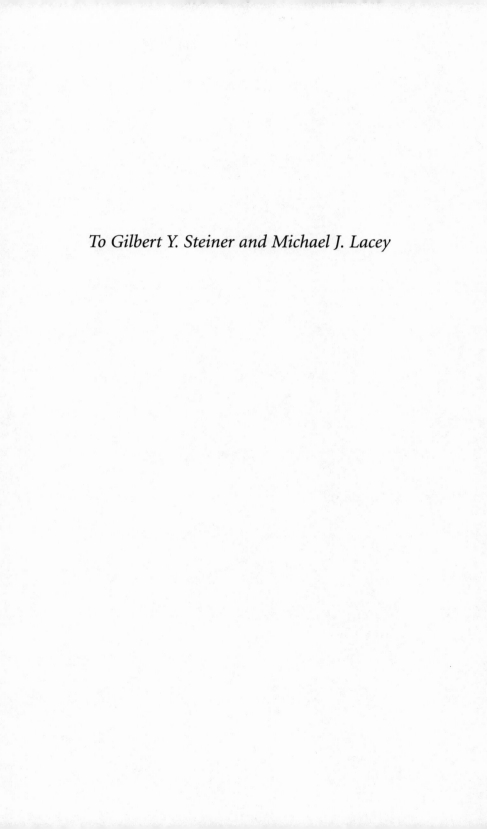

To Gilbert Y. Steiner and Michael J. Lacey

Contents

<u>THREE</u>

EVOLUTION

Preface

These essays were written in the quarter century from 1975 to 2000, beginning when I was on the staff of the Brookings Institution and ending after I retired from the faculty of the University of Virginia, to which I moved in 1983. In selecting them from a somewhat larger body of work, I tried to achieve both coherence and completeness. Still, I would not have included the essay on income support programs (published in 1975) had not an anonymous reviewer urged coverage of grants-in-aid. That seemed like good advice, so I attempted to bring that essay up to date, mainly through addition of explanatory endnotes. But that is unusual; most essays appear essentially as they did originally, with only minor changes for accuracy and copyediting to improve style and clarity. Only one, that on Roosevelt as Madison, was written specifically for this volume and has not been previously published. I concluded that I could not claim completeness in the historical part without covering the New Deal.

Most of the essays are more descriptive than prescriptive or normative, although it will be clear that I regard the compound republic as an appropriate form in principle for the United States, even if sometimes disappointing in practice. Mainly, the work grows out of a strong personal preference for a form of government that divides and disperses official power, ideally with the goal of making it representative and grounding its exercise in practicality as opposed to a political rhetoric that is all too often the demagogic style of mass democracy. More concretely, it grew out of a desire, as a professor of government, to improve my understanding of American federalism and to communicate that understanding to graduate and undergraduate students at the University of Virginia.

Some of those students proved to be very engaged in the subject of federalism, and I am grateful to them for encouragement and instruction. One such, John J. Dinan, who received his Ph.D. in 1996 and has since taught at Wake Forest University and Davidson College, is coauthor of the essay on progressivism. I am grateful also to colleagues who invited some of the work. The chapter on the 1960s was written in response to an invitation from Brian Balogh, a historian at the University of Virginia, to contribute to an edition of the *Journal of Policy History* that he was editing, and he is responsible for important improvements in that essay. Similarly, Sidney Milkis, then a professor of politics at Brandeis University and now at the University of Virginia, invited the chapter on progressivism and federalism for a conference and book, one of a series on American political development in the twentieth century that he was organizing with Jerome Mileur. At the time these two essays were written, I was benefiting from financial support from the White Burkett Miller Center of the University of Virginia, of which Kenneth W. Thompson was director. "Up to Date in Kansas City" resulted from my having been invited by the American Political Science Association to deliver the John Gaus Distinguished Lecture at its annual meeting in 1992. The Gaus Award Committee at that time consisted of Frank J. Thompson, chair, Beverly A. Cigler, and Francis E. Rourke.

The idea for collecting the essays came in the late 1990s from Nancy Davidson, who was then acquisitions editor for the Brookings Institution Press. No good deed goes unpunished, and Ms. Davidson's punishment was to emerge from retirement in 2001 to do the copyediting. I am extremely grateful to her, and also to Eric Patashnik, whom I have reason to believe suggested that she consider the project.

Christopher Kelaher, Ms. Davidson's successor at the Brookings Institution, presided over the emergence of the manuscript in published form and recruited several anonymous peer reviewers who provided encouragement and correction. I am grateful to all of them for improvements.

I have dedicated the book to Gilbert Y. Steiner and Michael J. Lacey, who headed research programs in Washington with which I have been affiliated. Both set high standards of scholarship and defended the intellectual independence and integrity of their employees and affiliates. Their programs excelled under their leadership, and I am fortunate to have been among the beneficiaries. As director of the Governmental Studies Program at

Brookings, Gil Steiner brought me to its staff in the early 1970s and over-saw much of my work there. Mike Lacey, as head of the Division of United States Studies of the Woodrow Wilson International Center for Scholars, invited me to be a guest at that institution, and thus was instrumental in enabling me to write the overview essay, "How Many Communities?" which appeared initially in a publication of the Woodrow Wilson Center that I edited, *Dilemmas of Scale in America's Federal Democracy* (1999). I am in the habit of describing that as the book on federalism that I induced my friends to write for me, and I could not have done it without Mr. Lacey's support.

This collection of essays turns out to be the book on federalism that I wrote by myself, and I am of course solely responsible for what is in it. No doubt, it lacks some of the smoothness and coherence of a single work written as such, but had I written a single work, it would have said the same things that I say here.

Introduction

I hold it for a fundamental point that an individual independence
of the States, is utterly irreconcileable with the idea of an aggregate
sovereignty. I think at the same time that a consolidation of the
States into one simple republic is not less unattainable than it would
be inexpedient. Let it be tried then whether any middle ground can
be taken which will at once support a due supremacy of the
national authority, and leave in force the local authorities so far as
they can be subordinately useful.[1]

So wrote James Madison to Edmund Randolph not long before the
Constitutional Convention of 1787. Agreeing on how to define the middle ground was the critical event of the convention, which nearly broke up
over the question. But the issue was not settled, and the search for a middle ground has continued. It has been a theme of American political experience ever since and is the central topic of this collection of essays.

The Framers found middle ground in a new form of federalism to which
Madison gave the name "compound republic." It is often said that the
Framers of the U. S. Constitution invented federalism. They most certainly
did not invent federalism in its classical form, under which formally independent and equal political societies enter voluntarily into a league for
specified common purposes, typically defense. Such leagues had existed for
centuries. The Articles of Confederation, which the Framers were seeking

1

to revise or replace, was an example of one. And it was in deep trouble. "Our situation is becoming every day more & more critical," Madison wrote in February 1787. "No money comes into the federal Treasury. No respect is paid to the federal authority; and people of reflection unanimously agree that the existing Confederacy is tottering to its foundation."[2]

What the Framers settled on was an implausible compromise between a pure federation and a pure unitary or national government. They designed a national government, deriving its powers directly from the people, and juxtaposed it with state governments that remained intact and had their own constitutions also deriving from the people. Thus the various governments coexisted with one another, constitutionally independent yet sharing territory and constituents. The national government incorporated some federal features, principally an upper house of the legislature, the Senate, in which the states were represented equally by two members, who were to be chosen by the state legislatures. The other house of a bicameral legislature, the House of Representatives, would represent the people directly, and within each state delegation be proportionate to their numbers. This was the critical compromise that enabled the founding to proceed. The Framers liked it so much that they reincorporated it in the electoral college, the body through which the new government's chief executive was to be picked. In the electoral college, each state was entitled to members "equal to the whole Number of Senators and Representatives to which the State may be entitled in the Congress."

In *Federalist* No. 39, one of the papers he and Alexander Hamilton wrote with John Jay to promote the new Constitution, Madison methodically dissected its various features in order to judge whether they were "national" or "federal," an exercise designed to assure opponents that the Constitution was sufficiently federal. The opponents feared that the Constitution would end in consolidation, their term for a unitary government. There were ample grounds for such apprehension, principally the sweeping grants of power to Congress in Article I ("to . . . provide for the common Defence and general Welfare of the United States" and "to make all Laws which shall be necessary and proper for carrying into Execution" the various powers specifically enumerated); the creation in Article III of a Supreme Court that was apparently intended to be the final arbiter of the Constitution's distribution of power between the nation and the states; and the supremacy clause in Article VI ("This Constitution, and the Laws of the United States which shall be made in Pursuance thereof . . . shall be the supreme Law of the Land").

As reassurance to those who feared that the new form was excessively national, the first Congress under Madison's leadership approved the Tenth Amendment, which stipulates that "the powers not delegated to the United States by the Constitution, nor prohibited by it to the States, are reserved to the States respectively, or to the people." But this was more admonition than applicable law, and it omitted the term *expressly* as a modifier of *delegated*. It did not alter the fact that the Constitution was weighted to the national rather than the federal side.[3]

It is a pity that Madison's term *compound republic* did not survive in our political language, for it conveys the complicated and ambiguous intent of the framing generation and helps to make comprehensible what otherwise is bewildering to the modern citizenry. The Framers hoped that centralization and decentralization of governments could coexist; they sought a mix of the two. And in thinking about how deliberation should be conducted at the national level, both in regard to legislation and in regard to the choice of presidents, they sought to assemble majorities of two different kinds: one composed of individual voters, the other, of the states as distinct political societies. To modern citizens, schooled in the ideology of one person, one vote, it takes an effort to conceive of assembling a majority in a different way, by aggregating the wills of subnational political communities.

Political commentators have also grown accustomed to associating federalism with decentralization and to supposing that political actors will favor either the national government or the state governments in a continuing contest between the two. They seem to imagine that this should be a principled choice, hence consistent over time and in different political situations. Media analysts therefore thought it ironic, even hypocritical, for Democrat Al Gore to take refuge in state law and courts during the contest in 2000 for Florida's electoral votes while Republican George Bush appealed to the federal courts. This was contrary to the positions commonly imputed to the two political parties. Yet a review of American history would show that the positions of leading politicians and the major political parties on the question of centralization versus decentralization have often been determined largely by expediency. Over time, the Republican and Democratic Parties have traded places on this question, and they could trade places once again if political circumstances were to change.

Such switches would be no shock to Madison, who rapidly executed one himself. Entering the convention as a nationalist, he emerged as advocate of the compound republic, and before long he was allied with Thomas

Jefferson in the leadership of a party that sought to employ the power of state governments in opposition to the reigning Federalists, who stood for a strong national government with a strong chief executive and judiciary. Madison had foreseen such strategic uses of the federal system in writing *The Federalist*, when he argued, in No. 46, that the "federal and State governments are in fact but different agents and trustees of the people," and thus equally subject to address by "the people," or, one might suppose— Madison does not say this—factions competing for the people's favor.

In the light of constitutional history, a *principled* stand in favor of federalism would not be a stand in favor of decentralization or states' rights, but rather for preservation of the compound. This would require pure nationalists and majoritarians to recognize that the United States is a nation made up of distinct political communities, and that citizens conduct their politics, including deliberations about national policymaking and president choosing, in part as members of those communities. A result of this is that the most sparsely populated places gain weight that their residents would not have in a purely majoritarian regime. On the other hand, it also requires defenders of states' rights to acknowledge that the distinct political communities, to be legitimate, cannot claim autonomy. They must honor constitutionally prescribed standards of the United States for citizenship and political participation. One of the principal justifications for the numerous separate political communities is that they multiply opportunities for officeholding and the practice of democratic citizenship. If they fail to meet a just and reasonable standard of democracy, the bargain at the heart of American federalism fails.

The bargain of American federalism has been hard to sustain over time precisely because a large part of the country was home to a racial caste system that, behind the shield of states' rights, flouted constitutional principles of liberty and equality. Racism has tainted American federalism for most of the nation's history. I describe some of the resulting tensions in the opening essay and the one on "crossing thresholds" in the 1960s (chapter 10). To the extent that power has been decentralized through American federalism, it has often resulted in protecting the privileges of local elites. But of course the reverse is true as well. To centralize power within the federal system does not escape the omnipresent peril of concentrated privilege; it just creates a different set of elites. Nationalization of politics and government has gone hand-in-hand with judicialization, professionalization, and media-ization. It has been associated also with the rise of intensely motivated minorities—what political scientists have come to call "single-issue interests"—that are able to wield more influence over policy-making than a moderate and reasonable majority of the public. I believe this to have been the case, in a perverse and complicated way, with tobacco politics (chapter 7), in which a minority of state attorneys general were able in the late 1990s to use the coercive power of lawsuits against the cigarette industry to construct a regulatory regime in the absence of legislation.

The effort to remove the racial taint from federalism resulted in a surge of nationalizing measures in the 1960s that left the compound republic profoundly changed. Yet many of its features endure. This is partly because some of them are embedded in a written constitution that is hard to amend. Article V of the Constitution provides that no state shall be deprived of its equal suffrage in the Senate without its consent. Article IV protects the boundaries of the states by providing that "no new State shall be formed or erected within the Jurisdiction of any other State; nor any State be formed by the Junction of two or more States, or parts of States, without the Consent of the Legislatures of the States concerned as well as of the Congress." Thus it is not possible that the rest of the country could decide to divide California (with a population of 33.8 million) into two states or to merge Wyoming (with a population of less than 500,000) with one of its neighbors.

The features of American federalism are also embedded in social and political reality. The United States is a vast, populous, and varied country that is hard to govern solely from the center. Politics should reflect the variegation of society. Acknowledging as much, Madison remarked on the floor of the Constitutional Convention that if the states did not exist they would have to be invented. Madison's opponents, the Anti-Federalists, warned of a concentration of power in the national capital, whose office-holding inhabitants would become detached from the populace and be prey to corruption. If such views had merit in 1787, they ring even more true today, when much more is expected of governments, more resources are placed at their disposal, institutions of accountability are hard to sustain in the face of greatly expanded activity, and thus more is to be apprehended from arrogant uses of official power.

Interest in federalism, not always and to everyone a gripping subject, is likely to rise in the wake of the election of 2000. There will be demands for reform of the electoral college, given heightened awareness that it does not strictly reflect the popular vote, and appointees to the Supreme Court may be scrutinized for their beliefs about federalism. One of the projects of a narrow Supreme Court majority under Chief Justice William H. Rehnquist in the past decade has been to mount an explicit defense of federalism. In a series of sometimes controversial decisions, it has sought to impose limits on Congress's power to regulate interstate commerce and to enforce the Fourteenth Amendment; to limit the power of Congress to "commandeer" state governments in order to implement federal law; to broaden the immunity of state governments to lawsuits under the Eleventh Amendment to the Constitution; to show increased deference to state courts; and to reduce federal judicial supervision of state and local institutions such as schools and prisons.[4]

Whether the Rehnquist court's jurisprudence will arrest or deflect the secular tendency toward centralization remains to be seen. On one hand, many of the Court's recent decisions on federalism and the reach of congressional power have struck students of constitutional law as "stunning" and "revolutionary."[5] On the other hand, they have not changed the day-to-day conduct of intergovernmental relations, having no effect, for example, on the ability of Congress to preempt state laws or to attach onerous and far-reaching conditions to grants-in-aid to the states. Nor are students of the Court agreed on just how committed it is to federalism principles, or whether it is motivated more by a desire to trim the sails of Congress and bring it back within what a majority sees as proper constitutional bounds.[6] Finally, the narrowness of many decisions on federalism suggests that they might not survive changes in the composition of the Court.

Whatever the Court may have achieved with its decisions on federalism, it definitely has encouraged Americans to contemplate the subject. It invites us to join it in weighing the importance of federalism as an institution of government. I like to think of these essays as a way in which a reader might begin to do that.

PART One

Overview

1

How Many Communities?

Everyone who knows anything about American government knows that it is federal. Asked what that means, most people say that functions are divided between one national government and many state governments. Politically sophisticated persons may add that the governments are constituted independently of one another. Their respective functions are constitutionally defined and thus cannot be altered by ordinary legislation.

This is, however, not the only and arguably not the most interesting way to conceive of federalism. In this essay I will borrow an idea from the late Martin Diamond and speak of federalism as an arrangement that is chosen by people who are unable to decide whether to be one community or many. To do justice to Diamond's subtlety, he put the point as follows:

> The distinguishing characteristic of federalism is the peculiar ambivalence of the ends men seek to make it serve. The ambivalence is quite literal: Federalism is always an arrangement pointed in two contrary directions or aimed at securing two contrary ends. One end is always found in the reason why the member units do not simply consolidate themselves into one large unitary country; the other end is always found in the reason why the member units do not choose to

This essay first appeared as "How Many Communities? The Evolution of American Federalism," in Martha Derthick, ed., *Dilemmas of Scale in America's Federal Democracy* (Cambridge University Press, 1999), pp. 125–53.

remain simply small, wholly autonomous countries. The natural tendency of any political community, whether large or small, is to completeness, to the perfection of its autonomy. Federalism is the effort deliberately to modify that tendency. Hence any given federal structure is always the institutional expression of the contradiction or tension between the particular reasons the member units have for remaining small and autonomous but not wholly, and large and consolidated but not quite.[1]

Federalism involves, then, a choice about how many communities to be, which is not merely a matter of legal arrangements but one of the most fundamental of political questions. I am assuming that "communities" take the form of "polities." Polities have institutions through which people define the objectives of their collective life, whether through deliberation—the democratic ideal—or through a struggle among power holders, which is always in greater or lesser degree the reality. Polities make and enforce laws, raise taxes, and provide public goods and services.

I will argue that Americans chose originally—in the late eighteenth and early nineteenth centuries—to be both one great nation and many relatively quite small, local communities. Beginning with the states as a base, the core polities of their federation, Americans moved paradoxically both to centralize and decentralize. They opted for nationalism *and* localism.

For some time, national and local political development progressed simultaneously, without serious tension (even if national development was challenging the states). Indeed, the most eminent social commentators on the United States, from Tocqueville to David Potter, have argued that local mores helped to sustain national patriotism: in the nineteenth century, the two were mutually reinforcing.[2]

Eventually, however, tension was bound to develop. In the Progressive and New Deal Eras, and then more purposefully during the rights revolution of the 1950s and 1960s, national power was deliberately employed to reduce the place of the local polity in American life. In pursuing the choice to be one great nation, Americans steadily abandoned their historic localism—but not without reluctance and regret.

Original Choices

Americans' choice to be one great nation must be one of the best documented political decisions ever made. It is manifest principally in two events: the framing and ratification of the Constitution in 1787–89 and the Civil War, with associated constitutional amendments, in 1861–68.

There was, of course, much more to it than that. The establishment of a national judiciary through Congress's enactment of 1789 and John Marshall's three decades of leadership was crucial. Had the Supreme Court not successfully asserted its role as constitutional interpreter and its superiority to state courts, there would have been no great nation. Crucial, too, was the early establishment of the practice of a loose, expansive interpretation of the Constitution, manifested in creation of the national bank and John Marshall's sweeping, pregnant defense of it in *McCulloch v. Maryland.* Less generally recognized, but hardly less important, was the early failure of the Senate to develop as a peripheralizing institution, in William Riker's phrase. Because state legislatures could not enforce instructions upon them, senators did not become spokesmen for the interests of state governments.[3] Neither in the Senate nor outside of it were state governments able to concert their actions vis-à-vis the national government. When state legislatures generally declined to endorse the Virginia and Kentucky resolutions in 1798–99, they set a pattern of inaction and noncooperation that augured well for nation building. Finally, one should note the prompt emergence—beginning with George Washington—of the president as a heroic leader and unifying symbol, the development of the presidential election as the central political ritual of the American people, and the development of rival political parties whose prime objective was the capture of that office.

The choice for localism is quite obscure by comparison and more diffuse in time. That it could be made at all depended on the fact that the states, though on balance losers in 1787–89, nonetheless emerged from the framing intact, with powerful claims to be vigorous polities themselves—"commonwealths," no less, some of them proclaimed. The principle on which American federalism was founded, which even leading nationalists accepted, was embodied in the Tenth Amendment: the national government had only those powers delegated to it, all else remaining with the states and the people. The states were the fundamental polities, possessing residual functions. They would presumably be the place of first resort when there was a need for domestic government. The burden of proof would rest on those who claimed jurisdiction for the national government.

But if states were in principle the core polities, they did not for long enjoy as such the confidence of the people. Constitutional revisions occurring periodically in the nineteenth and early twentieth centuries curbed the powers of their legislatures and limited the frequency and duration of leg-islative sessions.[4] As of the mid-1930s, only five state legislatures met annu-ally. All the rest met biennially except for that of Alabama, which met quadrennially.[5] While local governments enjoyed no legal independence, and in the case of big cities were frequently the object of intervention, they nonetheless benefited from these restrictions and the state governments' lethargy. They became the residual domestic governments of the American federal system. "Our local areas are not *governed*," Woodrow Wilson wrote in the late nineteenth century. "They act for themselves. . . . The large free-dom of action and broad scope of function given to local authorities is the distinguishing characteristic of the American system of government."[6] County and municipal debt, at $800 million in 1880, was three and a half times the size of the states' debt.[7]

Among the restrictions placed on state legislatures were some that reserved to the populace decisions about the creation and definition of units of local government. Following the lead of the Massachusetts consti-tutional convention of 1820, the local referendum spread to all parts of the country in connection with legislation affecting the forms, organizations, powers, and procedures of local government. It became common for state constitutions to forbid legislatures to enact measures to incorporate vil-lages and cities, to define the boundaries of counties or divide them into townships, to locate county seats or change county names or to alter the forms of local government without the consent of the people of the locali-ties affected.[8] This meant that Americans were allowed to create and define their small-scale governing communities for themselves.[9] That nineteenth-century Americans cared very much about such decisions is suggested, for example, by the fact that in the Midwest people fought pitched battles over where the county seat was to be located.[10]

Americans at the local level were also enabled to choose their own lead-ers. Jon C. Teaford has shown how the municipal corporation, upon being transplanted to the colonies and subjected to revolutionary influences, became republican. No longer a closed, self-perpetuating body, its officers were popularly elected and served fixed terms.[11] As the nineteenth century progressed, state constitutions were amended to provide for popular elec-tion of local officials where it did not already prevail. County governments in particular became more democratic as judges, sheriffs, and justices of the peace were made subject to election. At least in principle, the change was significant especially in the South, where oligarchical county courts had controlled local government.[12]

Hand in hand with their becoming more democratic, counties also became much more numerous. The increase, between the time of the Revolution and the early twentieth century, was from 12 to 61 in New York, 12 to 67 in Pennsylvania, 34 to 97 in North Carolina, and 8 to 146 in Georgia. Americans had come to treat counties as institutions of local self-government, entitled as such to representation in state legislatures, rather than as administrative subdivisions of the state, serving the convenience of state governments.[13]

Over time, local governments and their electorates gained more power to tax, a third crucial element of the formal founding of local self-government. At least in New York, early municipal charters, following the precedents of English borough charters, did not confer on municipal corporations the power of taxation. When the colonial legislature authorized the cities to levy taxes, those authorizations were at first only for limited amounts necessary for specific purposes, and the tax laws had to be re-enacted from year to year. Early in the nineteenth century, however, these special laws gave way to general authorizations, and new city charters allowed municipal corporations to levy taxes.[14] Having been lodged in local governments, decisions about taxing, spending, and borrowing then became susceptible to further decentralization to local electorates. State legislatures that had been made subject to constitutional limits on taxing and borrowing sometimes reacted by prescribing local referenda to check the powers of local governments.[15] Eventually it became common for state constitutions to limit the amount of tax that could be levied by local governments without popular approval in a referendum.

Resting on such foundations, local governments became for most Americans most of the time the most important domestic governments. As the twentieth century began, they administered and overwhelmingly financed schools, which as agents of socialization were the most important domestic public institutions. They predominated in the administration and finance of poor relief. They administered and overwhelmingly financed road construction. They financed and were responsible for police protection. They were raising more revenue and doing more spending than the federal and state governments combined. The bedrock of American domestic government was local.

To be sure, state governments retained a larger role than simple figures on revenue and expenditure might seem to indicate. Their courts created the framework of law within which American capitalism developed, family relations were structured, and the holding and transfer of real property took place. Their legislatures had promoted and subsidized economic development with measures for the construction of roads, canals, and reclamation works. They created penitentiaries, almshouses, orphan asylums, and reformatories in the early nineteenth century, in what one scholar has called "the discovery of the asylum."[16] Local governments were legally their creatures, and what local governments did was done under the authorization or command of state law. This gave local powers a contingent character. Whatever state constitutional conventions and legislatures gave, they could withdraw. On the other hand, the states' supervision of local governments' activity was initially minimal. As late as 1890, the median size of state departments of education was two persons, including the state superintendent.[17] Moreover, even where state governments had been most active—in regard to economic development—they tended over the course of the nineteenth century to become less so.[18]

In sum, the American choice—insofar as choice was made consciously through the medium of government—was for one large political community and many small ones.

The Erosion of Localism

The bedrock of local government was deeper and firmer than the preceding discussion implies, because it was constituted of custom as well as consciously decentralizing choices. The bedrock functions—roads, poor relief, police, schools—developed at the local level originally. Before they were carried out by local governments, they were provided privately or not at all.

Although state laws mandating such functions were often filled with exhortation and command early in the nineteenth century, state governments lacked organizations and practical means with which to supervise local governments and enforce instructions. Thus Massachusetts law in the late 1820s prescribed in considerable detail the duty of towns to support schools, specifying the subjects to be taught, the number of teachers per household, the qualifications of teachers, and the moral content of instruction (they should teach "the principles of piety, justice, and a sacred regard to truth, love to their country, humanity and universal benevolence, sobriety, industry and frugality, chastity, moderation and temperance, and those other virtues which are the ornament of human society, and the basis upon which the republican Constitution is structured"). Towns were obliged to create school committees, which were enjoined to visit the schools and to report to the secretary of the commonwealth information about how many schools they maintained and what they spent. He was to furnish them with a blank form on which to report these returns.[19] That appears to have been the extent of state supervision.

As urbanization progressed later in the century, the states of the Northeast—Massachusetts and New York especially—began creating agencies with powers at least of information gathering and advice and sometimes more formal oversight. The professions were beginning to develop and find a toehold in state governments. The new agencies could take the form of individual offices or multimember boards of varying sizes, such as state commissioners or superintendents of instruction, boards of charities, or boards of public health. States to the west then followed the lead of Massachusetts and New York.[20]

One turn-of-the-century sign of the states' growing role was a change in spending ratios. Whereas local governments spent fourteen times as much on education as the states did in 1902 and forty-three times as much on roads, by 1913 these ratios had fallen to 9 to 1 and 15 to 1, respectively. State-level centralization proceeded, however, in halting fashion, affecting states and functions unevenly and not very deeply. State-level administrative centralization became penetrating and widespread only when national action caused it to.

In intergovernmental relations, national action during the Progressive Era took the form principally of grants-in-aid with conditions attached. The conditions suited both the administrative convenience of the federal government and the ideology of Progressive reform, one strand of which was marked by the pursuit of efficiency and expertise. Two bedrock functions in particular were affected: roads, for which federal aid began in 1916, following introduction of the automobile, and poor relief, for which federal aid was enacted in 1935, in response to the Great Depression.

Grant-in-aid conditions were above all delocalizing, quite deliberately so. The county, one eminent professional social worker declared, was the "dark continent" of American public administration.[21] State governments were to be prodded and helped in a modernizing, civilizing mission. They were required to match federal grants with state funds, secure statewide uniformity in program operations, create agencies that would be responsible to the federal administration for meeting statewide standards, and create merit systems of personnel administration.

When federal highway aid began in 1916, sixteen states had "no highway department worthy of the name."[22] Federal law did not initially require the creation of state highway departments, but within five years was amended to do so. The U.S. Bureau of Public Roads suspended grants in Arkansas in 1923, Kansas in 1925, and Maine in 1929 "until the personnel of the State Highway Department . . . shall be so changed that this [agency] can have . . . confidence in the organization as a whole."[23] By 1922 the ratio of local-to-state spending for roads had dropped to 3 to 1, a change in nine years so precipitous that it must be attributable in substantial measure to the introduction of federal aid. The growth of state authority continued thereafter. In 1962, a student of highway policy succinctly summarized the experience of four decades in midcentury:

> In 1920 the local units of government occupied a dominant position in the over-all highway picture. Approximately 70 percent of all road work was undertaken by the political subdivisions of the states. Today over three quarters of the highway funds are channeled through state authorities. In short, the roles of the two levels of government in highway affairs have been reversed.[24]

Similarly, when federal grants for public assistance were enacted in 1935, local responsibility for that function was still entrenched. Although most states had enacted laws for aid to mothers and the aged, these were not necessarily backed with state funds, and they were not always mandatory for local governments. Only half of the counties in the country that were authorized to give mothers' aid were actually doing so as of 1934. In only ten states were old age assistance laws in effect statewide. Administrative structures were likewise varied and haphazard, for state welfare agencies had developed unevenly. Responsibility for administration rested predominantly at the county level, with boards of commissioners or judges. Only twelve states had set up county welfare agencies.[25]

The Social Security Act required state financial participation and mandatory statewide operation, which the Social Security Board, as the federal administering agency, chose to interpret as a requirement of statewide uniformity. Beginning in 1946, it successfully pressured states to establish statewide standards of need and assistance, such that benefits would no longer vary among local places.[26] The ratio of local to state spending for assistance, which had been 5 to 1 in 1932, dropped to 1.3 to 1 in 1942. By 1952 state spending surpassed local spending.

The federal requirement that a single state agency administer assistance or supervise administration of it contributed to the formation and strengthening of state welfare departments. Federal law also fostered the professionalization of welfare agencies after amendments to the Social Security Act in 1939 authorized the Social Security Board to require the establishment of merit systems. As attachments of welfare workers to a profession grew with federal encouragement, attachments to place weakened: professionalization meant delocalization.

While merit system requirements did not extend to all federally aided agencies, a companion measure—the prohibition of partisan activity by state and local employees—did. This was enacted in 1940 as an amendment to the Hatch Act and upheld by the Supreme Court in *Oklahoma* v. *Civil Service Commission* (1947), a case involving the federal government's decision to withhold highway grant funds in order to secure removal of a state highway commissioner who was also chairman of the state Democratic Party. Breaking the ties of state and local employees to state and local parties was crucial to the Progressive Era project of rationalizing state and local administrative structures and making them responsive to national leadership.[27]

Scholarship on the New Deal has generally stressed the extent to which it honored the traditional prerogatives of the states, accommodating to the institutions of American federalism.[28] It is true that few purely national agencies were created, and those that were created often found that the price of acceptance, if not survival, was to make adjustments at the grass roots. However, this interpretation overlooks the recasting that federal action achieved in state-local relations. Eroding slowly and steadily in any case, the bedrock of localism eroded much faster when federal grant programs came to bear.

Still, as the Progressive and New Deal Eras came to an end with World War II, much of the bedrock had barely been affected. Nothing that occurred before midcentury diminished the localism of police departments or, crucially, of schools. Neither function had been the beneficiary (or victim) of federal aid. The ratio of local to state spending for education, though tending to fall throughout the century, was 5 to 1 in 1942, at a time when state spending on roads had passed local spending. In one important respect the bedrock had actually been augmented. As urbanization progressed, state legislatures authorized zoning and land-use regulation, which became local functions. As such, they had considerable potential for defining the character of the local place, and hence sustaining a sense of community.

The Rights Revolution

In the first half of the twentieth century, the national government's direct challenge to localism had been relatively confined. It concentrated on administrative structures in functions where grants-in-aid gave the federal government an entree and a stake. Also, it was spearheaded by professional administrators, and while they benefited from the strength of centralizing coalitions in regard to road construction and poor relief, their independent power was modest. Congress did not always give them the statutory authority that they sought for state-level reforms.

The rights revolution in the 1960s brought an attack of greater scope, depth, and legitimacy, officially led as it was by the nation's highest court. It also had far greater mobilizing power. As political goals, efficiency and expertise did not excite large numbers of people. Equality excited many more. Besides, egalitarianism is the greater enemy of federalism. It exalts the autonomous individual, whereas federalism, in honoring communities, implies acceptance of distinctions among and even within them. When the Warren court met the bedrock of localism, an epic contest occurred.

I will focus on the Warren court for economy's sake, recognizing nevertheless that the modern rights revolution depended critically on constitutional and statutory foundations laid in the wake of the Civil War; that it had a morally potent social basis in the protest activity of African Americans; that even conceived of as the work of the national government, it was not the work of the Supreme Court alone, but was in due course embraced by Congress; and that even as the work of the judiciary, it did not begin with the Warren court. The Court's project of incorporating Bill of Rights guarantees into the Fourteenth Amendment dates at least to *Wolf* v. *Colorado* (1949) in regard to criminal procedures and to *Gitlow* v. *New York* (1925) in regard to speech.[29] As of the Warren era, though, the Court was very much in the lead.

Without articulating a philosophy of federalism, the Court nonetheless had a consistent attitude, born, apparently, of its struggle to achieve Southern school desegregation. It did not trust state and local governments. John Marshall Harlan, a sitting justice who dissented from some of its leading decisions, took note of the "fundamental shift" in its approach to federal-state relationships compared with that of its predecessors. He wrote:

> This shift must be recognized as involving something more than mere differences among judges as to where the line should be drawn between state and federal authority in particular cases arising under the Fourteenth Amendment. It reflects, I believe, at bottom a distrust in the capabilities of the federal system to meet the needs of American society.[30]

The most fundamental of the Court's challenges to localism were its reapportionment decisions. These were the decisions of which Justice Earl Warren himself was most proud and the Court's critics most critical. "There is no better example of the Court's egalitarianism," Robert Bork observed, and "its disregard for the Constitution in whose name it spoke than the legislative reapportionment cases."[31]

The challenge to localism was twofold. It lay first in the Court's rejection of the local polity as an entity meriting representation in the state legislature and second in its indifference to claims that the people of the states were entitled to devise their own representative arrangements. The Court laid down a doctrinaire rule—one person, one (equally weighted) vote— for which there was no warrant in custom or the Constitution. In a dissent in *Baker* v. *Carr*, the Court's first step down this path, Justice Felix Frankfurter protested that this "was not the colonial system, it was not the system chosen for the national government by the Constitution, it was not the system exclusively or even predominantly practiced by the States at the time of adoption of the Fourteenth Amendment, it is not predominantly practiced by the States today."[32]

The upper houses of state legislatures, analogous to the U.S. Senate, had typically represented units of local government, usually counties, even though this sacrificed strict proportionality to population. In *Reynolds* v. *Sims* (1964), the Court rejected the federal analogy as "inapposite and irrelevant" because the national choice had been a political compromise (as if that made it illegitimate!) and because counties, cities, and other local subdivisions, unlike the states, had never had any claim to be sovereign entities. In a companion case, *Lucas* v. *Forty-Fourth General Assembly* (1964), the Court majority struck down a Colorado apportionment that had been approved by the state's voters in a referendum, including majorities in every political subdivision. Colorado's voters had explicitly rejected a plan to apportion both legislative houses on the basis of population. The Court ruled that they had no right to depart from its prescribed standard.[33]

It was not just what the Court did in these cases, but the grounds on which it chose to do it, that showed disdain for federalism and locality. That malapportionment was severe enough in some states to warrant a federal judicial remedy is conceded even by some of the Court's critics. But whereas the Court grounded its holding on the equal protection clause— equal numbers of people must have an equal number of legislative representatives—it might have supplied a remedy and honored federalism nonetheless by relying instead on the clause that guarantees each state a republican form of government. This dead letter, ignored since the mid-nineteenth century, might have been given life and logically applied to cases in which the state legislatures' failure to enact reapportionments violated their own state constitutions and thwarted government by majorities.[34] Such an approach would have been less likely to culminate in the Court's prescribing a "sixth-grade arithmetic" rule as a straitjacket on the states.[35]

In the wake of the reapportionment decisions, social entities defined by space—local communities—are often sacrificed. Legislative districting has been turned into an arcane exercise for computers, consultants, and constitutional lawyers, along with the usual array of incumbents trying to save their seats or party politicians trying to protect or gain majorities. District lines now cut arbitrarily through local places that once would have been respected as such and represented intact.

The Warren court's other leading decisions came in those areas of local government activity—police and schools—that had earlier been least subject to nationalizing influences. One of the Court's great projects was the reform of state criminal law, which entailed the steady incorporation of Bill of Rights guarantees into the Fourteenth Amendment. Another, even more deeply challenging to local mores, was school desegregation.

Among the many decisions on criminal law, the most important for local government was *Miranda* v. *Arizona*, which in 1966 spelled out "a fairly complete code of behavior" for local police who were interrogating suspects. The Court said that the prosecution could not use as evidence in a criminal case a statement resulting from police interrogation of a person in custody unless he had been warned of his right not to be questioned, of the danger that any statement might be used against him, and of his right to have a lawyer present, either his own choice or one appointed at public expense. Moreover, these rights, though waived initially, could be invoked at any time.[36]

Also, the relatively obscure but profoundly important case of *Monroe* v. *Pape* (1960) arose out of police conduct, even if it had much broader ramifications. By expanding the use of one long-standing provision of federal civil rights law, *Monroe* v. *Pape* transformed the relations of the federal judiciary with state and local governments. Since 1871 the law had authorized suits against persons acting "under color of state law" who deprived anyone of a right secured by the U.S. Constitution or laws. In *Monroe* the Court held that this law—section 1983 of title 42 of the U.S. Code—would apply even though there had been no showing that the offending activities had been authorized or encouraged by state law, and the federal constitutional remedy was immediately available as a front-line remedy. It was not a backstop available only after efforts to get a remedy in state courts had been exhausted. The plaintiff could begin by coming into a federal court and claiming a constitutional violation. Previously, the relation between citizens and state and local governments had been governed by the large body of state tort law, administrative law, and criminal law. These rules were now superseded by federal constitutional rules, and federal courts were turned into supervisors of the whole of state and local government conduct. Thousands of cases began to be filed annually under section 1983.[37]

In regard to schools, the Court laid down its constitutional principle in *Brown* v. *Board of Education* in 1954—"separate educational facilities are inherently unequal"—and then, in a rare burst of practicality, acknowledged a year later in *Brown II* that full implementation "may require solution of varied local school problems." School authorities had primary responsibility for solving these problems. Courts would have to consider whether their implementation was sufficient. Because of "their proximity to local conditions," district courts would bear this burden primarily. The Supreme Court said that in fashioning their decrees, lower courts should be guided by the principles of equity, a specialized legal term meaning that they would have a great deal of freedom. The lower courts might consider "problems related to administration, arising from the physical condition of the school plant, the school transportation system, personnel, revision of school districts and attendance areas . . . , and revision of local laws and regulations which may be necessary in solving the foregoing problems."[38]

An extraordinary chapter in the nation's experience followed, as federal district courts struggled to realize racial integration. Faced with prolonged and inventive Southern resistance, federal courts ultimately endorsed drastically intrusive remedies. The key case was *Swann* v. *Charlotte-Mecklenburg Board of Education* (1971), in which the Supreme Court approved a plan for massive busing of students as well as a system of attendance zones marked by "frank—and sometimes drastic—gerrymandering." The Court observed that the remedy for segregation may be "administratively awkward, inconvenient and even bizarre in some situations . . . but all awkwardness and inconvenience cannot be avoided."[39]

Each city in which desegregation suits were filed produced its own story. Federal district judges on the front lines of the federal system took charge of local schools and sought to reconcile national ideals with local realities, sometimes at considerable risk to their safety. Charlotte, where busing got its start, made a success of it.[40] In Boston, it was a disaster, breeding neighborhood violence and white flight.[41] A study of school desegregation for the period from 1968 to 1980 found that as of 1980 the eleven states of the South had the lowest level of segregation of any region.[42] Southern schools had been reconstructed.

The Supreme Court gave leadership to the nation in this effort, and inspiration to the civil rights movement, but ultimately it needed the kind of help that only Congress could give. The Civil Rights Act of 1964 prohibited racial discrimination in the administration of federal grants-in-aid, and the Elementary and Secondary Education Act of 1965 authorized federal grants to elementary and secondary schools, giving the federal government enormous leverage over southern schools. They badly needed the federal money and stood to get a large part of it because it was designated for poor children. When the combined authority of all three branches of the federal government was brought to bear against the South after 1964, progress toward desegregation came swiftly.[43]

One subsequent instance of collaboration between Congress and the Warren court needs to be noted. Like reapportionment, voting rights produced a challenge to localism that was arguably more fundamental than that of school desegregation.

School desegregation got more publicity than any other action of the Court and affected the daily lives of ordinary people more deeply. The spectacle of federal judges deciding the most mundane details of local school administration, as in Boston, while ethnic neighborhoods turned into battle zones caused even the most ardent liberals to ponder whether the power of national judges was being appropriately employed.[44] Precisely because it did address social mores rather than forms of government, school desegregation would ultimately expose the limits of judicial power. It would be settled by the people themselves. They would achieve racial harmony or not, live and go to school where they could and would. Federal judges would not dictate such choices for them.

The policy issues that arose out of the Voting Rights Act of 1965 were far different. As interpreted by the Supreme Court and administered by the Department of Justice, this legislation, like reapportionment decisions, addressed who and what was to be represented in American legislatures and who was to have power to define the spatial boundaries and governmental structures of local communities. It led to unprecedented measures of national intrusion.

Two parts of the act have had potent implications for localism. One is section 5, which prohibits the implementation of any changes affecting voting in certain state and local (mainly southern) jurisdictions without the approval of the attorney general or a special three-judge federal district court in the District of Columbia. The Supreme Court construed this provision to extend far beyond mere changes in laws affecting the act of voting or running for office. Consequently, proposed annexations, redistricting plans, shifts from district to at-large representation, and changes in the location of polling places must be cleared in advance.[45]

Section 2, as amended in 1982, is the other significant part. It prohibits electoral practices resulting in "less opportunity [for minority citizens] . . . to participate in the political process and to elect representatives of their choice." It has elicited approximately 225 lawsuits a year attacking local representative structures. Both in response to such suits and in anticipation of them, there has been a widespread shift at the local level from at-large to district representation for county, city, and town councils and school boards.[46] Whereas the Voting Rights Act originally targeted the seven states of the old confederacy for the purpose of enfranchising southern blacks, it now is being used to secure proportional representation for racial and linguistic minorities everywhere in the country. To achieve this, local electoral arrangements are made to yield to national decision.

The States as "Winners"

The Warren court made deep inroads on localism, but if local government was changed in the course of this conflict, so was the Court. The election in 1969 of Richard Nixon, who ran for the presidency in part by running against the Court, brought a change in its composition. Warren Burger replaced Earl Warren as chief justice in 1969. Of greater long-run importance for federalism, William H. Rehnquist and Lewis F. Powell were named in 1972. Powell was a former chairman of the Richmond school board, and Rehnquist had been active in Arizona politics. Both were judicial conservatives with ingrained respect for local custom. The reconstituted Court recoiled from the recasting of local institutions.[47]

As one sign of this change, the Court moderated its position on state legislative reapportionment to acknowledge the legitimacy of representation for local communities. In *Mahan* v. *Howell* (1973), it held a 16.4 percent deviation from perfect proportionality in the lower house of the Virginia legislature to be justified by "the State's policy of maintaining the integrity of political subdivision lines." And, in *Brown* v. *Thomson* (1983), it upheld an apportionment plan of Wyoming's House of Representatives that allowed an average deviation from population equality of 16 percent and a maximum deviation of 89 percent, noting that "Wyoming's constitutional policy—followed since statehood—of using counties as representative districts and ensuring that each county has one representative is supported by substantial and legitimate state concerns."[48]

More telling signs came in cases dealing with school finance (*San Antonio v. Rodriguez*, 1973), school desegregation (*Milliken v. Bradley*, 1974), and exclusionary zoning (*Warth v. Seldin*, 1975). In each of these, the more conservative Court confronted the bedrock of localism and drew back.

In the school finance case, Demetrio Rodriguez and others had brought a class action on behalf of school children who were members of poor families residing in school districts with low property tax bases. They claimed that the Texas system's reliance on local property taxation favored the more affluent and violated equal protection requirements because of substantial interdistrict disparities in per-pupil expenditures that resulted primarily from differences in the value of assessable property. Texas had a state-funded program designed to provide a basic minimum education in every school, but it did not eliminate interdistrict disparities in expenditure or compensate fully for disparities in assessable property.

Justice Powell, writing for a five-man majority, rejected the attempt of plaintiffs to apply equal protection analysis to the case and deferred to state and local governments with a statement of judicial modesty in stark contrast to the posture and rhetoric of the Warren court:

> [This] case . . . involves the most persistent and difficult questions of educational policy, [an] area in which this Court's lack of specialized knowledge and experience counsels against premature interference with the informed judgments made at the state and local levels. . . . It would be difficult to imagine a case having greater potential impact on our federal system than [this], in which we are urged to abrogate systems of financing public education presently in existence in virtually every State. . . . The consideration and initiation of fundamental reforms with respect to state taxation and education are matters reserved for the legislative processes of the various States.[49]

In *Milliken v. Bradley*, one sees the same reluctance to disrupt the long-standing arrangements of local government and an even more explicit statement in their defense. The crucial issue in this case was whether a federal court could order a multidistrict, metropolitan area–wide remedy for central-city school segregation. A district court, besides ordering the Detroit school board to formulate a desegregation plan for the city, had ordered state officials to submit desegregation plans encompassing the three-county metropolitan area despite the fact that the eighty-five school districts in these three counties were not parties to the suit and there was no claim that they had committed constitutional violations. The district judge, contending that "school districts are simply matters of political convenience and may not be used to deny constitutional rights," appointed a panel to submit a desegregation plan encompassing fifty-three of the eighty-five suburban school districts plus Detroit. He had also ordered the Detroit school board to acquire at least 295 buses for the purpose of transporting students to and from outlying districts. The decision in *Swann* had endorsed massive busing, but it occurred within a single school district.

The Supreme Court invalidated this plan. Burger, like Powell before him in the *Rodriguez* case, wrote for a five-man majority. Boundary lines might be bridged, he said, where there had been a constitutional violation calling for interdistrict relief, but

> the notion that school district lines may be casually ignored or treated as a mere administrative convenience is contrary to the history of public education in our country. No single tradition in public education is more deeply rooted than local control over the operation of schools; local autonomy has long been thought essential both to the maintenance of community concern and support for public schools and to quality of the educational process.

Noting that the plan would in effect consolidate fifty-four districts into a vast new superdistrict, the opinion asked rhetorically what would happen as a result, to the status and authority of popularly elected school boards, or to financing arrangements, for example. Perhaps such operational questions would be resolved by the district court, but the Supreme Court majority rejected that idea:

> It is obvious from the scope of the interdistrict remedy itself that absent a complete restructuring of the laws of Michigan relating to school districts the District Court will become first, a *de facto* "legislative authority" to resolve these complex questions, and then the "school superintendent" for the entire area. This is a task which few, if any, judges are qualified to perform and one which would deprive the people of control of schools through their elected representatives.[50]

In *Warth* v. *Seldin*, individuals and organizations in Rochester had sued the adjacent town of Penfield and members of its zoning, planning, and town boards, claiming that Penfield's zoning ordinance excluded low- and moderate-income persons, in violation of federal constitutional and statutory rights. Powell, writing again for a five-man majority, denied standing. While most of the opinion deals with that issue, there is more than a hint of the new majority's reluctance yet again to supplant state and local governments and to tamper with the established institutions of localism. Without standing requirements, Powell wrote, "the courts would be called upon to decide abstract questions of wide public significance even though other governmental institutions may be more competent to address the questions." And, in a footnote, he added: "We also note that zoning laws and their provisions, long considered essential to effective urban planning, are peculiarly within the province of state and local legislative authorities. . . . Citizens dissatisfied with provisions of such laws need not overlook the availability of the normal democratic process."[51]

The result of the Supreme Court's newfound restraint was not, however, that the issues presented in these cases languished. Rather, they were deflected to state governments, most particularly courts, some of which seized them with a will that had presumably been fed by the Warren court's example. All across the country, state supreme courts have acted on suits for equalization of school finance, while a smaller number have attacked exclusionary zoning and considered interdistrict remedies for racial imbalance in the schools. As of 1994 education finance systems had been overturned by courts in more than a dozen states, including California and Texas.[52] In California, which pioneered this movement, statewide equalization of per-pupil spending has been achieved. On exclusionary zoning, Pennsylvania's Supreme Court was the first to act, with a relatively cautious ruling in the late 1970s.[53] New Jersey's Supreme Court has gone farthest, with two rulings (1975 and 1983) in *Southern Burlington County NAACP v. Township of Mount Laurel.* The second, coming after the first had brought no response from the state legislature or local governments, imposed numerical fair shares of low-income housing on local places. In response, the state legislature passed the Fair Housing Act of 1985, which incorporated much of the judicial decree in statutory form. Zoning has ceased to be a local function in New Jersey.[54]

Seeking to build on the success of state-level constitutional cases in school finance, the National Association for the Advancement of Colored People in 1989 brought suit in a Connecticut court to compel racial desegregation of public schools in the city of Hartford and its suburban districts. A similar suit also developed in New Jersey. In 1996 the Connecticut

Supreme Court ruled in *Sheff* v. *O'Neill* that racial segregation in Hartford's schools violated the state constitution and called on the state legislature to remedy the racial discrepancy between central-city and suburban schools.[55]

All of this action (and much more) has led numerous scholars to remark on the revival of state constitutional law, which is but one manifestation of the post-1960s renaissance of state governments generally.[56] At the heart of this renaissance is expansion of the states' role in education. Schools, the most durably local of the bedrock institutions, were very much changed by centralizing forces in the 1970s.

State spending for schools began to exceed local spending in the mid-1970s and continued to gain thereafter.[57] Federal aid, introduced on a large scale in the mid-1960s, may have given impetus to the change, but that is less clear in the case of education than it was for welfare and highways several decades earlier. If centralizing influences emanated from the national government above, some also rose from below, in the form of resistance from local property taxpayers to bearing the rising costs of education. Possibly the two forces were linked. Per-pupil spending more than doubled between 1960 and 1980, responding in part to national mandates such as that to provide a "free and appropriate education for all handicapped children." Taxpayer resistance to school spending measures rose in the late 1970s, and the passage of Proposition 13 in California in 1978 marked the start of a multistate property taxpayers' revolt. As states moved to assume a larger share of school costs, they did so with revenues from other sources: income and sales taxes.

Because federal grants-in-aid and the rights revolution reached local schools as companions to each other, the effects of the two are hard to sort out. Grants to schools in the 1960s and 1970s, designated for the poor and the disabled, were driven by the aim of substantive equality and placed less emphasis on centralizing the state and local administrative structure than was true in the Progressive Era. Indeed, showing the liberals' want of confidence in state governments at this time, one title of the Elementary and Secondary Education Act created a grant program administered directly to local districts for the development of "supplemental educational centers." These were conceived of in Washington as a means to outflank the state educational agencies, which were presumed to be stagnant and conservative.[58]

Nevertheless, the introduction of federal aid did a great deal to change state education agencies. If they stagnated after 1965, it was not for lack of federal money. The act of that year and its subsequent amendments required them to approve local projects requesting federal funds for educational innovation and education for disadvantaged, disabled, bilingual, and migrant children. One percent of the money in such programs was earmarked for state administration. Also, one title of the 1965 act provided general support for state education agencies, giving priority to planning and evaluation. From these sources, state agencies underwent a sizable expansion between 1964 and 1970. As of 1972, three-fourths of the staff members in such agencies had been in their jobs for less than three years. Seventy percent of the funding for the Texas agency, for example, was coming from the federal government.[59]

Federal court decisions in many areas—not just racial segregation, but also education for the disabled, bilingual education, and due process guarantees for individual students and teachers—elaborated statutes and the Constitution so as to weave an intricate web of restriction around the daily conduct of local administrators. Michael Kirst has captured the change, writing from experience as president of California's board of education as well as a professor of education. There had been a time, he says—a "golden era" from 1920 to 1950—when the local superintendent could set an agenda and shape decisions. No more: "Now, the local superintendent and administrative staff have become mostly reactive, as they try to juggle diverse and changing coalitions formed around different issues and operating across different levels of government." Students can no longer be expelled without "due process," meaning lengthy hearings with carefully defined procedures.[60]

Grants-in-aid were just one means of national influence, and they did not grow very much, in contrast to the earlier pattern of federal spending for welfare and highways. Federal aid reached 10 percent of school spending in 1970 but began to fall in the early 1980s and stood at less than 7 percent in 1987. Ironically, in regard to schools, federal *retrenchment* may eventually have increased pressure on the states to spend, coming as it did after federal action had fostered organization and heightened expectations among a number of constituencies that were the beneficiaries of federal mandates.

Despite two centuries of national development, states remain the central polities of the United States in form. Under some conditions and for some functions, form becomes fact. The states are the "default setting" of the American federal system. To the extent that other levels of government lack the resources to act—authority, revenue, will power, political consensus, institutional capacity—the states have the job. They retain a vitality born of the limits of national institutions' capacity, limits that the Warren court's clash with the bedrock of localism helped to reveal. The national government did not seize control of the schools, nor did local governments maintain control of them. Neither possessed the resources that would have been required to do so. The states, possessors above all of clear constitutional authority, picked up the pieces and began to pay more of the costs. The result, as Kirst shrewdly observes, is not so much centralization as fragmentation. Everyone and no one is in charge of the schools.[61]

Today's Choices

To borrow once again from Diamond, the history I have sketched is that of the national political community's struggle to attain "completeness . . . the perfection of its autonomy." Resistance came from a set of deeply rooted local institutions that were themselves not mere historical accidents. They were shielded by the original choice of federalism, embraced by nineteenth-century America, and given up to central authority (both state and national) slowly and reluctantly.

To argue that communities have been shaped by deliberate choices is not to deny that other forces shape them as well. If localism lacks vitality in modern America, that is not because it was killed by the Warren court, still less by technicians crusading for civil service reform from within the Social Security Board in the 1930s. Both did their part, especially the Court, but the nation's numerous wars and rise to great-power status did more, both to enlarge the claim of the national government on public resources and to stimulate the geographic and social mobility of the populace. Economic development brought specialization and interdependence, creating national and international markets and exposing local economies to forces far beyond their power to control. Urbanization was followed by suburbanization and the separation of place of work and place of residence. Transportation and communication technologies changed in ways that helped integrate the national society while attenuating local ones. If World War II assaulted the local place metaphorically, in the abstract, the interstate highway system literally assaulted it with concrete, while federally sponsored urban renewal gutted its physical core, not always replacing what it destroyed. The many acts with which the national government directly attacked localism, such as *Reynolds* v. *Sims* and the later-model Voting Rights Act, were compounded by many more that did not have that purpose but produced that effect as an inescapable by-product of the exercise of national power.

As American federalism has steadily grown more centralized, it is tempting to attribute the change to the influence of such (presumably uncontrollable) forces and to overlook the extent to which choices steadily present themselves nonetheless. A leading example is the debates currently raging over the schools, localism's last bastion, only recently breached. Egalitarians attack what remains of local distinction with measures for equalization of per-pupil spending. They would erase the effects of interlocal differences in taxable wealth, denying people one of the most compelling reasons for attachment both to schools that excel and the places in which they excel. On the other hand, libertarians—the proponents of the more extreme forms of choice—would enable parents to select whatever schools they prefer, public or private, freeing them from an obligation to support the public schools in the place where they live. Policy choices about schools are choices as well about the nature and function of local communities, to which schools have been central, even defining.

There is also the question of whether the formation of private communities should be encouraged or discouraged. Private substitutes for public local governments have been proliferating since the 1960s. There were about 150,000 community associations in the United States as of the early 1990s, helping to administer the lives and property of 32 million people—one of every eight Americans. In the fifty largest metropolitan areas, 50 percent or more of new home sales were in "common interest developments" or CIDs, as privately run communities have come to be called. In the metropolitan area of Washington, D.C., the figure was around 80 percent.[62]

The impetus for the formation of CIDs comes partly from developers, who, because of dwindling supplies of land, are under pressure to develop with greater density and who gain from putting playgrounds, pools, and tennis courts on commonly owned land. It also comes from financially pressed local governments that lack the capacity to supply services to large new developments and therefore welcome proposals that promise to relieve them of this burden.

While some CID associations are confined to responsibility for a single building, the vast majority administer territory as well as a building. They levy fees that are in effect taxes, and they provide a variety of services, such as roads, bus routes, television stations, security forces, parks, and swimming pools. Some of them are walled. Although most are associated with new developments, others have become established in older settings. St. Louis is laced with privately owned streets, complete with gatehouses.

Analysts of these quasi governments disagree about their implications for citizenship. They may be merely one more organized place in which Americans engage in "political" activity, arguing over how to define their shared interests. Even if most CID residents are apathetic, the figures on participation are impressive: 750,000 persons serve on the boards of directors. Dissident homeowners, chafing under restrictions about pets, alterations to their dwellings, and the like, resort to legal actions, counterorganization, and vocal assertions of their rights. All of this looks like normal American politics; people have merely invented a new setting in which to practice it. On the other hand, what is at issue here, even more precisely and narrowly than usual, are rights and responsibilities associated with the ownership of real property. These are thoroughly private-regarding places. Maintenance and protection of private property, to the exclusion of more encompassing purposes, unite (or divide) the members of the CID.

While exclusive, property-centered private community associations multiply, local public places continue to come under attack for not being inclusive enough. In the summer of 1991, President Bush's Advisory Commission on Regulatory Barriers to Affordable Housing (the Kemp commission) recommended a series of federal actions that would compel local jurisdictions to relax restrictions on construction of low-cost housing. It proposed denial of federal housing assistance to state or local governments that failed to reduce regulatory barriers and denial of tax-exempt status to state and local bonds issued to finance housing construction in such jurisdictions.[63]

Such policy proposals and choices raise in turn a series of larger, underlying questions: How important is it to the well-being of society that spatially defined communities be sustained? Are they entitled to primacy, or may race under some circumstances supplant place, as it has come to do in the ideological framework of the Voting Rights Act? How important is it that spatial communities have a general-purpose public character? If they are to have a public character, to what extent, to what ends, and with what instruments should higher levels of government regulate their capacity to define themselves as communities? May federal judges impose taxes on states and localities (the issue raised in 1990 in the Kansas City school desegregation case, *Missouri* v. *Jenkins*)?[64] Should any autonomy remain to the local place in an America that increasingly searches for equality, including interjurisdictional equality? Should any autonomy be restored to the local place in an America that laments the loss of a sense of community, fears for personal safety, and worries about the alienation of citizens from politics?

Underpinning any answers to such questions are a series of value judgments and facts that political theory and behavioral social science ought to be able to help clarify. They ought to be able to illuminate the value and social function of the small-scale public place and weigh the differences in the citizen's relation to places of different scale. The starting point for any such effort remains today, as for 150 years, Tocqueville's argument for the importance of decentralization in democracies—not just of the execution of centrally framed laws, but of deliberation and lawmaking in matters of daily consequence to ordinary citizens.[65]

What Tocqueville sought to decentralize, according to Martin Diamond's interpretation, were "the daily things, the intra-regime things, that make up the vast bulk of a government's business—the little things, immensely interesting to most men . . . which may be done safely and salutarily by the locality in whatever way it chooses, because the doing of them affects the whole not at all or only insignificantly."[66] Yet in a society where a high school teacher's refusal to wear a tie can rise to the level of a constitutional question, it is hard to see what can be safeguarded to the local citizen who might have the time, taste, or temperament for participating in the labor of democratic governance.[67]

PART Two

Properties and Functions

2

Enduring Features

It is a commonplace of scholarship that American federalism constantly changes. And it is a commonplace of contemporary comment that the states are enjoying a renaissance. Their historic role as laboratories of experiment is acknowledged with praise. Their executives and legislatures are increasingly active, seizing issues, such as economic development, that the federal government has failed to come to grips with. State courts are staking out positions on individual rights in advance of those defined by the U.S. Supreme Court, while state attorneys general pursue consumer protection and antitrust cases that federal agencies have ignored. The states' share of government revenue has gained slightly on that of the federal government in the 1980s, and considerably surpasses that of local governments, contrary to a pattern that prevailed until the 1960s. The states' standing with the public and with prospective employees has improved. The governors are getting their share of good press and, what may be almost as important, of presidential nominations. As a result, state governments are perceived to have improved their position in the federal system.

Yet it is worth recalling how different the impression was but a short time ago, and how little has changed in some respects. Early in 1984 the Advisory Commission on Intergovernmental Relations published a much-noticed report, *Regulatory Federalism,* detailing a wide range of new or

This essay first appeared as "The Enduring Features of American Federalism," in *Brookings Review,* vol. 7 (Summer 1989), pp. 34–38.

expanded federal controls over state governments.[1] In 1985, in the case of *Garcia v. San Antonio Metropolitan Transit Authority*, the Supreme Court declined to protect the state governments from congressional regulation under the Constitution's commerce clause and seemed to wash its hands of this crucial federalism question.[2] In the spring of 1988 the court removed the constitutional prohibition on federal taxation of income from interest on state and local government bonds (*South Carolina v. Baker*).[3]

Certain regulatory excesses of the federal government vis-à-vis the states have been modified in the past several years; rules regarding transportation of the disabled and bilingual education are two examples. Yet not even under Ronald Reagan did the federal government step back from the new constitutional frontiers mapped out in the 1960s and 1970s, such as the Clean Air Act of 1970, which addresses the states with the language of outright command ("Each state shall . . ."). The president's executive order of October 1987 on federalism may be interpreted as an attempt to draw back, with its rhetorical statement of federalism principles and its instructions to executive agencies to refrain from using their discretion to preempt state action.[4] But to read it is to be reminded of how little unilateral power the president has. The drawing back can succeed only to the extent the national legislature and courts concur. Nor did the Reagan administration consistently adhere to its professed principles. Substantive policy goals often were in tension with discretion for the states; the Reagan administration could be counted on to opt for discretion only when that tactic was consistent with its pursuit of a freer market and lower federal spending.[5]

American federalism is a very large elephant indeed, and it is hard for a lone observer to grasp the properties of the whole beast. One needs to be abreast of constitutional doctrines; of legislative, judicial, and administrative practices over the whole range of government activities, from taxation to protection of civil liberties to pollution control; of the development or disintegration of political parties (are they decaying at the grass roots? at the center? both? neither?); of the volume and locus of interest group activity; of trends in public opinion and public employment, and more. To understand the condition of federalism, one needs to comprehend the functioning of the whole polity.

Granting that the federal system is always in flux, it is harder than one might suppose even to detect the dominant tendencies. While most academic analysts probably would assert that centralization is the secular trend, such distinguished scholars as political scientist Richard P. Nathan and historian Morton Keller have argued that centralization is not inexorable and that the evolution of American federalism follows a cyclical pattern, with the federal government and the states alternately dominating.[6]

Fighting the customary temptation to concentrate on change, I want to try to identify some elemental and enduring truths of American federalism. I want to map the features of the terrain, a metaphor that may be in fact apt. Our federalism is much like a piece of earth that is subject to constant redevelopment. It can be bulldozed and built up, flattened and regraded, virtually beyond recognition. Yet certain elemental properties of it, the bedrock and the composition of the soil, endure. I will start with propositions that I take to be purely factual and then proceed to others that are more analytical and normative, hence debatable.

THE STATES ARE GOVERNMENTS IN THEIR OWN RIGHT. They have constitutions that derive from the people and guarantee specific rights. They have elected legislatures that make laws, elected executives that enforce laws, and courts that interpret them—and not incidentally interpret the laws of the United States as well. State governments levy taxes. Their territorial integrity is protected by the U.S. Constitution, which also guarantees them equal representation in the Senate and a republican form of government. These creatures that walk like ducks and squawk like ducks must be ducks.

NEVERTHELESS, THE STATES ARE INFERIOR GOVERNMENTS. In our pond, they are the weaker ducks. The stubbornly persistent mythology that governments in the American federal system are coordinate should not obscure that fact. The two levels of government are *not* coordinate and equal, nor did the winning side in 1787 intend them to be. One cannot deny the existence of the Constitution's supremacy clause and the prescription that state officers take an oath to uphold the Constitution of the United States, or the fact that the Framers of the Constitution fully expected an instrumentality of the federal government, the Supreme Court, to settle jurisdictional issues in the "compound republic," as James Madison called it. See *Federalist* No. 39, in which Madison makes a feeble, unsuccessful attempt to deny that the court's having this function gives the federal government a crucial advantage.[7]

Whether the federal government has always been superior in fact can certainly be debated. At various times and places its writ did not run very strong. The full impact on federalism of the post–Civil War amendments on civil rights was long delayed. Only recently has the South ceased to have a deviant social system. But on the whole, the federal government has won the crucial conflicts. Surely its ascendancy is not currently in dispute. Not only are the states treated as its administrative agents; they accept such treatment as a fact of life. Not since *Brown* v. *Board of Education* (1954) and *Baker* v. *Carr* (1962) have truly strenuous protests been heard from the states against their palpably inferior status.[8]

THE STATES' STATUS AS GOVERNMENTS, EVEN THOUGH INFERIOR ONES, GIVES CONGRESS A RANGE OF CHOICE IN DEALING WITH THEM. It may choose deference, displacement, or interdependence. In domestic affairs Congress always has the option of doing nothing, knowing that the states can act whether or not it does. Sometimes Congress consciously defers to the states, judging that the subject properly "belongs" to them. Perhaps just as often, Congress today is not deliberately deferential but fails to act for lack of time or the ability to reach agreement. It defaults. The area of congressional inaction, be it through deference or default, is reliably quite large. It normally includes new issues, such as AIDS or equal pay. States remain on the front lines of domestic policy, the first to deal with newly perceived problems. Congress tends to defer or default on particularly difficult issues, such as the amount of support to be given to needy single mothers with children.

Congress rarely employs its second option, complete displacement, although explicit invocations of it, using the term *preemption,* are more frequent now than they used to be. The third option, interdependence, is very common, I would think predominant. Through some combination of inducements, sanctions, or contractual agreements, Congress enters into collaborative arrangements with the states in the pursuit of national ends. The most common techniques are conditional grants-in-aid, which are characteristic of programs for income support and infrastructure development, and qualified preemptions, which are typical of the "new" regulation, including environmental protection and occupational health and safety. Congress sets standards but tells states that if they meet or exceed the national standards, they may retain the function, including administration.

THE VIGOR AND COMPETENCE WITH WHICH STATE GOVERNMENTS PERFORM FUNCTIONS LEFT TO THEM DOES NOT PROTECT THEM AGAINST CONGRESSIONAL INCURSIONS. Here I mean to challenge one of the leading canards of American federalism. Whenever Congress takes domestic action, that action is rationalized as a response to the failures of the states. Congress has had to step in, it is said, because states were not doing the job. The only thing one can safely say about the origins of nationalizing acts is that they are responses to the power of nationalizing coalitions.[9] When Congress acts, in other words, it is not necessarily because states have failed; it is because advocates of national action have succeeded in mustering enough political force to get their way. State inaction may constitute part of their case, but state actions that are offensive to their interests may do so as well. Pathbreaking states have often demonstrated what can be done.

Congress's usual choice, moreover, is to cooperate with the states, not displace them, and in the relationships of mutual dependence that result, it is a nice question just whose deficiencies are being compensated for. The federal government typically contributes uniform standards and maybe money. The states typically do the work of carrying out the function. The more they do and the better they do it, the more they are likely to be asked or ordered by Congress to do.

IN COOPERATING WITH THE STATES, CONGRESS AGAIN HAS A CHOICE. It can emphasize their status as governments, or it can emphasize their inferiority as such. Our ambiguous constitutional system enables Congress to view the states as equals or as agents. Congress gradually has abandoned the former view in favor of the latter. In making this change, at critical stages it has had the acquiescence of the Supreme Court, which once tried to defend "dual federalism"—that is, the notion that the states were sovereign, separate, and equal—but abandoned that doctrine during the New Deal.[10] And Congress does not indulge its agents. Ask any federal bureau chief. Congress is very poor at balancing the ends and means of action. All major federal executive agencies—the Environmental Protection Agency, the Social Security Administration, the Immigration and Naturalization Service, to cite just a few—are laboring under a burden of excessive obligation.

BECAUSE STATES ARE GOVERNMENTS, THEY MAY BARGAIN WITH CONGRESS. Bargaining is the usual mode of intergovernmental relations. State governments, even when treated by Congress as administrative agents, are agents with a difference. Unlike federal executive agencies, they are not Congress's creatures. Therefore they can talk back to it. They can influence the terms of cooperation.

THIS BARGAINING BETWEEN LEVELS OF GOVERNMENT IS GOOD, DEPENDING ON HOW THE STATES USE IT. Here again I mean to challenge what I take to be a conventional view. Fragmentation of authority in the federal system is ordinarily portrayed, at least in academic literature, as a severe handicap to the federal government's pursuit of its goals. The federal government would be more effective, it is commonly said, if it did not have to rely so heavily on other governments. I believe, to the contrary, that the federal government needs a great deal of help, of a kind that can best—perhaps only—be supplied by governments. It needs help with all aspects of governing, that is, with all the functions that legislatures, courts, and executives perform. Beyond that, it needs a great deal of help quite specifically in adjusting its goals to social and economic realities and to the capacities of administrative organizations.

Madison may be cited in support of this view—not the famous passage in *Federalist* No. 51 that one might anticipate, in which he argues that "the different governments will control each other, at the same time that each will be controlled by itself," but a passage less remarked, yet perhaps more prescient, in No. 62. In this essay on the Senate, Madison wrote:

> A good government implies two things: first, fidelity to the object of government, which is the happiness of the people; secondly, a knowledge of the means by which that object can be best attained. Some governments are deficient in both these qualities; most governments are deficient in the first. I scruple not to assert, that in American governments too little attention has been paid to the last.[11]

The deficiency in our attention to the means of government is glaring. All institutions of the federal government—Congress, presidency, courts—have far more to do than they can do, but the executive agencies as the instruments of government action are arguably the most overburdened of all. Through most of the post–World War II period, the federal government has also had a shortfall of fiscal capacity. It has had financial obligations in excess of its willingness or ability to meet them.

State governments help fill the federal government's performance gaps. They do much of the work of governing, as Madison anticipated. Even as an ardent nationalist, at the time of the Constitutional Convention, he held to the view that the national government would not be suited to the entire task of governing "so great an extent of country, and over so great a variety of objects."[12] But if the states help fill the federal government's implementation gaps, they also are very much at risk of being victimized by them. Congress will try to close the distance between what it wants and what the federal government is able to do independently by ordering the states to do it.

The states are entitled to talk back. As governments in their own right, they have an independent responsibility to set priorities and balance means against ends. Because they are closer to the practical realities of domestic problems and because they lack the power to respond to deficits by printing money, state governments are in a superior position to do that balancing.

This appeal to the states to talk back is not a call to defiance, but a call to engage federal officials in a policy dialogue—and, having done so, to address those officials with language suitable to governments. If states habitually present themselves as supplicants for assistance—like any other interest group—they will inevitably contribute to the erosion of their own status.

I believe that the states *are* increasingly using the language of governments, rather than supplicants, in their dialogue with the federal government. The enactment in 1988 of welfare reform legislation, which a working group of the National Governors Association helped to shape, is an example. The governors drew on the state governments' experience with welfare programs to fashion changes that would be both politically and administratively feasible, besides containing improved assurances of federal funding for welfare.

There are numerous explanations for the new, more authoritative voice of the states. One is that individually the states have heightened competence and self-confidence as governments, whatever the range among them. Another is that the decline of federal aid under Presidents Carter and Reagan compelled greater independence. A third is that self-consciousness and cohesion of the states as a class of governments have increased, as indicated by the development of organized, well-staffed mechanisms of cooperation. Their shared status as agents of Congress and objects of its influence has caused the states to cooperate with one another today to a degree unprecedented in history, even if they remain intensely competitive in some respects, such as the pursuit of economic development.

I have concentrated on relations between the states and Congress to keep the subject focused and relatively simple. But the federal judiciary rivals the legislature as a framer of federal-state relations. Federal courts, like Congress, can choose to emphasize the states' standing as governments or their inferiority as such. Like Congress, over time the courts have come more and more to embrace the latter choice, so that states have been routinely commanded to implement the detailed policy decisions of national courts as well as the national legislature.

For the states, it is one thing to talk back to Congress, quite another and much harder thing to talk back to the federal courts. Yet here as well, they have been trying to find ways to talk back more effectively. The National Association of Attorneys General and the State and Local Legal Center, both with offices in Washington, now offer advice and assistance to state and local governments involved in litigation before the Supreme Court. Such governments in the past have often suffered from a lack of expert counsel.

These developments in federal-state relations do not transgress the Framers' intentions, at least if one takes the *Federalist* as the guide to those intentions. Alexander Hamilton foresaw with evident satisfaction the federal-state relation that obtains today. In *Federalist* No. 27, he wrote that

> the plan reported by the convention, by extending the authority of the federal head to the individual citizens of the several States, will enable the government to employ the ordinary magistracy of each, in the execution of its laws. . . . Thus the legislatures, courts, and magistrates, of the respective [states], will be incorporated into the operations of the national government . . . and will be rendered auxiliary to the enforcement of its laws.[13]

This is exactly what has happened.

3

The Paradox of the Middle Tier

State administrators—particularly good state administrators and good governors and people who want to do things well—feel that they are on the receiving end of a very, very long pipeline that has no feedback loops whatever; that there is no way in which Washington understands what they need; that there is no way in which Washington is systematically learning from them and from the serendipitous way . . . things happen.

This comment comes from a veteran student of federalism and social welfare policy, Forrest Chisman.[1] I will assume that the Washington of which he speaks—the Washington that is so oblivious to the states—is primarily Congress, or at least Congress in the first instance. Federal administrators would probably not be indifferent to the states if Congress instructed them not to be.

For Congress to be obtuse or indifferent to state governments is genuinely baffling. The Senate, after all, was constituted initially to represent the states as such, a fact still signified by their being represented in it equally, with two members each. The authors of *The Federalist* fully expected members of the national legislature to be highly localistic.

This essay first appeared as "The States in American Federalism: The Paradox of the Middle Tier," in Forrest P. Chisman, Lawrence D. Brown, and Pamela J. Larson, eds., *National Health Reform: What Should the State Role Be?* (Washington: National Academy of Social Insurance, 1994), pp. 3–10.

Madison wrote in *Federalist* No. 46—a paper devoted to explaining why the advantage in federal-state relations would lie with the states—that "the prepossessions, which the members themselves will carry into the federal government, will generally be favorable to the States. . . . A local spirit will infallibly prevail much more in the members of Congress, than a national spirit will prevail in the legislatures of the particular States."[2] At least when I was growing up, textbooks in American government routinely portrayed Congress as being highly sensitive to the interests of state and local governments. What has happened to change this?

The answer is not to be found simply in the attitudes or behavior of incumbent members of Congress or of the small army of ideologically charged, fresh-faced congressional staff who are innocent of the history of American federalism. More fundamentally, it lies in the place of the states in our complicated and ambiguous constitutional system.

Two facts are pertinent. First, within the federal system, the states have had a formal and chronological primacy. They were the first governments, and the mediums, therefore, for creating the national and local governments. This primacy was embedded in the original constitutional theory: the national government possessed only those limited powers granted by the people. All else remained with the states and the people. This is what the Tenth Amendment says. For a long time, Americans took it very seriously. Second, the states are inferior governments. That is what the supremacy clause says, and it is reinforced by an implicit constitutional principle of surpassing importance: the United States Supreme Court, a national institution, determines what the Constitution means.

Juxtaposed, these two facts appear somewhat paradoxical, and in this paradox lies the explanation for the states' predicament. On one hand, they are governments "on the rise," as much journalistic and academic punditry over the past decade would have it. Their responsibilities are large and, arguably, growing. On the other hand, they receive a stream of orders from Washington, as Chisman says, and as the state governments themselves constantly complain. How can they be reviving and falling under the federal yoke at the same time? I hope to provide a plausible, if partial, answer with an excursion into constitutional history.

The States in Constitutional History

State governments, emerging out of the colonial ones, were, as I have said, the first fully constituted governments on the American scene. Except for Connecticut and Rhode Island, which clung to colonial charters that had provided for an exceptional measure of self-government, all of them prepared constitutions after the Declaration of Independence and before the framing of the United States Constitution. As the first governments, they were at least the mediums and, arguably, the agents for creating other governments, national and local, that would soon surpass them in functional importance.

The national government fought wars, including a civil war, to secure its own existence, promoted economic development with tariffs, and represented the hope for fulfilling America's destiny as a great republic, exemplar to the world. Local governments, which were well established in the colonial period and given a great deal of freedom by state constitutional conventions, legislatures, and courts in the mid-nineteenth century, built and maintained roads, maintained public decency and order, provided relief to the poor, taught children, and raised taxes. In short, they did the things that connected people to the polity on a daily basis. The bedrock of American domestic government for a very long time was local. At the opening of the twentieth century, American local governments were raising more revenue and doing more spending than the federal and state governments combined. "As compared either with the federal government or with local authorities, the central governments of the states lack vitality," Woodrow Wilson wrote in his textbook, *The State*, in the late nineteenth century. "[They] do not seem to be holding their own in point of importance. They count for much in legislation, but, so far, for very little in administration."[3]

Historically, then, the states did not actually do very much. Having created a framework of law within which local governments functioned, they did not closely supervise its application. At the same time, with respect to what they and their local subdivisions did, the states enjoyed a great deal of autonomy. There prevailed the concept of separate and equal sovereigns, to which the late Edward S. Corwin, a distinguished constitutional scholar, gave the name "dual federalism." Corwin identified four operative constitutional postulates as the components of dual federalism: (1) the national government is one of enumerated powers only; (2) the purposes which it may constitutionally promote are few; (3) within their respective spheres, the two centers of government are "sovereign" and hence "equal"; and (4) the relation of the two centers to each other is one of tension rather than collaboration.[4]

The doctrine may be found in stark form in such decisions as *Collector v. Day*, in which the Supreme Court ruled in 1871 that the federal government could not tax the salary of a county judge because he was a state officer; the *Civil Rights Cases* in 1883, which struck down congressional enactments regulating private conduct because they invaded the domain of local jurisprudence; and *Hammer* v. *Dagenhart*, which ruled in 1918 that Congress could not forbid the shipment in interstate commerce of the products of child labor because to do so invaded state authority. Justice Day wrote in *Hammer* v. *Dagenhart* that "if Congress can thus regulate matters entrusted to local authority by prohibition of the movement of commodities in interstate commerce, all freedom of commerce will be at an end, and the power of the States over local matters may be eliminated, and thus our system of government be practically destroyed."[5] To put it mildly, such rulings have an antiquarian ring today.

Equally antiquated is the constitutional doctrine, associated with the Civil War–era case of *Kentucky* v. *Dennison*, that the federal government may not give commands to officers of the states. Consider the following observations of Henry M. Hart, late professor of constitutional law at Harvard, written in 1954:

> Federal law often says to the states, "Don't do any of these things," leaving outside the scope of its prohibition a wide range of alternative courses of action. But it is illuminating to observe how rarely it says, "Do this thing," leaving no choice but to go ahead and do it.

Hart goes on to elaborate his point and to cite Justice Taney in *Kentucky* v. *Dennison*:

> "And we think it clear," said Chief Justice Taney, ". . . that the Federal Government, under the Constitution, has no power to impose on a State officer, as such, any duty whatever, and compel him to perform it." Taney's statement can stand today, if we except from it certain primary duties of state judges and occasional remedial duties of other state officers.[6]

Taney's statement does not stand today. It is in ruins. Formally overruled by the Supreme Court in 1987, it had been rendered obsolete by congressional practice long before.[7]

The Transformation of American Federalism

Clearly, something drastic happened to American federalism. Several things, actually.

First, beginning in the late nineteenth century, the states slowly asserted themselves vis-à-vis local governments, taking over at first more supervision, and then more actual performance, of the bedrock domestic functions: road construction, relief for the poor, schooling, public safety, and tax collection.

The process was uneven and, not accidentally, was given impetus by federal grants-in-aid whose conditions fostered state-level centralization. By 1950, state spending surpassed local spending for highways and welfare, functions that, unlike schools and the police, received heavy federal funding. Local spending continues even now to exceed state spending for schools, but states nonetheless play a much expanded role through bigger, more active education agencies and judicial and legislative action addressed to finance. Overall, state-raised revenue began to exceed locally raised revenue in 1965—a critical date for American federalism—and the gap has steadily widened. Although local employment still far surpasses state employment, the gap between the two has sharply narrowed. In 1929, state governments had only 318,000 employees, compared with 2 million for localities. As of 1987, the states had 4 million compared with the localities' 10 million.

Second, great nationalizing surges destroyed the old constitutional doctrines. The milestones are well known: the Civil War and two world wars, the New Deal, the Great Society. Dual federalism fell, as did the precept that state officers were not subject to federal commands. The warfare and welfare states rose on a national scale to consume the bulk of public resources. The civil rights and environmental revolutions, also national, produced a mass of tangled, nuanced regulation that is one of the numerous battlegrounds fought over in the federal judiciary. Constitutional commands emanating from the courts, statutory commands emanating from Congress and reinforced by judicial interpretation, and regulations emanating from federal agencies flood the land, constraining virtually every state and local act.

Finally—and this concludes my excursion into history and returns to Chisman's point—in recent years the national government has seemed to approach the limits of its power and political will. This development is too recent to know whether it is temporary or enduring. To understand why it has happened, for a start one may speculate commonsensically that bigness and its by-products have brought their own costs.

The war power, which historically was very advantageous to the national government, eliciting vast amounts of revenue and popular support, ceased to be so with Vietnam. When war turned unpopular, it impaired the legitimacy of both the government and its chief executive, who was seduced by his exalted place in the warfare state into deeply damaging abuses of power. Americans generally have embraced the welfare state: they have proved to have an undisciplinable appetite for entitlements. Costs of the major welfare state programs, income support and health care, have proved very hard to contain or predict.

As the national government's debt grew in the late twentieth century and its capacity for direct action waned, federal officeholders began looking habitually to get help with governing, and to get it on the cheap. They did not lose the urge or political incentive to act, only the capacity to do so effectively, with adequate political, financial, and administrative foundations. Under these circumstances, they turned increasingly to the state governments because of the states' peculiar combination of strength and vulnerability, which is a legacy of our federalism. This reliance on intergovernmental techniques is not new—far from it—but it is more pervasive, intrusive, routinized, and burdensome for the states than ever before.

Because the states are governments, yet subordinate, Congress can—or can try—to put much of the burden of governing on them. Because they are governments, they have the capacity to raise revenues and execute laws. Of themselves, even leaving local subdivisions aside, they have more employees than the federal government, although it is worth noting that this is a relatively recent development. State employment, at a mere 318,000 in 1929, was barely more than half of federal civilian employment. It surpassed federal employment between 1970 and 1975, and the gap has continued to widen. As governments, states are headed by elected officials who have to take heat from the public when hard choices are to be made. On the other hand, because they are subordinate governments, they have also to take orders from Washington.

President Clinton's health security plan, proposed in the fall of 1993 but never enacted, suggested the extremes to which federal intrusiveness might go. When the foundations of national health insurance were laid in 1965 with passage of Medicare, a national program financed with a payroll tax, most students of American social policy would probably have predicted that Medicare would grow incrementally until it covered the whole of the population. How many would have predicted what President Clinton laid before the country: a measure designed to achieve universal coverage, but with only marginal and obscure increases in federal taxation? Rather than a payroll tax, the president proposed to secure his objective with a pervasive and highly coercive increase in national regulation of individual consumers of health care, providers of care, employers, and state governments.

Must state governments submit to the national government as it commands them to perform administration and finance on its behalf? How have they responded historically to their paradoxical situation? Broadly, state governments can try to cling to their status and prerogatives as such, or they can accept subordination.

The States' Response

Madison devoted two numbers of *The Federalist*, 45 and 46, to explaining why the advantage in federal-state relations would lie with the states. Among the several reasons he adduced was that a state could more easily defeat unwarranted encroachments than could the national government. And the states collectively would be still more effective:

> Ambitious encroachments of the federal government on the authority of the State governments would not excite the opposition of a single State, or of a few States only. Every government would espouse the common cause. A correspondence would be opened. Plans of resistance would be concerted. One spirit would animate and conduct the whole.[8]

On the whole, that has not been true. Historically, state governments as such have not been able to concert action in defense of prerogatives within the federal system. States as polities have been divided within and among themselves in ways that have impeded their ability to collaborate as governments. And even when they have banded together in the name of states' rights, the cause has been patently disingenuous. Not states' rights, but the interests of various minorities—New England's Federalists in the War of 1812, southern slaveholders in the nineteenth century, and their descendants into the twentieth—were crucially at stake. As a doctrine espoused by minorities, states' rights has suffered devastating defeats. Even if southern state governments succeeded in fighting a war together, they did not win it. Moreover, their having waged a war elicited a use of national power so great as to transform the Constitution.

To organize cooperation among independent state governments in pursuit of a common goal is difficult, but the states have also failed historical tests far less exacting. Even when the Constitution offers formal mechanisms of protection—namely, in the amending process—state governments as a class have not used them to secure governmental prerogatives.

The Fourteenth Amendment is perhaps a poor example because southern states were coerced into accepting it, but no such coercion obtained in regard to the Seventeenth Amendment. By providing for popular election of senators, it formally removed from the structure of American government one of the principal protections of state governments' interests. To be sure, the Seventeenth Amendment merely confirmed a change that had already taken place, but that change itself was rooted in the early nineteenth-century failure of state governments to enforce instructions upon their delegates to the United States Senate.[9]

In modern times, following development of the welfare state and very high levels of governmental interdependence, the state governments have succeeded in organizing to voice their interests vis-à-vis the national government. Government action often stimulates the formation of interest groups, and the involvement of the national government in state government affairs through regulation and grants-in-aid has either stimulated the formation, or heightened the activity, of such groups as the National Governors Association, the National Conference of State Legislatures, the National Association of Attorneys General, the State and Local Legal Center, and other, more specialized organizations of state officials. These organizations purport to articulate the interests of state governments before Congress and the courts.

Even thus organized, state governments continue to find it difficult to concert their interests beyond a relatively narrow range of issues. Threats to financial prerogatives unite them. When revenue sources are jeopardized, as in issues over national taxation of the interest income from state and municipal bonds, they find it easy to collaborate. Clearly, governmental prerogatives are crucially at stake also in regard to abortion, yet the states are unable to come together in opposition to *Roe* v. *Wade* in order to retain their prerogative to legislate on the subject. As in the past, the differences within and among them as political societies override what unites them as governments with prerogatives to defend in a federal system.

If the states have a very limited ability to cooperate in asserting themselves as independent governments with shared interests, do they accept a role as subordinate governments, in which they become agents of nationally defined purposes? On the whole, they do. When Congress sets standards for clean air and provides that states shall prepare implementation plans to achieve them, the states do it. When Congress authorizes grants-in-aid for highway construction and maintenance but attaches to them all kinds of conditions, some of which are onerous and extraneous, the states accept the money and the conditions. It is almost unheard of for state governments to decline to participate in a nationally prescribed regulatory regime or grant-in-aid program, even though the option of not participating is technically available.[10]

When President Clinton's health care plan was drafted calling for the states to "assume primary responsibility for ensuring that all eligible individuals have access to a health plan that delivers the nationally guaranteed comprehensive benefit package," states did not protest. Among the functions prescribed for them in the administration's proposal were administration of subsidies for low-income individuals, families, and employers; certification and financial regulation of health plans; establishment and governance of health alliances; data collection; and quality management and improvement programs. In short, the states were to do everything but make the rules, which would have been up to Congress and a presidentially appointed National Health Board.[11] A reasonable response to this incredibly difficult assignment might well have been: "Are you kidding? You do it." Publicly and collectively, at least, the states said no such thing.

The failure of state governments to be more assertive probably is to be accounted for by combined considerations of politics and organizational maintenance. Much of what Congress prescribes has strong popular or organized interest group support, or Congress would not prescribe it. (In the end, it is worth repeating, Congress did not prescribe the Clinton health plan.) Theoretically and practically, perhaps Madison's most telling point in *Federalist* Nos. 45 and 46 was that "the federal and State governments are in fact but different agents and trustees of the people . . . substantially dependent on the great body of the citizens of the United States." As elected politicians themselves, governors and members of state legislatures are not very likely to defy a Congress that is legislating on behalf of causes and constituencies as deserving as clean air, the disabled, or pregnant women. Nor are they very likely to surrender functions affected by federal commands when those functions include most of what their governments do.[12]

In theory, states might try to take refuge in constitutional tradition. They could claim that mandates are unconstitutional because they violate the prerogatives of coordinate governments in a federal system. Seven states did bring suit unsuccessfully against enforcement of the National Voter Registration (Motor Voter) Act of 1993, which required states to provide all eligible citizens the opportunity to register to vote when they applied for or renewed a driver's license. More modestly, in 1995 they succeeded in getting Congress to enact the Unfunded Mandates Reform Act, which requires the Congressional Budget Office to report to Congress concerning the effects of any intergovernmental mandate estimated to impose annual costs on state and local governments of $50 million or more.[13] Yet for the most part, state officials merely grumble that mandates come without money. Their typical posture vis-à-vis the national government is that of financial supplicant. They want more money. Typical newspaper stories on the states' reaction to the Clinton health proposals were headlined "Health-Care Reform May Seem Like a Bitter Pill to Localities Sick of Unfunded Federal Mandates," and "States Trying to Ferret Fiscal Impact Data Out of Clinton Health Plan."[14]

The high priority that state governments individually and collectively attach to maximizing receipt of national government funds perhaps accounts for the fact that they are often treated in Congress not as governments at all, subordinate or otherwise, but as one more lobby—a mere interest group to be given no more recognition and access to decision processes than any other interest group.

Should this decline be a source of dismay? Has anything important been lost to American government generally as a result of the state governments' degeneration into something less than governments?

The Mismatches in Modern Federalism

At least three undesirable consequences are evident. I will call them "mismatches": between prescription and practicality; between the locus of responsibility for generating public benefits and for paying costs; and between the locus of responsibility for defining public goals and for making trade-offs among them.

National law and regulation often fail to come to grips with practicalities. They tend to be abstract and utopian, or, if concrete and particular, as when environmental laws set detailed, explicit standards, they turn out to be irrational when applied to particular places. State governments, converted into national administrative agents, are often called upon to enforce laws that do not suit the circumstances of their societies, be they the value preferences of their publics, the technology of their industries, or their geography or demography. When these mismatches result from differences of prevailing values—for example, if the national polity is pursuing egalitarian goals and the smaller-scale polity is defending hierarchical ones—the resolution one prefers will depend on value preferences or views of which political community ought to be superior. But often no very important value preferences are at stake; "mere" practicalities are. Mismatches between national prescription and on-the-ground practicalities turn up with such frequency in journalistic accounts and tales told by state and local officials that I am inclined to think the problem is real and serious, though I know of no attempt to document it rigorously.[15]

Accountability and fiscal responsibility are undermined when elected politicians in one government can create new benefits while elected politicians in many other governments are obliged to finance them. There is more involved here than Congress's being unfair to other governments because it gives them "mandates without money." To the extent that Congress is freed from the obligation to fund what it enacts, it is also free to act irresponsibly, without facing true tests of the public's preferences or being accountable for results.

Having been liberated by today's federalism from an obligation to fund what it enacts, Congress is more able to avoid weighing the relative urgency of, or demand for, different activities. It defines goals of public policy for one policy area at a time. The national government mandates innumerable environmental protections and educational programs and health programs without making the trade-offs among them that rational policy must entail. States and their local subdivisions receive commands for each policy area separately and are obliged to pay the costs of all, without having the freedom to weigh independently either the total cost or the allocation among those functions to which mandates apply. Did the public really want local governments to spend an additional $110.6 billion for sewage handling facilities by February 19, 1995, as federal environmental laws and regulations required?[16] Given the way in which intergovernmental relations have evolved, the American political system cannot yield answers to such a question.

It might be argued that while this critique of Congress may be valid, federalism does not fundamentally determine Congress's behavior. Mandates without money are not confined to state governments; Congress treats agencies of the national government the same way, obligating them to perform tasks for which it fails to provide enough, or sometimes any, appropriations. Nor has Congress ever been good at making trade-offs among competing programs, even when those programs are purely national. Perhaps the appropriate question to ask of contemporary American federalism is whether government in general is better by reason of Congress's relying so heavily on administrative agents that, though no longer fully governments, nevertheless have government-like properties. How do regimes of intergovernmental cooperation compare with direct federal administration?

One of the original justifications for federalism was that the task of governing a great nation would be too much for one government alone. If that was true in 1787, it remains so today. One may think of governmental tasks in conventional terms, such as taxation, education, defense, income support, public safety, public health, and development and administration of a system of private law (family relations, real property, corporations, contracts, torts). Or one may think of such tasks in the terms that social scientists have come to use, such as management of conflict, mobilization of consent, and policymaking and implementation.

Whatever concepts one employs, there is more to be done than a single set of representative institutions operating in the national capital is likely to do well. The United States is a sprawling, populous nation in which citizens have very high expectations of access to public power and responsiveness on the part of public officials. It is appropriate in this society that there should be many dispersed sets of representative and accountable institutions with powers of lawmaking, adjudication, and taxation. That is, there should be many governments, and the subnational governments should exist as creatures of the people rather than as creatures of the national government (that is what makes the system "federal" rather than "unitary"). The ultimate justification for the existence of all those governments is that it makes the system as a whole more truly republican, more truly "of the people," which is the touchstone for government in the United States.

When the national legislature enacts mandates without money and without ordering priorities, the resulting dilemmas are dealt with elsewhere in the governmental system, and it is arguable that they are more properly dealt with by subnational governments, which have representative properties, than by national administrative agencies, which do not. Subnational governments have more potential for considered response, resistance, and a legitimate (that is, popularly and deliberatively based) ordering of priorities. Whether such a response now occurs is debatable. There has been relatively little scholarly analysis of how states in fact respond to the various federal mandates: to what extent they actually implement them despite strains, or ignore them, or selectively adapt and revise them to fit particular circumstances, and through what processes.

For state governments to respond to the federal government assertively, entering into dialogue over policy ends and administrative means, puts a very heavy burden on them. It presumes that, in addition to reflexively ask-ing Washington for more money, they will exert themselves to influence national policymaking so as to inject more realism and pragmatism into it. It also presumes that they will assert claims to governmental prerogatives, as indeed they have been seeking to do through the State and Local Legal Center. It requires them to be as inventive in their own defense as Congress has been inventive in devising new techniques of influence over them.

The customs of intergovernmental relations change constantly. One thinks, for example, of the post–Civil War decline of the practice of state legislatures formally addressing their representatives in Congress. In the nineteenth century, it was quite common for state legislatures to speak to Congress as follows: "Be it resolved that our senators in Congress are hereby instructed, and our representatives are hereby requested, to vote for . . . ." The practice of instruction, never having been successfully institu-tionalized even in the nineteenth century, is not likely to be revived today, but this old custom may help remind states that they are constitutionally entitled to at least a voice.

They need to keep developing their voices and to use them vigorously and responsibly on behalf of policy objectives they articulate, if they are to retain a credible claim to governmental status.

4

Congress, the States, and the Supreme Court

When the Supreme Court early in 1985 reversed a decision of 1976 and decided that state and local governments must, after all, abide by federal regulation of wages and hours, it developed two main lines of argument. One was that it is difficult to define a sphere in which state governments are protected from the reach of the commerce clause. The other, and more fundamental of the two, was that the Supreme Court has no business trying.

The second argument asserted that structural features inherent in the national government, principally the representation of states in the U.S. Senate, provide adequate protection for the states' interests. And it pointed to alleged successes of the states, principally the volume of grants-in-aid, as

Published in 1986, before the Supreme Court mounted its contemporary defense of federalism, this is one of the earliest essays in the collection. It first appeared as "Preserving Federalism: Congress, the States, and the Supreme Court," in *Brookings Review*, vol. 4 (Winter–Spring 1986), pp. 32–37. It is included because the argument—that political processes do not adequately protect the state governments as members of the federal system—remains timely. For more recent statements of this argument, see Steven G. Calabresi, "Federalism and the Rehnquist Court: A Normative Defense," in Frank Goodman, ed., *The Supreme Court's Federalism: Real or Imagined? Annals of the American Academy of Political and Social Science*, vol. 574 (March 2001), pp. 24–36, and Marci A. Hamilton, "The Elusive Safeguards of Federalism," ibid., pp. 93–103.

concrete evidence of their power in national politics. For scholarly support, it drew on one relatively old law journal article, "The Political Safeguards of Federalism," by Herbert Wechsler (1954), and one much newer book, *Judicial Review and the National Political Process* (1980), by Jesse H. Choper.[1]

One wonders why, if the states' interests are so well protected by the political branches, the issue of Congress's right to regulate the wages and hours of state employees reached the Supreme Court at all. It arose because Congress in 1974 extended the Fair Labor Standards Act, which since 1938 has regulated wages and hours in much of the private economy, to cover all state and local government employment as well. An earlier Congress had covered certain categories of state and local workers—those employed in schools, hospitals, and other institutions—and in 1968 the Supreme Court had upheld the validity of its action in a case brought by Maryland.[2] But when Congress extended the act again, a 5-4 majority of the Court found its action unconstitutional, ruling in *National League of Cities* v. *Usery* (1976) that Congress could not "operate to directly displace the states' freedom to structure integral operations in areas of traditional government functions."[3] In the interim, the Court had been significantly altered by the addition of four Nixon appointees—Chief Justice Warren E. Burger and Justices Lewis F. Powell Jr., William H. Rehnquist, and Harry A. Blackmun—who joined with Potter Stewart to constitute the majority in the case. (President Ford's one appointee to the Court, Justice John Paul Stevens, was in the minority.)

Although congressional debate over the legislation in 1973 and 1974 did not completely ignore its likely effects on state and local governments or the implications in principle for federalism, it paid far more attention to the economic and social consequences of the bill as a whole—for example, its effects on youth unemployment and the rate of inflation. Not surprisingly, Congress generally enacts social policies with an eye mainly on social and economic outcomes, giving only secondary consideration to the consequences for constitutional principles or the structure of government institutions.[4] The legislation abolished exemptions from the Fair Labor Standards Act generally, not just those applying to state and local government, besides increasing the minimum wage. President Nixon's successful veto of it in 1973 rested mainly on the grounds that it would contribute to inflation and unemployment and harm the disadvantaged. That it was "an unwarranted interference with state prerogatives" entered late and only incidentally into his veto message.[5] During the debate of 1974, spokesmen for state and local governments in Congress made no effort to preserve a general exemption for them but sought merely to exempt firemen and policemen from the provisions governing overtime. The House agreed to this exemption, but the Senate defeated it by a vote of 65-29, and this time Nixon signed the bill.

Taking note of the Senate's vote, Choper carefully constructs an argument that, because senators must stand the test of election, their votes more truly reflected the "opinion" of the "states" than briefs filed by twenty-two attorneys general who asked the Court to invalidate application of the Fair Labor Standards Act to state and local employees. Choper looks specifically at the votes of the senators from those twenty-two states and finds that in seven of them both senators voted to cover the overtime of police and firemen; in ten the vote was split; and in only three did both senators vote to exempt police and firemen.[6]

Choper does not acknowledge the possibility that the senators who voted for coverage were responding to the interests of active, well-organized public employee unions, or at least that they were deferring to a committee with a pronounced pro-labor bias, the Committee on Labor and Public Welfare. Nor does he argue that "truly" representing the "opinion" of the "states," if that is what the senators were doing, is the equivalent of adequately protecting the states' role and interests as governments in the federal system. Let us grant that senators are sensitive to the preferences of the states' voters; what ground is there for supposing that the voters, or the portion of them that is active and concerned on any given issue, will attach value to preserving the federal system?

The Court's opinion of 1985 in *Garcia* v. *San Antonio Metropolitan Transit Authority,* in which a 5-4 majority overruled *National League of Cities* v. *Usery* (Blackmun having joined the other side), raises fresh doubt about the value attached to federalism within the Court. The plaintiff was a local transit authority employee seeking to collect overtime pay. A federal district court ruled against him, finding that San Antonio's operation of a mass transit system was a traditional governmental function and thus exempt from the Fair Labor Standards Act under the Court's ruling in 1976. Although the majority in *Garcia* said that there are undoubtedly limits on the federal government's power under the commerce clause to interfere with state functions, it was unwilling to carry on an effort to define what they might be. "State sovereign interests," it said, ". . . are more properly protected by safeguards inherent in the structure of the federal system than by judicially created limitations on federal power."[7] Choper, whom the opinion cited in support of this point, asserts that federalism cases raise questions of practicability only, whereas individual rights cases are matters of principle.[8]

The defenders of federalism within the Court—in this case a minority consisting of Burger, Powell, Rehnquist, and President Reagan's first appointee, Sandra Day O'Connor—insisted that federalism is indispensable to the constitutional scheme, that it promotes democratic self-government, and that the Court has a constitutional responsibility to define and protect the essentials of state sovereignty. If it abdicates, the only protection for the states will lie in Congress's "underdeveloped capacity for self-restraint," in Justice O'Connor's caustic phrase.[9]

To the extent that this dispute within the Court turns on differing interpretations of our constitutional history and differing perceptions of the value of federalism, there is probably not much an outsider can add. However, to the degree that it revolves around the political propensities of the contemporary Congress, political scientists ought to be able to help. Can Congress be relied on to protect the states? Is the large volume of grants-in-aid a credible indicator of the states' power in national politics? As a practical matter, who is more nearly correct? Is it Justice O'Connor, believing that the balance of power in our governmental system has shifted to the national side, or the *Garcia* majority, asserting that "the political process ensures that laws that unduly burden the states will not be promulgated"?[10]

The Forces of Centralization

The founding generation recognized that the government it had created, being a compound of unitary and federal features, could prove unstable. "It will be fortunate," James Madison wrote in 1828, when instability was already manifest, "if the struggle should end in a permanent equilibrium of powers."[11] The Anti-Federalists had gloomily predicted that the national side would win out, and, from the perspective of 1986, surely everyone must agree that they were right.

The Constitution itself, if only by incorporating the supremacy clause, has a national bias, reflecting the outcome of the original contest. The Tenth Amendment has proved a weak defense for the states, being not a rule of law, but merely, as Walter Berns has written, an "accessory to interpretation."[12] Not even the warmest friends of the states rely heavily on it but often resort instead to "principles inherent in the constitutional scheme."

The Supreme Court has stood with the national side through much of our history—plainly before 1837 and for several decades, at least, after its famous New Deal switch of 1937, and much more ambiguously in the intervening century. Yet even in that constitutional era to which Edward S. Corwin applied the curious label "dual federalism," the Court endorsed many extensions of the reach of the commerce clause. With the end of that era, it ceased acting as an impartial arbiter between the two levels of government and instead emerged, in the Warren years, as an aggressively nationalizing force in its own right.[13]

Economic, social, and technological developments have been powerful forces for centralization as well. Federalism is not only a constitutional principle. It rests on social and economic foundations, and as the country becomes more homogeneous socially and interdependent economically, federal legislation follows inexorably.

Against such forces (and my list does not even mention the application of military power in the Civil War, followed by constitutional amendments with immense nationalizing potential), the structural protections for the states built into the Constitution appear unavailing and badly eroded by time. Though Choper argues that the presidency contributes to protecting the states, even he discounts the importance of today's electoral college in that respect. The president sympathizes with the states, Choper argues, because he must do so in order to maintain good relations with a Congress that retains "binding local ties." He cites President Carter's early conflict with Congress over funding of federal water projects as an example of continued congressional vigilance in defense of localities.[14] Such vigilance is not in doubt. What is dubious is Choper's casual propensity to presume that any constituency-based interest can be equated with the interests of state governments as elements of the federal system.

Those who argue that Congress reliably protects the states' interests emphasize the structure of the Senate, in which the states are formally and equally represented, but they rarely pause to inquire whether equal representation assures effective representation. It did not do so in the case of the Fair Labor Standards Act amendments in 1974, when the House was more responsive to the states' interests than was the Senate, and there is really no reason why it ever should. After popular election replaced election by state legislatures in 1913, senators ceased to be under any constraint to protect the functions of state governments. Even though their electorates are defined by state boundaries, senators need not define state governments as crucial components of their constituencies. Moreover, by giving these state delegates long terms and freeing them from the necessity of voting as units (as senatorial delegations had been required to do under the Articles of Confederation), the Founders intially gave them more freedom than is generally recognized.

In sum, the forces of centralization, barely sketched here, appear to be overwhelming, while the built-in protections for the states are enfeebled. In view of this, it is necessary to ask why the states remain vigorous. At least since Woodrow Wilson's time, the states have repeatedly been declared to be dying, yet they seem never to be dead. Recurrently, commentators detect in them a "new vitality." "The States Are Leading as Washington Wallows," said a headline in the Outlook section of the *Washington Post*. Beneath the headline, two resident scholars at the American Enterprise Institute proceeded to document the competence and energy of today's state governments.[15] Surely this capacity for survival testifies to the states' power at the national level.

In a sense it does, but that power, which I believe to be great, does not flow from the scheme of representation. It flows from Congress's dependence on the states. Congress needs them to share the burdens of governing.

Sources of the States' Power

Congress attempts so much that it is easy to overlook how much it ignores. While few important matters escape it forever, even fewer are not dealt with first in the states. They remain laboratories. Consider the following items:

—In October 1985 Montana became the first state to implement legislation requiring that prices and benefits for all forms of insurance be the same for men and women. A proposed federal law mandating unisex insurance policies nationwide passed a House subcommittee in 1983, but then died. "Montana will be the laboratory for this policy idea," an attorney with the American Council of Life Insurance told the *Washington Post*.[16]

—The *Wall Street Journal*, in a story on the unreliability of computer software, reported that efforts were under way in five states to pass consumer protection laws specifically for the benefit of computer users. A member of the California State Assembly had proposed a bill to set truth-in-advertising standards, require refunds and warranties, and, in some cases, allow civil damage suits.[17]

—As of 1985 thirty-three states had begun to restore wildlife species to former habitats. The states were spending millions of dollars, most of it raised from residents who agreed to divert part of their income tax refunds to the purpose. As a result of this effort bighorn sheep are back in Oregon's mountains, beavers in Ohio's rivers, and peregrine falcons in California's skies.[18]

—Andrea Bonnicksen and Edward Brazil reported in 1985 that twenty-four states had adopted laws dealing with artificial insemination by donors, several states had laws directly or indirectly regulating in vitro fertilization, and ten states forbade women to sell a fetus for experimentation. All were laws that could be construed as forbidding ovum transfer, which Bonnicksen and Brazil identify as a third method of "alternative conception."[19]

These examples should suffice to demonstrate that the states remain active on the frontiers of domestic questions, but it is not only the frontiers that occupy them. Consider yet another news story: an alliance between liberals and conservatives in California has initiated a work-for-welfare program that "many experts expect to become standard nationwide," the *Washington Post* reported. Californians had been inspired in part by a tour of "innovative welfare programs in Massachusetts, West Virginia, and Pennsylvania." Hardly a new issue, welfare is a traditional responsibility of the states, in which federal involvement has grown steadily since passage of the Social Security Act in 1935. However, major efforts at completing the process of nationalization were unsuccessful in the 1970s and left the Washington participants exhausted. It is remarkable to see welfare reform rising anew from the states, albeit in this instance under federal prodding.[20]

If news stories seem an insufficiently dependable source of information about what the states are doing—subject, conceivably, to the influence of the states' own publicists or to journalism's tendency to exaggerate what is "new"—then consider a study of the California legislature by William K. Muir Jr. In what is surely one of the best books ever published about a legislative body, Muir writes that the California legislature in 1975–76 passed over 2,570 laws, among which were the nation's first agricultural labor relations act; a complete restructuring of prison sentencing; public school teachers' collective bargaining legislation; a $600 million increase in annual unemployment insurance taxes; a significant tort and professional reform in medical malpractice; a program to subsidize the contruction of low-income, privately owned housing; a complex scheme for regulating all building construction within a thousand-mile-long coastal zone; a comprehensive reform of eminent domain legislation; a pathbreaking and stringent nuclear energy safety act; the first euthanasia (or right to die) law in the United States; elimination of an oil-depletion income tax deduction; a new basis for taxing timber; decriminalization of both marijuana use and private adult sex acts; and provision of unemployment insurance to farm-workers. In summary, the author says, its agenda outside of foreign affairs, defense, immigration, and monetary power was "boundless." It made laws relating to every domestic matter except the post office.[21]

California's legislature is not typical, nor was 1975–76 a typical year even for it. Still, this information is reliable enough as an indicator of the scope of the legislative burden from which Congress is routinely relieved by reason of the state legislatures' existence.

In short, the states help Congress by tackling novel policy issues and by continuing to handle many familiar problems that Congress either chooses to ignore or, as with welfare, fails to find a national solution for. And, of course, the states can adapt policy to local preferences and circumstances: the laws California enacts governing private sex acts and coastal development need not suit Georgia.

Congress is already overwhelmed. Consider how much worse off it would be if the state legislatures did not exist. The inability of Congress to do more is an important source of protection for the states and in a certain sense stems from their power. They are powerful simply because they are functioning, legitimate governments in a country that now requires, or at any rate submits to, a very large amount of governing indeed.

Congress depends on the states for more than legislation. It also relies on them for administration, an aspect of the grant-in-aid relation overlooked by those who interpret the volume of federal grants as simply a measure of the states' ability to raid the federal treasury.

Congress has habitually chosen the medium of grants not so much because it loves the states more as because it loves the federal bureaucracy less. Congress loves action—it thrives on policy proclamation and goal set-ting—but it hates bureaucracy and taxes, which are the instruments of action. Overwhelmingly, it has resolved this dilemma by turning over the bulk of administration to the state governments or any organizational instrumentality it can lay its hands on whose employees are not counted on the federal payroll.

Upon examination, the power of the states in the governing sphere comes to resemble the power of the corporation in the private sphere. Political scientists of left-liberal views are fond of pointing out, quite correctly, that the need to keep the economy functioning introduces a subtle and pervasive pro-business bias into our politics.[22] There is a similar bias in favor of the states, arising out of the need to keep our governmental system functioning. The bias arises both from the legislative actions Congress does not take and from its deliberate choices of administrative strategies.

The Need for Judicial Scrutiny

The fact that Congress needs the states is no guarantee, however, that it will not abuse them, just as its dependence on corporations for productivity is no guarantee that it will not abuse them. In particular, there is a danger that Congress, in striving to close the gap between its desire to define large goals and its unwillingness to provide the administrative means to achieve them, will try to conscript the states. That is, it will give orders to them as if they were administrative agents of the national government while expecting state officials and electorates to bear whatever costs ensue. In a number of the new regulatory programs of the 1970s, Congress moved distinctly in that direction. In the Clean Air Act of 1970, for example, it addressed the states with the language of command—each state "shall" adopt a plan for controlling air pollution—a striking departure from customary constitutional forms.[23]

Like Congress, federal courts have been uninhibited by federalist principles as they have ordered the states to conform to newly discovered requirements of the equal protection and due process clauses of the Fourteenth Amendment. In the process, they have often imposed heavy burdens of expenditure—as in the "institution" cases, in which numerous states were required to overhaul institutions for the mentally ill or retarded, prison systems, and juvenile detention systems.[24] Yet courts have also protected states from the more extreme commands of Congress or, at any rate, of an administrative agency acting under what it took to be authority granted by Congress.

Under the transportation and land-use provisions of the Clean Air Act of 1970, the Environmental Protection Agency tried to compel the states to impose stringent regulations on private parties. These included such measures as gasoline rationing, parking surcharges, and review and approval of construction of parking facilities. The EPA claimed that the states' failure to comply would justify the imposition of such sanctions as "injunctive relief, imposing a receivership on certain state functions, holding a state official in civil contempt with a substantial daily fine until compliance is secured, and requiring a state to allocate funds from one portion of its budget to another in order to finance the undertakings required by the agency."[25]

Whether Congress had authorized this approach was unclear. One circuit court concluded that it had, whereas three others preferred to believe that it had not. Beyond ruling that the EPA had exceeded its statutory authority, the three strongly intimated that its actions were unconstitutional as well. In a lengthy discussion of constitutional issues, the Ninth Circuit held that a state could decline to enforce a federally prescribed program of regulation without becoming liable to sanctions and hinted that the EPA's effort to compel state action in this instance might have violated the Tenth Amendment and Article IV, section 4, which obliges the United States to guarantee to every state a republican form of government.[26]

The circuit courts stood in the way of federal conscription of the states on this occasion, and by the time any of the cases reached the Supreme Court, the EPA had retreated far enough to make them moot. But it would be rash to assume that the Supreme Court need not be ready to respond to comparable challenges to the states at other times.

To admonish the Court to be ready of course constitutes no help with the practical question of what standards it should apply to the states' defense. For those who believe, in contrast to Professor Choper, that federalism *is* a constitutional principle of the United States, the articulation of such standards ought to be an intellectual objective of high priority.[27]

5

Income Support Programs and Intergovernmental Relations

The rising interest in intergovernmental relations threatens to distort our view of the subject. Scholars have come to think of it as a discrete area of activity. New fiscal or administrative measures are advanced for the purpose of improving intergovernmental relations, and students of federalism naturally concentrate on such measures. They have spent a great deal of time in the last few years talking about revenue sharing, block grants, A-95 (the designation of a circular of the Office of Management and Budget relating to intergovernmental coordination), and Federal Regional Councils.

One should not lose sight of what is going on elsewhere. Wherever there is government in this society, there are relations among governments; fed-

This essay first appeared as "Income Support Programs and Intergovernmental Relations," in Walter F. Scheffer, ed., *General Revenue Sharing and Decentralization* (University of Oklahoma Press, 1976), pp. 41–55. This is the oldest essay in the collection and therefore the most at risk of being out of date. Nonetheless, I include it with confidence that the general points about intergovernmental relations remain valid even if specific facts have changed. By far the most important change is that in 1996 Congress replaced Aid to Families with Dependent Children (AFDC) with Temporary Assistance for Needy Families (TANF). Unlike AFDC, under which the federal government promised to pay a share of the cost of supporting all families found to be eligible, TANF is a block grant, under which the federal government promises to pay the states a stipulated sum. TANF was designed to promote work, for example, by imposing time limits on receipt of assistance. Throughout this essay, I have used endnotes to update some of the most important facts, but the reader should keep in mind that except for a great deal of material added to the notes (see pages 172–74), it was written a quarter century ago. The text is virtually unchanged.

eralism is a pervasive fact of our public life and institutional arrangements. In studying intergovernmental relations, it is a good idea at least occasionally to start with what governments are doing in general rather than with what is going on specifically in intergovernmental relations. A-95 and even general revenue sharing matter much less to most Americans than what is happening in the schools, or the welfare department, or the police department.

Governments in general are doing what governments have always done, only much more so. They are protecting the national security; managing the economy; instructing children; maintaining public order; supporting the poor; building public works for transportation or recreation, flood protection or agricultural development; protecting the public health; and regulating economic activity. Probably the most striking feature of government activity in general today is the sharp rise in spending for social welfare.

The staff of the Office of Research and Statistics of the Social Security Administration does periodic analyses of trends in social welfare expenditures, in which they include social insurance, public assistance, health and medical programs, veterans' programs, education, housing, and such relatively minor items as vocational rehabilitation, institutional care, and child nutrition. They found that in 1973 half of the federal budget was going for social welfare. For all governments (federal, state, and local) this category's proportion was 55 percent. The total expenditure was $215.2 billion, which becomes comprehensible only when translated into a per capita figure. Public social welfare spending amounted to $1,007 for every man, woman, and child in this country. Only a decade earlier, in 1965, the first year of Lyndon Johnson's Great Society, the comparable figure was a mere $391, which adjusted for inflation was $508. Thus per capita spending for social welfare doubled in less than a decade. National priorities have changed quite dramatically.[1]

I cite these figures as background, in order to remind us of where governmental action is and where, therefore, we should direct much of our attention as students of intergovernmental relations. In this essay, I want to look at one component of social welfare spending: those programs devoted to income support. I refer to a large and amorphous bundle. Any definition is at least a little bit arbitrary. Roughly speaking, I will be referring to the programs found in the Social Security Act, the basic federal statute for income support programs, plus food stamps. The Social Security Act covers the following major programs: social insurance—in official language, OASDI (old-age, survivors, and disability insurance), in common parlance, "Social Security"; Supplemental Security Income (SSI); Aid to Families with Dependent Children (AFDC); Medicaid; unemployment compensation; and grants to the states for social services.

To this bundle, I propose to add for present purposes food stamps, the fastest-growing single program of income support.[2] It is a major addition to the federal government's measures for income maintenance but has not been much publicized until recently. One might argue that I should include housing programs or veterans' pensions or should exclude grants for social services, which do not directly support the incomes of poor individuals. One has to draw the boundary lines of the subject somewhere. The contents of the Social Security Act make a convenient and logical, if large, bundle. At the same time, to exclude food stamps would be a gross and distorting omission.

My purpose is to inquire into the state of intergovernmental relations in this very large sphere of governmental activity. What are the main features of intergovernmental relations? What are the trends?

Features of Intergovernmental Relations

The first feature to note is the high degree of interdependence among governments. The main point about intergovernmental relations is their pervasiveness. I can say this even though I have included in my bundle the Social Security program, which is presumed to be a purely federal program. On inspection, however, it is not purely federal after all. The federal government relies on state governments for much of the administration of the disability portion of the Social Security program. It is up to state agencies to make the initial determinations of disability through which an individual qualifies for monthly payments from the Social Security Administration.

This is an important function. Today it seems more important than ever before, because disability recipient rates are climbing fast, at a high cost to Social Security payroll taxpayers. Until 1969, the number of disability insurance recipients grew steadily but slowly. Since then a sharp, unexpected increase has occurred. This is one reason for the much-publicized financial troubles of the Social Security system. No one knows what the explanation is, but one theory has to do with intergovernmental relations. At one time, the Social Security Administration reviewed 100 percent of the state determinations of eligibility. (It can deny state approvals but not reverse state denials.) A few years ago it started to review only a small sample (5 percent). Perhaps this change in intergovernmental relations has contributed to the sharply rising cost of the disability portion of the Social Security program, which is turn is contributing to the rising cost of Social Security, which soon will require higher than anticipated taxation of virtually all Americans.[3]

The second notable feature of intergovernmental relations in the field of income support is variety. Interdependence appears in a wide range of forms and patterns. Sometimes state governments are administrative agents of the federal government, as in the case of the disability insurance portion of Social Security that I just described. State agencies make determinations of disability using standards and guides provided by the federal Department of Health, Education, and Welfare.[4] No implementing state legislation is involved. HEW contracts with the state agencies to administer its standards. The same kind of relationship obtains in the food stamp program. Uniform standards of income eligibility are promulgated by the secretary of Agriculture in consultation with HEW. State agencies administer those standards on behalf of the federal government.[5]

More surprisingly, the reverse relationship also exists. The federal government sometimes acts as the administrative agent for state governments. This happens in the Supplemental Security Income program, under which Congress has set national minimum standards for the income of elderly, blind, and disabled persons. The federal government pays a standard amount. State governments then may supplement the federal payment. States may administer the supplement themselves or have the secretary of HEW do it for them. The federal government will carry out administration in accordance with state-prescribed standards, even if these standards incorporate certain intrastate variations. Sixteen states and the District of Columbia have chosen federal administration of their supplementary payments.[6]

Other types of relationships are also possible. There is of course the familiar form of federal grants-in-aid to the states. The federal government offers money to the states in return for carrying out a national purpose, but the states are not mere administrative agents of the federal government. In principle they may accept the aid or not, and they carry out the aided programs under their own statutes.

This is the pattern in AFDC, Medicaid, and social services, but within this cluster there are significant differences. AFDC and Medicaid conform to the pattern of the categorical grant. Statutes and regulations spell out the federal intent in fairly specific terms.[7] Grants for social services under title 20 of the Social Security Act, which became law in January 1975, are given under more permissive terms. Officials in Washington view this as an example of a block grant or special revenue sharing. The statute sets forth some very general goals that the states are supposed to pursue, and it prohibits certain uses of funds. States may do anything with the money that is not prohibited, whereas with AFDC and Medicaid they are told much more clearly what kind of activity may qualify for federal support.

Unemployment is yet another case, unusual though not unique in American experience. It uses the method of tax credits. The federal government levies a payroll tax on employers to finance unemployment compensation but authorizes credits to employers in states that have enacted such taxes themselves. The effect was to induce state unemployment compensation programs.[8]

A third main point about intergovernmental relations in the area of income support is that they are unstable. There is hardly an intergovernmental relation that has not recently been changed or that someone is not trying to change.

There may soon be a campaign for a national program of unemployment compensation. A recent staff report of the House Ways and Means Committee points out the drawbacks of state administration of disability determinations. Major amendments to the food stamp act in 1971 very much altered federal-state relations that had prevailed since 1964. The Supplemental Security Income program, which substantially altered federal-state relations in the field of public assistance, was passed in 1972, and Congress keeps tinkering with it. A program of national health insurance, which appears to be high on the public agenda, would end the Medicaid program. President Nixon's family assistance plan would have replaced AFDC. Though defeated, it may have made welfare reform a more or less permanent item on the national agenda. Social services grants have agitated federal-state relations for several recent years, and laws were passed in 1962, 1967, and 1974.

Trends in Intergovernmental Relations

This particular pot is always boiling—which brings me to my final and most difficult task, that of assessing trends. The trend in this most important area of government activity is toward centralization. Leave aside proposed changes, such as national health insurance, and look just at what has actually happened. Major steps have been taken toward nationalization of income support programs.[9]

Historically, state governments or their local subdivisions in this country have made the most important decisions about giving poor relief, to borrow an old-fashioned term. They decided how poor someone had to be in order to qualify for aid, and how much aid that poor person should be given. Since enactment of the Social Security Act in 1935, the federal government has given grants-in-aid to help the states support most poor persons, but until very recently it left to the states the fundamental decisions, namely, those about standards of eligibility and size of payments.

This has changed for a good many of the poor. The federal government now guarantees that elderly, blind, or disabled persons will have monthly incomes of a certain level ($146 if they are living alone, or $219 for a couple).[10] The federal government makes such payments itself, directly, rather than giving grants-in-aid to the states. Such payments constitute the federal government's Supplemental Security Income program, enacted in 1972, put into operation in 1974, and under fire from Congress in 1975 because of innumerable administrative problems.[11]

In addition, the federal government now offers an income subsidy in the form of food stamps to everyone in the country who receives public assistance or whose income and assets fall below a certain level. Participants must purchase stamps; in return for their purchases they get stamps worth more than what they have paid. They may then use these stamps to buy food. The difference between what they pay and the value of the stamps is provided by a federal subsidy. Federal spending for food stamps jumped from $251 million in 1969 to about $4 billion in 1975.[12] This is a form of national guaranteed income, given to the working as well as to the non-working poor, though it comes in coupons, not cash.

The contemporary food stamp program dates from 1964. When it began, it followed the traditional pattern of public assistance in that state governments set standards of need and eligibility. They decided who should qualify for food stamps. In this program, a centralizing trend set in very fast. State eligibility standards were superseded by federal standards in 1971. The federal government now makes the big decisions here, as it does in regard to cash support for the aged, blind, and disabled.

With Social Security, which is predominantly federal, SSI and food stamps make up a bundle of big and important programs in which the federal government makes the big and important decisions, even if it relies selectively on the state governments for administration.

Yet it would be a careless analyst who would claim that the United States has federalized welfare functions. It is one thing to identify trends and quite another to describe reality. It is hard to describe in a clear and succinct way the balance of functions between federal and state governments because that balance, as always in our history, is subtle and complicated. While change in the direction of centralization is discernible, so also one can discern the persistence of important areas of power and discretion for the states and of important differences among states in the way the poor are treated.

For one thing, national standards of need and payments have not been imposed in AFDC, the biggest single category of aid to the poor. There the pattern of federal grants-in-aid to the states persists, and the states are free to make basic decisions as they always have been, except that federal courts have increasingly intervened to set standards for determinations of eligibility.[13] Thus in a recent month the average payment for an AFDC family ranged from $50.87 in Mississippi to $304.12 in New York.[14] The same is true in Medicaid. There are as many programs as there are participating states. States do very different things and provide medical assistance of widely varying liberality with the federal grants that they get.[15]

For another thing, even where federalization has taken place—with regard to payments for the aged, blind, and disabled—there is no uniform national program. Far from it. There is a national floor, a common minimum payment, but beyond that, things are more chaotic than ever. Interstate differences in payments persist, and now are compounded by intrastate differences among individuals, some of which are the freakish result of the transition from a state to a national program.

Let me try to convey some of the complexity of SSI. This will be confusing, but my main point, which is that we do not have a uniform national program, will be clear even, or especially, to those who get a bit lost in the labyrinth of program detail.[16]

The federal government provides a standard minimum payment. But a first rule of American politics—probably a wise rule, conducive to domestic tranquillity if not to fairness—is that a privilege or benefit once granted shall not be withdrawn. Accordingly, when Congress enacted SSI, it stipulated that no one's grant should be cut. Anyone who was receiving old-age assistance, aid to the blind, or aid to the permanently and totally disabled in 1972 was to continue to receive at least as much as he or she had received before. That meant that states which had been paying more than the new federal minimum were required to continue to pay the additional amount to those persons who were already on the rolls. However, they did not have to pay the additional amount to persons who came on the rolls henceforth.

A second rule of American politics is that special favors shall be granted to groups with the power to extract them from Congress. Our lawmakers

are not much embarrassed by exceptional provisions of laws that in principle are supposed to apply uniformly. I have just said that states are required
to supplement payments if, before enactment of SSI, they had been paying
the poor more than SSI provides. This federal requirement for supplementary payments does not apply, however, if a state constitution contains provisions that prevent compliance. As it happens, the constitution of Texas,
and of Texas alone, prevents compliance.

States also may freely choose to supplement the federal minimum. As I
have said, all are required to supplement to the extent that such supplements will hold individuals harmless against enactment of SSI. But beyond
that, many choose to guarantee their elderly, disabled, and blind residents
a higher standard of living than the federal SSI program provides. As of
1971 thirty-three states and the District of Columbia were providing
optional supplementation, that is, were meeting a higher standard than the
federal standard for all eligible persons. Sixteen states were providing
mandatory supplementation, that is, were assuring, out of their own funds,
that no one lost by reason of enactment of the federal program. Then there
was Texas, in a class by itself.[17]

Among the states that are providing optional supplementation, there is
a very wide range in the size of the supplement. Massachusetts adds $123 a
month to the federal payment for an aged person, $113 a month for a dis-
abled person, and $146 a month for a blind person. Oklahoma adds $15 a
month to the federal payment for each. Oklahoma's $15 exceeds by $1 the
amount that Michigan pays monthly as a supplement. I will not take time
to explore the intrastate differences that have developed in the wake of SSI.
The basic point—that interstate differences survive—should be clear.[18]

Let me turn briefly to food stamps. Again, there is a national program.
Yet for the categories of poor supported by SSI, states are permitted to "cash
out" food stamps, that is, give recipients cash instead of stamps. Five states
do so. This national program begins to look not quite so national after all.
And it does not look national enough to Washington watchdogs, liberal
critics who note that not all eligible persons are actually benefiting from
food stamps and that the proportion of the eligible population participating shows great differences among states.[19]

The participation rate falls below 20 percent in Alaska, North Dakota,
and Wyoming. It rises above 50 percent in California, the District of
Columbia, Illinois, New Jersey, Rhode Island, and Washington. Offhand, it
looks as though this difference is accounted for by differences in the degree
of urbanization, but can one be sure? Differences in urbanization would
not seem to account for the discrepancy between Washington State, with

one of the highest participation rates in the country, and my own adopted state of Virginia, which has one of the lowest rates, barely above 20 percent. Is this difference perhaps partly accounted for by the fact that Washington relies mainly on post offices as food stamp outlets, whereas Virginia relies primarily on banks? That is a tempting explanation, yet other states, such as Connecticut and Pennsylvania, which rely even more heavily on banks than Virginia, have relatively high rates. Interstate differences persist; no one knows why they are as great as they are.[20]

Finally, as a third instance of the complexity of federal-state relations and of the persistence of some independence of the states, I cite briefly the case of social services grants. They are an interesting case for students of intergovernmental relations.[21] In 1962 the federal government began making grants to the states for social services. A decade later, expenditures suddenly jumped, approaching $1.7 billion in 1972. Social services grants had turned into what the *Washington Post* called "back-door revenue sharing." States had discovered a loophole in the law and were exploiting it for purposes of fiscal relief. This was done primarily by Illinois and New York, but other states did it too. Between 1972 and 1974 the federal administration struggled, with moderate success, to close the loophole, bring spending under control, and direct it toward purposes that responded to federal preferences in at least a general way. Today the states are getting $2.5 billion a year, and getting it on very permissive terms.[22] Is this a case of centralization or decentralization? Federal aid to the states increased, on terms that the states found very much to their advantage.

I wish I might end on a less ambiguous note, with a finding of fact that would ring in the ears. However, the realities of American federalism are ambiguous in the extreme. In intergovernmental relations, it is often hard to tell in which direction influence runs and whether the federal government is controlling the states or states are raiding the federal treasury. On the one hand, we seem constantly to be moving in the direction of a national community with one government. On the other hand, we seem never to get there. State governments persist. They retain vital functions. Important differences in public policies among states persist.

The trend systemwide is centralization. Beware of statements to the contrary. Revenue sharing and less significant acts of decentralization in the past few years have not reversed that trend, in my judgment.[23] But the movement toward a centralized system is slow and uneven and must advance over and around a thousand institutional barriers, visible and invisible. Those of us who call ourselves experts are not sure—at least, I am not—of just where we stand at any given time.

6

Up-to-Date in Kansas City

My title, as anyone over the age of fifty will recognize, is from Rodgers and Hammerstein's *Oklahoma*. My mode of analysis is from the James boys: James Madison and James Q. Wilson. My purpose is to ask what difference American federalism makes. It was Wilson and our common mentor, Edward C. Banfield, from whom I learned to ask the "what difference does it make" question. I take Madison to have been an early practitioner of the kind of analysis that the question calls for.

By American federalism I mean an arrangement whereby the functions of government are divided between one national government and numerous subnational ones, all resting on popular consent and written constitutions. American states are not creatures of the national government. State governments derive authority from their respective constituent communities. When the people of the United States created the government of the United States, they included in the Constitution various protections for the states. Some of these—the guarantee of a republican form of government and the reservation of powers soon declared by the Tenth Amendment—have proven to be of the parchment sort. Others are more deeply rooted and effective: the assurance of equal representation in the Senate, which is secured against amendment, and the assurance that the states' boundaries will not be changed without the consent of their legislatures.

This essay first appeared as "Up to Date in Kansas City: Reflections on American Federalism," *PS: Political Science and Politics*, vol. 25 (December 1992), pp. 671–75.

Federalism importantly affects the setting within which American public administrators operate. I am tempted to say that it *is* the setting within which they operate. Yet political scientists have not done as much as they might to explain what difference federalism makes either to the work of administrators or, more broadly, to the political life of all Americans. What are the consequences of distributing the work of government among many governments that are formally independent of one another?

There is a helpful literature that explores the consequences of locating functions at one or another level. In effect, it asks what difference scale and inclusiveness make. I have in mind the work of Paul Peterson and his associates in *City Limits* and *When Federalism Works*, as well as a chapter on "The Constituency" in Grant McConnell's *Private Power and American Democracy*. Robert Dahl and Edward Tufte's *Size and American Democracy* is also pertinent.[1] My question here is different from theirs. I am not asking how the allocation of functions among jurisdictions of different scale affects policy outcomes or citizen participation. Rather, I want to inquire into the consequences of having so many jurisdictions.

Madison's most celebrated observation on this subject appears in *Federalist* No. 51:

> In the compound republic of America, the power surrendered by the people is first divided between two distinct governments, and then the portion allotted to each subdivided among distinct and separate departments. Hence a double security arises to the rights of the people. The different governments will control each other, at the same time that each will be controlled by itself.[2]

Federalism is justified for its contribution to securing rights. The argument had been made earlier by Hamilton in *Federalist* No. 28:

> In a confederacy the people, without exaggeration, may be said to be entirely the masters of their own fate. Power being almost always the rival of power, the general government will at all times stand ready to check the usurpations of the state governments, and these will have the same disposition toward the general government. The people, by throwing themselves into either scale, will infallibly make it preponderate. If their rights are violated by either, they can make use of the other as an instrument of redress.[3]

This is the starting point for defenses of federalism. Citing both passages, the Supreme Court in *Gregory* v. *Ashcroft* (1991) observed that perhaps the principal benefit of the federal system is that it constitutes a check on abuses of government power. The court discerned other advantages as well: sensitivity to the diverse needs of a heterogeneous society; increased opportunity for citizen involvement in democratic processes; more innovation and experimentation; and heightened responsiveness that results from competition among the states for a mobile citizenry.[4]

This is the received wisdom about federalism, the text in the textbooks. It is what youthful law professors incant when they write articles defending federalism, as they occasionally do. It is what a task force of the Reagan administration said when it set out to argue that federalism should be preserved, an effort that culminated in an executive order of little or no consequence.[5] Does anyone really believe it? Can any of it be seen happening? Surely political science has—or can have if it tries—something to say on this subject.

For help in thinking about the consequences of federalism, I propose to repair again to Madison—not to *Federalist* No. 51, the force of which is blunted by an excess of familiarity, but to a less well known essay on "consolidation" that he published in Philip Freneau's *National Gazette* late in 1791. The piece was unsigned. Madison was writing as a partisan, the congressional leader of the group that would soon become the Republican Party. I see no more reason therefore to discount what he said than to discount the essays of *The Federalist*, which in their own way were partisan as well.

The piece is cast as an argument against consolidation of the states into one government. He raises two objections, thus sketching out two broad defenses of federalism. First, he says that consolidation would increase the power of the president by compelling a legislative delegation on practical grounds: "the incompetency of one Legislature to regulate all the various objects belonging to the local governments, would evidently force a transfer of many of them to the Executive department." Second, he says that consolidation would make it hard for the people to maintain control over the national legislature. "Were the State governments abolished, the same space of country that would produce an undue growth of the executive power, would prevent that control on the Legislative body which is essential to a faithful discharge of its trust." The people of the nation could not act as a whole, and this would raise the danger of "partial expressions of the public mind" or, ultimately, "a universal silence and insensibility, leaving the whole government to that *self directed course* which . . . is the natural propensity of every government."[6]

The Madison of 1791 thus points us in two directions: he invites us to look at how federalism affects the roles of and relations among the institutions of the national government, and, second, to consider how federalism affects the relation between the people and the national government, its legislature in particular.

I plan to borrow Madison's outline. In regard to the first point, I will argue that whatever federalism may have done to limit the powers of the president pales by comparison with what it did to enlarge those of the federal judiciary. In regard to the second point, the results have been more obscure, but I will argue that, on the whole, federalism did not evolve in a way that helped to sustain popular control of national governing institutions.

The Effects of Federalism on National Institutions

The extraordinary power of the American judiciary has numerous sources. To explain it, one would turn first to culture and ideology: to the common law tradition, higher law doctrines, the place of lawyers in American intellectual life, and the force of John Marshall's mind. But in its application, judicial power has been broadened enormously by the specific structural influence of American federalism.

Most obviously, federalism enhances judicial power in two main ways. First, by dividing power among governments, it necessitates an umpire. Courts often, although not necessarily, perform that function.[7] They do so in the United States, as the byzantine history of commerce clause interpretation amply attests. Second, American federalism has been characterized by sweeping constitutional prohibitions against the states, which are cast in language that invites judicial interpretation: "No State shall . . . pass any . . . Law impairing the Obligation of Contracts. . . ." "[No state shall] deprive any person of life, liberty, or property, without due process of law; nor deny to any person within its jurisdiction the equal protection of the laws." Without federalism, there would be no Fourteenth Amendment. Without the Fourteenth Amendment, the judiciary would have a far narrower ambit. Judicial power derives in large measure from the exercise of judicial review, but it is easy to forget how rarely, relatively speaking, judicial review has been used against Congress.[8] There have been spectacular exceptions, but in general government by judges is government at the expense of the states, whose combination of inferior constitutional status and broad, bedrock functions has made them a target at once easy and irresistible.

To understand why Madison expected the institutions of federalism to help control the national legislature, one needs to look both at what he said and what he did. He anticipated that state legislatures would address the national one. In the essay on consolidation, he wrote that "neither the voice nor the sense of ten or twenty millions of people, spread through so many latitudes as are comprehended within the United States, could ever be combined or called into effect, if deprived of those local organs, through which both can now be conveyed." I assume that by "local organs" he meant state legislatures primarily. He and Jefferson used them in 1798 and 1799 to protest the Alien and Sedition Acts. This was a pure case of seeking to secure rights by pitting the power of state governments against that of the national government. It did not work very well. When the Virginia and Kentucky legislatures asked other state legislatures to join them in protest, they got no help.[9] Early on, parties and elections proved more efficacious than address by the state legislatures to deter Congress from pursuing "a self-directed course."[10] And the people eventually would learn that they were supposed to look to courts for protection of their rights.

Nevertheless, until the Civil War it was quite common for state legislatures to address the members of Congress with the following form: "Be it resolved that our senators in Congress are hereby instructed, and our representatives are requested, to vote for. . . ." They acted as if congressional delegations were in some degree accountable to them. Then this expectation waned, a victim both of the war and of the rise of popular election of senators. Significantly, as William Riker showed in an article in the *American Political Science Review* in the mid-1950s, even when state legislatures chose members of the Senate, they were not able to enforce instructions upon them.[11] Intergovernmental communication between elected, representative bodies about what policy should be did not become institutionalized in American federalism. Nor have state and local officials sat in the national legislature, as they do in Germany.

The direct intergovernmental dialogue that does take place—and a great deal takes place as the levels of government become ever more engaged and interdependent—is largely within the less popular parts of government: courts and administrative agencies. Under federalism, advantage flows to those interests or institutions that are able to collaborate across the intergovernmental divide. Judges, administrators, and, often, judicial-administrative combinations have such an advantage. Judges talk to judges and administrators to administrators across the jurisdictional boundaries of federalism with relative ease, their shared roles and specialized vocabularies facilitating such talk. Hence the complaint, prominent in the literature on federalism not many years ago, about "vertical functional autocracies," in reference to professional administrators.[12] Hence, too, I believe, the growing resemblance in recent decades between federal and state judicial policy outputs. State judges became more liberal and activist partly by attending to what federal judges had to say and emulating or surpassing it.

Of course, the intergovernmental dialogue does not always consist of like institutions talking to each other. Much of intergovernmental communication consists of federal courts admonishing various state and local officeholders about schools, prisons, mental health institutions, or the conduct of police forces in enforcing criminal law. In effect, the judges are instructing whole polities, which are internally differentiated.

Some very important policy choices have emerged from these exchanges. Busing did. So did the Kansas City alternative to busing, in which a federal judge, Russell Clark, ordered extreme spending on city schools, far beyond anything that an elected body would have secured approval for from its electorate. Sometimes in these exchanges judges are at odds with state and local administrators—as, say, in the conflict between Judge William Wayne Justice and W. J. Estelle Jr. in regard to the Texas prisons—but it may also happen that administrators invite courts to order them to do things that they would like to do but cannot get popular endorsement for doing.[13]

However much we have come to rely on them, courts are ill equipped to govern. They lack not only the purse and the sword, but personnel and practical knowledge. They need advice about what to prescribe in their decrees. Sometimes they get this from experts independent of any government, but often they find it in what expert administrators, the functional specialists within governments, have proposed to do in particular places or have enunciated as the standard for what should be done everywhere. Judges become parasitic on administrators and vice versa. In the Texas prison case, Judge Justice ordered the U.S. Department of Justice to appear as *amicus curiae* and instructed it "to investigate fully the facts alleged in the prisoners' complaints, to participate in [the] civil action [before the court] with the full rights of a party thereto, and to advise this court at all stages of the proceedings as to any action deemed appropriate."[14] In this, Judge Justice was borrowing a technique that Judge Frank M. Johnson had used in a prison case in Alabama. Publics and the officials whom they have elected to office await the results of these judicial-administrative combinations, and then they have to devise a response.

That so much of the talking from the federal side of intergovernmental relations is done by judges means that many state and local actors feel excluded from the talk. They resent having to submit to authority that is both unelected and inaccessible. This is evidenced by the anger and frustration among, say, neighborhood opponents of busing in Boston, or citizens of Mobile, Alabama, who objected to having a ward-based local government decreed for them under the Voting Rights Act, or the Kansas City residents who tore up their voter registration cards and mailed them to Judge Clark, brandished tea bags at protest meetings, or paid their taxes under protest, forcing Jackson County to put the collections in escrow.[15]

For their part, judges sometimes seem not to be particularly comfortable with the prolonged dialogues that intergovernmental policymaking forces upon them. They like to decide—and by deciding, settle—cases and controversies, not engage in lengthy conversations with an aroused populace or its elected representatives. The *Roe* majority in the Supreme Court developed a palpable resentment at the way that state legislatures kept coming back at them in the matter of abortion. Judge Justice remarked before an audience at Harvard's Kennedy School that "I would as soon have a live rattlesnake thrust at me as a lawsuit dealing with constitutional claims against an administrative organization."[16]

Madison's idea of 1787—that the veto on state laws that he so badly wanted be lodged in the national legislature—was surely not very practical. One's mind boggles at the thought of today's congressional staffs poring over the output of state legislatures, deciding which laws they will recommend to the members for veto. But that idea at least had the virtue of symmetry. The people's representatives at one level would have been overruling the people's representatives at the other. Instead the veto over state laws is lodged in judges appointed for life, and it has been expanded into a much broader function of general supervision over state institutions and administrative practices. The often tense exchanges between federal judges and state and local polities, whose members do not fully comprehend—how could they possibly comprehend?—why the judges have the power they do, are artifacts of American federalism, or more precisely of America's peculiar mix of federalism and constitutionalism.

Madison would have reason to be disappointed by the evolution of federalism—and the disappointment would go much deeper than anything my analysis so far would suggest. While he argued in 1791 for many governments, he argued more passionately for one society. He wrote: "But if a consolidation of the States into one government be an event so justly to be avoided, it is not less to be desired . . . that a consolidation should prevail in their interests and affections."[17]

One hardly needs to offer reasons for advocating social harmony, but it is worth noting the three that Madison gave. If there were a harmony of interests in the nation, then it would be easier for Congress to legislate and, correspondingly, it would be less necessary to make delegations to the executive: limiting executive power was very much on Madison's mind in 1791, at the height of the Jeffersonians' conflict with Hamilton. Second, it would be easier to concur in the choice, through election, of a president. Finally, it would be easier for the people to unite in opposition to oppression.

Alas, the consolidation of interests and affections that Madison hoped for did not soon take place. Federalism had developed in the first place because of Americans' uncertainty about whether or to what extent they wished to be one political community. In the short run that uncertainty grew more acute, until it had to be resolved by force, which of course did not resolve it fully, but left its own legacy of animosity.

As Madison anticipated, disharmony in the society made it hard for the national legislature to legislate. Regional differences, represented within it and exacerbated by overrepresentation of the South, limited what it could do. For decades after Reconstruction it could not act at all on civil rights legislation, while on other subjects it was often unable to achieve policy coherence, let alone precision. Grant-in-aid statutes typically stated national objectives only in the most general and permissive terms. Regulatory statutes were silent on the question of preemption, leaving courts to decide, in their role as umpire, whether state governments had been superseded. Other institutions acted instead: to some extent, as Madison feared, the federal executive, which benefited from discretion under congressional enactments yet remained relatively weak; to a great extent the state governments, exercising residual constitutional powers; and, once again, crucially, the judiciary.

National courts stepped, or were drawn, into the vacuum. It became their function to make national policy where the national legislature could not. More, it became their mission in the 1960s under the leadership of Chief Justice Earl Warren to assail the social differences that underlay federalism and even the institutions of federalism itself, as in the reapportionment decisions.

Again, one sees how federalism has enlarged the role of the courts, here subtly and indirectly, by institutionalizing interjurisdictional differences that courts are the institution apparently best able to correct when social forces develop to demand correction. The legislatures' default, deriving from their structure, becomes the courts' opportunity or obligation.

Federalism and Popular Control of Government

In closing, let me take up once more, briefly, the second and more elusive strand of my argument: that federalism has been disappointing as a means for the people's limiting the power of government. Two factual premises are, I think, indisputable. First, federalism has conspicuously failed to do what might most confidently have been expected of it. It has not provided a stable set of understandings about how to distinguish the national from the local. Americans are forever searching for that distinction without finding it. It is no sooner declared to have been found than it is lost in a sea of social, economic, and ideological change. Interdependence among governments, always great, constantly grows. The national relentlessly encroaches on the local.

Nonetheless—and this is the second factual premise—large numbers of governments survive, with structures intact even if their functions are hopelessly indistinct. Disliking government, Americans nonetheless seem to like governments, for they have so many of them. And these many governments provide many potential arenas for political action and policy innovation. What are the consequences for popular control of having so many places in which to engage in governing?

One could make out a case, I suppose, that checking and balancing does occur, in part passively, as the mere by-product of the separate governments' existence, but in part effectuated by the people through an instrumental choice of governments. One thinks of the tax revolt that began in the 1970s, a political event of surpassing importance.[18] It profoundly changed the political context of policy discourse, warning governments against pursuing a self-directed course. Effectuated through California, Massachusetts, and other states, it affected national politics as well. Perhaps it would have emerged eventually out of interparty competition at the national level; Howard Jarvis, who led the grassroots tax revolt in California, may not have been indispensable to Ronald Reagan. I do not think that that is a foregone conclusion, however. At the very least, it reveals something about American government; the revolt against big government that in certain European unitary states was manifested in conservative victories in national elections started here at the subnational level.

Yet the dominant pattern of policymaking in our federalism of pervasively shared functions seems to me, not so much checking and balancing by design of the people, but opportunistic cost shifting and benefit distribution by design of elected officeholders in the context of a general obfuscation of responsibility and the constitutionalization of everything.[19] The upshot is that the electorate can have no idea who is in charge, and is caused either to cease caring and to lapse into "universal silence and insensibility," or, if it dares to care, to become disillusioned when the president, upon whom its expectations innocently focus, fails to deliver, as fail he must in respect to most domestic matters. Presidential candidates campaign as if they were to be the national superintendent of schools, while local superintendents, if they are prudent, will keep for ready reference a handbook of law and education, in which many Supreme Court decisions are entered.

The existence of the large number of governments provides wonderful opportunities for forum shopping, which national elites with policy agendas engage in. Not all forums are equal, of course. I am thinking of petitioning a federal judge for a right to vote in California. Sacramento is a long way from Charlottesville, but I have begun to notice that as a citizen of the United States I am often governed by California. It gives us much of our air pollution policy. It started the tax revolt. The first court to rule that the constitutional right to privacy extended to the woman's decision to have an abortion was the Supreme Court of California. When I studied welfare programs, I learned that federal administrators lived in fear of California, never knowing what it would invent to exploit federal law. What it does not exploit, it often defies, as, for example, nursing home regulations under Medicaid.

Our federalism makes many governments accessible to many interests, but there are bound to be biases in this wildly unsymmetrical system. Some governments do more and some interests do better than others.

The social functions of federalism may be more significant than the political and governmental ones. By sustaining subnational communities with some residual degree of governmental independence and distinctiveness, federalism gives individuals choices about where to live. This gives inequality a spatial form, because of course the better-off use their freedom to congregate in communities that suit their tastes and use the power of local governments to protect their property values and life-styles. Thus federalism in its social form, helping to give definition to distinct communities, is a leading ground of the continuing American battle between liberty and equality. Equalization of school finance is the issue that currently epitomizes this struggle.

How one judges federalism may well depend on where one stands in this fight—not school finance specifically, but the larger and longer-lasting fight, begun at the framing of the Constitution and even before, about whether there should be one political community or many, and how much freedom the many communities should have to define and govern themselves. What makes federalism a most interesting subject is that it is entwined with the issue of community. It is inseparable from one of the most fundamental of political questions: what constitutes a community? As an institutional form, federalism arises out of the difficulty that people experience in giving an unambiguous answer to that question.

Thus federalism gains interest and importance for political scientists and public administrators and ordinary citizens as one views it in social terms. Madison may have been uncharacteristically wide of the mark in supposing that there could be one society with many governments and that there would be any point in such an arrangement. Unless federalism does sustain communities that feel themselves to be such, it is hard to justify. The American version, at least, is hard to justify today on grounds purely governmental, as a means of achieving an optimal balance among branches of the national government and of enabling the people to maintain control over government generally by making instrumental use of one or another level of government.

7

Federalism and the
Politics of Tobacco

In the fall of 1998, the United States acquired a new regime of tobacco
control. It developed in a most unusual way: not through action of the
national legislature or a national regulatory agency, nor through a uniform
code of state governments, but rather through lawsuits filed by more than
forty state attorneys general against the major cigarette manufacturers.
These lawsuits, which rested mainly, though not exclusively, on claims for
recovery of Medicaid costs allegedly attributable to smoking, resulted initially in four individual settlements by state governments (Mississippi,
Florida, Texas, and Minnesota) and then one comprehensive settlement
embracing all of the remaining forty-six states.

The settlements required the manufacturers to pay more than $240 bil-
lion to the state governments and the National Association of Attorneys
General in the next twenty-five years and imposed numerous restrictions
on their advertising and marketing practices, such as prohibition of bill-
boards and mass transit posters.[1] Their most important effects on the market were a sharp rise in the price of cigarettes, which was intended by
tobacco's opponents to discourage consumption, and cartelization of the
industry, which was designed by framers of the master settlement to pro-

This essay first appeared as "Federalism and the Politics of Tobacco" in *Publius: The
Journal of Federalism*, vol. 31 (Winter 2001), pp. 47–63.

tect manufacturers from competition by new entrants who were not bound by the agreement.

To their proponents, principally the attorneys general who engineered them, the settlements were a great victory for the American people in the war on tobacco, which is "the leading preventable cause of death" in the United States.[2] To critics, a relatively small number of persons located mostly in university faculties, think tanks, and business associations such as the U.S. Chamber of Commerce, the settlements were deeply flawed public policy, framed in private by the contestants to serve their respective interests, contrary to the Constitution and antitrust laws. Arguably, they violated the constitutional grant of power to Congress to regulate interstate commerce; the constitutional provision that requires Congress to approve interstate compacts; First Amendment prohibitions against restraints on speech and assembly (because of certain prohibitions on advertising political activity by the cigarette industry); and Fifth and Fourteenth Amendment prohibitions against deprivation of property without due process of law. By signing the master settlement, the industry agreed not to mount a challenge to the constitutionality of any of its provisions. In addition, students of the legal profession have condemned as unethical the billions of dollars in fees realized by private tort lawyers who prepared the cases of the attorneys general.[3]

There is not space here to weigh fully these competing arguments, nor is that my purpose. I intend two things. First is to ask an empirical question: how did forty-six quite different polities manage to concur in the master settlement agreement of 1998? The second is to explore the implications of the agreement and its individual predecessors for the workings of American federalism.

What Brought the States Together?

It is perplexing that forty-six different polities would agree on the terms of a legal settlement with Big Tobacco. As political communities, they vary widely in their social and economic structures, cultures, prevailing political orientations, and stakes in the tobacco industry. Accordingly, they have varied widely in their policies toward cigarette use. Those who are home to the industry, whether as growers or manufacturers of tobacco or both—North Carolina, Kentucky, Virginia, Georgia, and Tennessee—have defended its interests in Congress, imposed light excise taxes, and shied away from burdensome prohibitions on use. At the other extreme, states with no direct interest in tobacco products but with populations harboring strong antitobacco movements or prohibitionist cultures—California, Utah, Oregon, and Massachusetts, for example—have enacted high excise taxes, adopted early and strict prohibitions on place of use, and contributed leaders to the antismoking movement in Congress.

Cigarette excise taxes in 2000 range all the way from Virginia's 2.5 cents a pack to New York's $1.11, an extraordinary gap. The proportion of adults who smoke ranges from a low of 13.7 percent in Utah to a high of 30.8 percent in Kentucky. Less than 1 percent of the population chews tobacco or dips snuff in the heavily urban northeastern states, whereas 15 percent of the population does so in West Virginia.[4] A fundamental reason for Congress's historic aversion to tobacco control legislation lies precisely in this feature of tobacco politics. The very sharp interregional and interstate differences of culture and interest make it much easier to do nothing and default to the states. But then how could political communities so different come together in support of a common policy in the 1998 settlement?

Part of the answer lies in the fact that, in respect to the tobacco litigation, the states did not act as political communities or even as whole governments. The suits were brought by the attorneys general, many of whom had broad discretion to act independently of the other parts of their governments.

Much of the explanation for their autonomy lies in the formal properties of their office. All fifty states have attorneys general, and in nearly all the office is defined in the state constitution and located in the executive branch. In forty-three states the attorney general is elected. Typically, the attorneys general have common law authority allowing them to represent "the public interest," which is a very broad charter indeed.[5] The U.S. Fifth Circuit Court of Appeals explained this authority in 1976:

> The attorneys general of our states have enjoyed a significant degree of autonomy. Their duties and powers typically are not exhaustively defined by either constitution or statute but include all those exercised at common law. There is and has been no doubt that the legislature may deprive the attorney general of specific powers; but in the absence of such authority he typically may exercise all such authority as the public interest requires.[6]

The activities of the attorneys general expanded very rapidly in the 1970s and 1980s, along with the size of their staffs. They tried many more cases and filed many more *amicus* briefs in the Supreme Court, where they appear more frequently than anyone except the U.S. solicitor general.

In addition to their capacious formal authority and growing record of activism, the attorneys general in the tobacco cases enjoyed another source of autonomy. They did not have to ask legislatures to finance their lawsuits because private tort lawyers were available to prepare the cases. In general, the lawsuits were developed by private lawyers performing under contingency fee contracts entered into by the attorneys general. As America's new class of venture capitalists, the tort lawyers were able to finance this particular venture with profits recently gained from lawsuits involving contraceptive devices, silicone breast implants, and, above all, asbestos.[7]

That the attorneys general who sued were not necessarily acting on behalf of their governments is suggested by the fact that the first one to file, Mike Moore of Mississippi, was in turned sued by his governor for suing. Kirk Fordice, the governor, claimed that the state's Medicaid Division was part of the governor's office and that the attorney general was the governor's lawyer, and therefore could not bring suit for recovery of Medicaid expenses without his permission. The Mississippi Supreme Court rejected the governor's petition while declining to rule on the merits.[8]

Nonetheless, even if one thinks of the attorneys general as largely independent actors within their governments, the more than forty who attain office by election cannot be independent of their constituencies. One would not expect the attorneys general of Virginia, Kentucky, and North Carolina to bet their political futures on assaulting the tobacco industry. On the other hand, one might wonder whether, having brought suit, each and every attorney general would want to settle with an industry that has been as reviled as the makers of cigarettes. Some might have wanted to appeal to antitobacco sentiment by refusing to deal with the devil. Also, in addition to constituency differences, one would expect partisan differences to appear. Presumably Democratic attorneys general would on the whole, after making allowance for constituency differences, be more inclined than Republicans to attack the industry.

In fact, the predictable differences among attorneys general were manifest. Led by Mississippi's Moore, Democrats initiated the campaign to sue cigarette manufacturers. Moore flew around the country encouraging others to join him. Ten Democrats filed and more than two years passed before any Republicans followed. Even within the parties, there were "outliers." Bill Pryor, the articulate, up-and-coming young Republican attorney general of Alabama, stood out in opposition to the suits. He wrote op-ed pieces for the *Wall Street Journal* and *New York Times* and gave a speech to the Cato Institute denouncing them as partisan and unprincipled.[9] At the opposite pole, Democrats Hubert H. Humphrey III of Minnesota and Scott Harshbarger of Massachusetts, both involved in gubernatorial campaigns that appealed to antitobacco sentiment, proclaimed principled opposition to settling with the industry.[10] Attorneys general in six states—Virginia, North Carolina, Kentucky, Tennessee, Delaware, and Wyoming—never did sue, but signed the master settlement agreement nevertheless.

The explanation for the unanimity is fairly simple. The first attorneys general to sue and settle created a situation in which there were mounting incentives for the rest to join. The individual settlements of the four "flagship" states—Mississippi, Florida, Texas, and Minnesota—had the effect of securing billions of dollars for those states' treasuries and imposing a tax, in the form of higher cigarette prices, on smokers everywhere in the country, not just in the settling states. As a matter of interstate equity and practical politics, other attorneys general could not thereafter refrain from seeking a share of the tobacco bounty for their own states. Officeholders cannot refuse a windfall, particularly when doing so does not provide any gains for their own constituents. Those who sued late or not at all did pay a price; the settlement gave higher monetary returns to those states that had made "strategic contributions" to achieving it.

By the end of May 1997, three years after Moore filed his pathbreaking suit, thirty-one states had followed Mississippi to the courthouse, and windfalls appeared to be in prospect. Because of a series of favorable pretrial rulings by a chancery court judge in Jackson County, Mississippi, it appeared certain that Moore could win his case. He and his litigating partner, tort lawyer Richard Scruggs of Pascagoula, had chosen their venue with the aim of avoiding a jury trial.[11] Juries had consistently ruled against individual plaintiffs in those few tobacco product liability cases that had reached them, and polling in anticipation of the state's suit indicated that this pattern would continue.

Scruggs commissioned a poll in four Mississippi counties (Hinds, Jackson, Smith, and Jones) by Dick Morris, who was also the pollster for President Clinton and Scruggs's brother-in-law, Senator Trent Lott of Mississippi. When it showed that a jury was not likely to return a verdict favorable to the state, Scruggs asked Morris to repeat the poll and remove respondents who were hostile to all lawsuits. Morris did so, and got the same result. Moore and Scruggs thereupon chose to file in one of the state's judge-ruled chancery courts, which are courts of equity rather than common law. Beginning in February 1995, the chancery court judge who heard their case issued a series of rulings adverse to the industry.

First, he kept jurisdiction of the case, denying a plea from the industry to transfer it to a common law court. In the spring of 1997, with a trial only three months away, he ruled that the industry could not argue economic benefit to the state from tobacco tax revenues or premature deaths from smoking in order to counter the state's argument of economic harm. This essentially left the industry defenseless. Finally, he rejected a last-ditch plea to permit a jury, even if he remained the presiding judge. These rulings, in combination with the defection of one renegade tobacco executive, the head of financially weak Liggett and Myers, compelled the remaining defendants to settle. In July 1997 Moore stood in the rotunda of the Mississippi capitol and announced to a bank of microphones that the state would receive $3.6 billion from its "little ol' lawsuit."

Events in Florida, which settled in August 1997 for $11.3 billion, intensified the threat to the industry. In April 1994, as Moore was getting ready to file in neighboring Mississippi, the Florida legislature was amending the state's Medicaid Third-Party Liability Act to ensure that any such suit in Florida would end in a victory for the state. Applying only to suits brought by the state government, as distinct from individuals, the law provided at its core that "assumption of risk and all other affirmative defenses normally available to a liable third party are to be abrogated to the extent necessary to ensure full recovery by Medicaid from third-party resources." Assumption of risk was the defense that the industry had traditionally relied on in individual cases. Other crucial provisions enabled the state to prove causation and damages through statistical analysis rather than having to establish a link between a smoker's illness and that person's use of tobacco products and relieved it of the burden of identifying sick individuals. This law was drafted by a plaintiff's lawyers, tacked onto an obscure bill in the last week of the legislative session, and passed without debate. After he signed it, Governor Lawton Chiles issued an executive order providing that it would apply only to the tobacco industry and sellers of illegal drugs. A four-man majority of the state's supreme court upheld this law over three dissenters who protested vainly that cigarette manufacturers "are entitled to just as much constitutional protection as anyone else."[12]

Big Tobacco's enemies were delighted with this development. "Mississippi filed its suit under existing common law, whereas Florida has changed the law to make it easier to bring this sort of case," a spokesman for the Tobacco Products Liability Project, an antitobacco group based at

Northeastern University in Boston, told a reporter. "It basically tilts the playing field in favor of the state and streamlines the process of getting money from the tobacco companies."[13] Project officials urged other states to follow Florida's lead.

At this stage of the assault on tobacco, both the industry and the attorneys general under Moore's leadership were hoping that Congress would enact the terms of a settlement. On June 20, 1997, the two sides had reached their first master settlement, which took the form of a wide-ranging proposal to Congress for legislation, including authority for the federal Food and Drug Administration (FDA) to regulate cigarettes as an addictive drug. But when Congress set to work on this proposal early in 1998, it quickly unraveled.

Senator John McCain, chairman of the Commerce Committee, whom the Republican leadership picked to manage the legislation, began by revising it to meet the demands of antitobacco activists inside and outside of Congress, led by former Surgeon General C. Everett Koop and former FDA Commissioner David A. Kessler. Once it was revised in this fashion, it was unacceptable to the industry, which in April 1998 opened a well-financed advertising campaign against McCain's bill. As the prospect of congressional legislation evaporated, lawyers for the industry and the attorneys general began to meet privately to resume the search for an inclusive settlement on which their clients could agree. Thereafter a working group of nine attorneys general was formed, representing different regions, degrees of hostility to the industry, and stages of progress in the lawsuits. What emerged in the fall of 1998 was a more moderate version of what had been agreed to in the summer of 1997. It was less costly to the industry and imposed fewer restraints, but also provided fewer protections against liability.

When the McCain bill died, there still remained a challenge of getting the attorneys general to agree with one another as well as getting them as a group to reach agreement with the industry. Despite the several early individual settlements, the strength of the remaining cases was in doubt and varied from state to state. No case had yet reached a jury. West Virginia's case had foundered early in the Kanawha County Circuit Court when tobacco defendants successfully challenged the attorney general's authority to file suit unless on behalf of a state-agency client. In late July 1998, a superior court judge in Marion County, Indiana, dismissed the suit of Attorney General Jeffrey Modisett, ruling that Indiana could not seek damages from harm to individual smokers because "the injuries are derivative and too remote." He also dismissed allegations of conspiracy, antitrust violations, and unjust enrichment.[14] The case of Washington, which had been filed relatively early (June 5, 1996) and was scheduled to go to trial in September 1998, had been dismissed in part. The state's effort to recoup Medicaid expenses had been thrown out, so that the case would have to depend entirely on antitrust and fraud claims. Early in September a judge dismissed Idaho's case. In five states with suits pending, the industry's potential liability was limited by a ban on punitive damages in civil cases, and ten other states imposed limits on such damages. Only two states, Maryland and Vermont, had followed the example of Florida and amended their laws so as to undermine the industry's defenses.

Nationwide, the remaining forty-six attorneys general were divided into three groups: hard-liners such as Harshbarger in Massachusetts, Joseph Curran in Maryland, Jim Doyle in Wisconsin, and Richard Blumenthal in Connecticut, whose cases had good prospects and who felt little pressure to settle; those whose chances in court were poorer; and those who had never brought suit at all, such as North Carolina's Michael F. Easley. In the end, the attorneys general could agree to settle with the industry because the number with weak cases and the number who had never sued constituted a sizable majority of the forty-six.

The severest critics of the attorneys general called the assault on Big Tobacco an abuse of government power. A professor at the Cardozo Law School in New York said:

> Contingency fee lawyers and the attorneys general used bare, brute force to bludgeon the tobacco companies into submission. Even though there were filings in state courts and one [Texas's case] in federal district court, the object was not to litigate. The object was to raise the threat level high enough to coerce tobacco companies into suing for peace. The lawsuits had no basis in law. They were not founded on any tenable legal theory or precedent. This was simply state terrorism. The tobacco companies feared that state courts, when faced with the choice of fidelity to law versus transferring enormous amounts of wealth from out-of-state corporations to the states' coffers, would embrace the golden rule, namely, let's get some of that gold.[15]

Insofar as this interpretation of the tobacco lawsuits is sound, federalism obviously posed no barrier to governments' abuse of power. It did not "guard the society against the oppression of its rulers," in a phrase that James Madison employed in *Federalist* No. 51. On the contrary, the dynamics of interstate relations encouraged all attorneys general to sue once the prospect of a revenue windfall became manifest and compelled even attorneys general who never sued to join ultimately in the settlement and claim a share of tobacco's gold. Madison had argued in *Federalist* No. 51 that federalism and separation of powers constituted "auxiliary precautions" against governments' abuse of power, reinforcing the principal safeguard, which is "dependence on the people." He wrote:

> In the compound republic of America, the power surrendered by the people is first divided between two distinct governments, and then the portion allotted to each subdivided among distinct and separate departments. Hence a double security arises to the rights of the people. The different governments will control each other, at the same time that each will be controlled by itself.[16]

No such result is evident in the tobacco case. The different governments did not control one another. They urged one another on, and eventually the federal government, following the example of the attorneys general, filed its own suit against the tobacco industry.

It is possible, of course, to advance an alternative interpretation of the suits and settlement. As the attorneys general and their tort-lawyer allies saw it, they were liberating the people of the United States from the tyranny of tobacco, which the national government had failed to do. Public opinion demanded that something be done about the scourge of cigarettes, and when the national legislature failed, tort lawyers stepped in. According to tort lawyer John Coale:

> Tobacco reached a threshold when it became so unpopular that the country was willing to have just about anybody, including us, do something to discourage its use. . . . What has happened is that the legislatures . . . have failed. They failed to regulate tobacco. . . . The polling data is overwhelming: Congress is not doing its job.[17]

One might find warrant for Coale's implicit theory of federalism in *The Federalist*. In No. 46, Madison asserted that

> notwithstanding the different modes in which they are appointed, we must consider both [the federal government and the state governments] as substantially dependent on the great body of the citizens of the United States. . . . The federal and State governments are in fact but different agents and trustees of the people, constituted with different powers and designed for different purposes.[18]

If the national legislature were to ignore the will of the people, this suggests, the people could turn to other trustees and agents, the state governments, to exercise their will. Coale was claiming that the attorneys general and tort lawyers were responding to a popular demand, which legislatures—he named only Congress—were ignoring because of the political power of the tobacco industry. In 1997–98 this was a common view of opponents of the industry, including the editorial pages of the *New York Times* and *Washington Post* and President Clinton.

There is, however, no evidence to substantiate it. Although the public was concerned about youth smoking and favored certain measures designed to discourage it, such as regulation of vending machines, there was no popular demand for a major new regime of tobacco control. Still less was there a popular demand for lawsuits against the industry.

In addition to the history of jury decisions favoring the industry, which the tobacco litigators were obviously well aware of but reluctant to credit, there were poll results. Polls done in 1997, roughly contemporaneous with the first settlement between the industry and the attorneys general, showed that respondents by large margins believed that the cigarette companies should not be held legally or financially responsible for smokers' illnesses. In five different polls, 64 to 76 percent of respondents said that smokers themselves were mainly to blame.[19] In late July 1997, immediately after Mississippi had settled its suit against the industry for several billion dollars, more than half of the respondents to a Hart/Teeter poll disagreed "somewhat" or "strongly" with the statement that "tobacco companies should be required to refund states for the cost of medical care for poor people who contract diseases related to smoking."[20] Polling also showed resistance to regulation of cigarettes by the FDA, which was a central goal of antitobacco activists.[21]

When tobacco legislation unraveled in Congress in the spring of 1998, the public reacted by favoring "voluntary restrictions that the tobacco companies would accept" (33 percent) or leaving things "as they are now" (31 percent) rather than "force a settlement on the tobacco companies" (28 percent), with 8 percent "unsure."[22] A large majority of respondents to a National Journal/NBC poll said that they thought the government was doing too much (28 percent) or about the right amount (31 percent) to regulate tobacco, while 38 percent thought it was doing too little.[23]

Other kinds of evidence about public attitudes support the poll results. In the mid-1990s, two social scientists under the auspices of the Rand Corporation did a study of the implementation of tobacco control laws at the state and local levels. They interviewed a variety of sources—state and local officials, restaurant owners, tobacco vendors, antitobacco activists, and industry representatives—in seven states that had strong control programs. Sympathetic to the cause of tobacco control, they were "particularly surprised" to find that "the relative salience of the smoking issue appeared to be low in comparison with other public policy issues. Implicitly or explicitly, respondents indicated that tobacco control often failed to ignite the passions of state legislators or city council members or even of the public at large."[24]

Election results in the fall of 1998, as the tobacco settlement was being concluded, likewise gave no sign that the public was clamoring for stricter regulation of cigarettes. Two attorneys general who were particularly aggressive in their pursuit of the lawsuits—Humphrey of Minnesota and Harshbarger of Massachusetts—failed in attempts to be elected governor. Bill Pryor, who had outspokenly opposed the suits after being appointed to office by Governor Fob James, was returned to the attorney general's office by the Alabama electorate.

In the mid-1990s, the tobacco companies had come under a savage propaganda assault from a coalition of antitobacco activists in Congress, the White House, the FDA, the public health professions, the health voluntary associations such as the American Cancer Society, the Robert Wood Johnson Foundation, the National Center for Tobacco-Free Kids, and the media. Central to this campaign was publicity given to internal documents of the industry that reached the public either through theft or discovery processes associated with lawsuits.

It was easy to impute to the public, which was the object of the campaign, the attitudes of the campaign's sponsors. There was in fact some effect on the public, which was more hostile to the companies at the end of the decade than at the beginning. Still, even after this propaganda onslaught, during which "shocking secrets" from industry files were regularly revealed, the public was definitely not as enraged or hostile to cigarette manufacturers as the activists were. Therefore, it is impossible to claim that the federal system provided an alternative channel—state governments—for expressing the popular will when that will was thwarted by the national legislature.

The Traditional Politics of Legislative Policymaking

Is there, then, no feature of tobacco politics that affirmatively illustrates the functions that federalism performs in the American constitutional system?

In fact, there are such features, but to discern them it is necessary to fore-sake the focus on the suits and settlements of the 1990s and look instead at legislative activity, which is the more usual form of policymaking and also the form more firmly grounded in constitutional precept. This requires also a broader perspective in time, because the modern era of tobacco con-trol began in the mid-1960s following the appearance of an advisory report to the U.S. surgeon general that documented the health hazards of tobacco use. In the thirty years that followed, many governments in the United States took many steps to discourage tobacco use. A rough division of labor emerged among these governments, consistent with a division that histor-ically has characterized public policymaking.

The federal government took charge of gathering and disseminating information of public importance, including the results of scientific research. Congress required annual reports by the surgeon general on the health consequences of smoking, which have become compendia of scien-tific knowledge on the subject. It also required health warnings on cigarette packages. Sometimes public health officials in the executive branch have used their offices as platforms for inveighing against cigarette use. President Carter's secretary of health, education, and welfare, Joseph Califano, who was the first to do so, described the federal government's role in tobacco control:

> Make no mistake, our efforts are to reduce smoking. But they are efforts grounded in persuasion and information that appeal to the common sense of our citizens. They are not efforts based on coercion and scare tactics. I have the greatest empathy for the millions of Americans who want to stop smoking, but who find it very, very dif-ficult to do so . . .
>
> . . . If our citizens . . . are given all the facts from government, or other sources, and still do not wish to give up a personal habit, how-ever hazardous, then, except for protecting the rights of non-smok-ers, I think government can properly do no more.[25]

Also at the federal level, Congress and independent regulatory agencies with jurisdiction over industries in interstate commerce used regulation to discourage cigarette use. Congress banned smoking on airline flights and cigarette advertising on radio and television. The Interstate Commerce Commission banned smoking on buses and segregated smokers on trains. When the Federal Trade Commission (FTC) threatened to require health

warnings in advertisements, the industry agreed to include them "voluntarily." Even before the surgeon general's report, the FTC was prohibiting
health claims in cigarette advertising, using its power to regulate "unfair or
deceptive acts or practices in commerce."[26]

Complementary to the federal government's actions, at the state and
local levels, grassroots antitobacco activists were demanding prohibitions
on places of cigarette use, beginning with public buildings and private
workplaces and eventually reaching even bars and restaurants. The purpose
of this activity was not just the proximate one of creating smoke-free physical environments. More broadly, for the most committed activists the goal
was to stigmatize the act of smoking everywhere. It was to turn smokers
into social outcasts. These activists were aggressively employing a traditional power of subnational governments, the "police power," appropriate
to governments of smaller scale, with which the health, morals, and order
of the community are regulated.[27] No nineteenth-century campaigner
against alcohol or prostitution performed with greater zeal than did the
late twentieth-century leaders of GASP (Groups Against Smoking Pollution) in California or the New York City policemen who put people in jail
overnight because they were smoking on Manhattan subway platforms.
The charge was "disorderly conduct."[28]

State and local laws against tobacco use spread, gaining momentum in
the 1980s. By 1995, the U.S. Centers for Disease Control and the National
Cancer Institute identified 1,238 state laws that addressed tobacco control.
Forty-one states restricted smoking on government work sites. Twenty-six
restricted it in private work sites and thirty-two states, in restaurants.
Forty-five states restricted it in a variety of other locations, such as day care
centers, shopping malls, grocery stores, enclosed arenas, vehicles of public
transportation, and hospitals.[29] Local ordinances might apply even when
state legislatures had not acted.

Such activity varied by region. In general the antismoking movement
started earliest and attained greatest strength in the Far West and Upper
Midwest, although Massachusetts has also been in the forefront. It has been
weakest in the Deep South and the border between North and South. A
growing dispersion in cigarette excise taxes illustrates the differences. All
states have excise taxes, having enacted them beginning in the 1920s,
although Virginia (1960) and North Carolina (1969) came late to this form
of revenue raising. As of 1995 the rates remained nominal in the tobacco
states—2.5 cents in Virginia, 3 cents in Kentucky, 5 cents in North
Carolina—but climbed to 50 cents or more in Connecticut, Massachusetts,

Rhode Island, New York, Washington, and Hawaii. Michigan topped all states with a tax of 75 cents, though it would later be passed by New York. One of the historic functions of federalism, richly illustrated by tobacco policies, has been to facilitate local adaptations to differences of interest and culture.

This old (prelitigation) regime of tobacco control was not ineffective. On the contrary, smoking was stigmatized, as the familiar sight of smokers huddled outside of workplaces shows. Cigarette consumption and adult smoking rates dropped by roughly half between the mid-1960s and early 1990s. The Centers for Disease Control counts the decline in smoking as one of the leading public health achievements of the twentieth century.[30]

Nor can it be said that at century's end this customary, legislation-centered regime was stymied. In 1992 Congress broke new ground by applying the familiar technique of grant-in-aid conditions to one of the most intractable obstacles to tobacco control, cigarette sales to minors. When it renewed mental health, drug, and alcohol abuse programs, some of which use grants-in-aid, it included language requiring the states to have and enforce laws prohibiting the sale of tobacco to anyone under the age of eighteen. All but three states already had such laws, but they were not being enforced. Now states were threatened with the loss of up to 40 percent of their mental health and substance abuse grants if they failed to enforce tobacco control laws effectively. Specifically, the law, which was called the Synar amendment, required them to conduct random, unannounced inspections—stings, in other words—to test vendors' compliance and also to make annual reports on the progress of enforcement.

A study of tobacco-control enforcement in the mid-1990s concluded that the states were taking the requirements of the Synar amendment seriously. No state completely banned vending machines, but thirty-two had enacted restrictions by 1995. Thirty-three states had required retail licensing for cigarette vendors, with accompanying penalties for failure to honor laws against sales to minors. The Synar amendment had "served as a rallying cry for progressive tobacco control states, such as Minnesota and New York, and has forced the hand of those states that have heretofore shunned responsibility for tobacco control (e.g., Texas and Arizona)."[31] States also began late in the decade to crack down directly on teenage smokers. In 1997, Florida, Idaho, Minnesota, North Carolina, and Texas all passed laws that threatened stiff penalties for minors who bought or possessed tobacco products. They could lose their driver's licenses, suffer fines of up to $1,000, or be imprisoned for six months. These extreme measures had more backing from the tobacco industry and retailers than from public health advocates, nearly all of whom preferred punishing the industry to punishing young smokers.[32] Between 1995 and 1998 eleven state legislatures raised cigarette excise taxes. In Alaska and Hawaii, the tax reached $1 a pack. By September 1998 there were sixteen states in which it was 50 cents or more.

The rate at which legislatures were acting raises the question of why litigation developed as an alternative strategy. The answer lies largely in the choices of actors who were primarily litigators, the tort lawyers. For years they had suffered defeat at the hands of the tobacco industry, which they hated for its product, its litigating tactics, and its arrogance in victory. Hungering for revenge, they discerned in class actions and alliances with the attorneys general a way to achieve it. For the sick individuals whom they had historically represented in court, they would substitute many thousands of sick individuals (a strategy that on the whole did not work) or state governments (a strategy that worked much better). The suits of the attorneys general began with a tort lawyer's approach to Mike Moore rather than the other way around, but Moore was receptive. The attorneys general as a whole had been active on behalf of consumer protection, a goal well suited to officials who need to develop electoral appeals.

Tort lawyers looking to defeat Big Tobacco are only part of the story. The other part is the ferocity, rage, and improved financing—thanks mainly to the Robert Wood Johnson Foundation, the National Cancer Institute, and a tax referendum in California—of antitobacco activists, for whom any strategy holding any prospect of success was attractive, the more so if it promised to punish the cigarette manufacturers, as litigation could. In particular, a litigation strategy was advocated by Richard Daynard, a law professor at Northeastern University who in the mid-1980s founded the Tobacco Products Liability Project. Presciently, Daynard argued that litigation could be used to force an increase in the price of cigarettes and to embarrass the cigarette companies by forcing release of internal documents, which might influence both juries and a broader public.[33]

For most antitobacco activists (except, to some extent, those in California), the regime of legislation by many governments was profoundly unsatisfactory because it was slow, halting, incomplete geographically, incomplete also in its scope of regulation (because it had not reached cigarette manufacture), prone to compromise, and historically ineffective in restricting youth access. To assertions that regulation had succeeded because adult smoking rates had been cut in half, the enemies of tobacco could reply that a quarter of the adult population of the United States still smoked.

If one's standard for judging the legislative regime is an ideal antitobacco outcome—abolition of tobacco use—then the regime was obviously flawed. If, however, one's standard is procedural and incorporates a principle of accountability to the electorate—indeed, to the many electorates of the American federal system—then the legislative regime was, and remains, superior. This is more than an a priori judgment, resting on the plain fact that legislatures are elected and composed of many members, which gives them a claim to being superior both to the attorneys general and to private tort lawyers as instruments of the popular will. It also rests on poll results that show support for the wide-ranging but less than total antitobacco regime that the fifty-one major legislatures of the United States had produced and were on their way to extending in the mid-1990s.[34] Smoking not only dropped sharply under legislative regulation, it fell with relatively limited use of government coercion, in a process that made it very hard to discern where official regulation ended and the development of a new social norm began. This is a tribute to democratic policymaking.

The core principle of American government is self-government. Federalism helps sustain it by multiplying the number of polities in which the institutions of representative government exist and by requiring elaborate, complex networks of intergovernmental cooperation to develop if national policies are to be framed and made effective. The tobacco litigation, in bypassing representative institutions in order to create a regulatory regime, undermined both Madison's "principal safeguard," dependence on the people, and the "auxiliary precautions" of federalism and separation of powers. Separation of powers was gutted when executive officials, the attorneys general, managed to commandeer the judiciary for purposes of policymaking without, however, permitting judges and juries to perform their putative functions. Courts became a medium for making a threat rather than an instrument of deliberation and judgement. Once separation of powers was gutted as a check on the power of governments, so too was federalism. The states, whatever their underlying interests and constituency preferences, were constrained to join a "race to the trough" of tobacco profits.

Three

Evolution

8

Progressivism and Federalism

with John J. Dinan

Progressivism left a greater legacy of political thought about federalism than of deliberate change in the working of the institution. Perhaps ironically, given the large amount of institutional reform that is associated with the Progressive Era—expansion of the civil service, strengthening of chief executives, reorganization of municipal governments, numerous measures of direct democracy—there is relatively little reform of intergovernmental relations that can be ascribed specifically to it.

Direct election of senators, which replaced election by state legislatures through the Seventeenth Amendment in 1913, was of transcendent importance to federalism, marking as it did the abandonment of one of the main constitutional protections of state governments. But this was only superficially a Progressive achievement; it had been many decades in the making.[1] The same may be said of the Sixteenth Amendment, which enabled Congress to impose income taxes, though here the implications for federalism, if no less profound, were less manifest.

Otherwise, unless it would be the development of uniform state laws or, less plausibly, the initiation of governors' conferences, the Progressive Era produced no milestones in the practice of intergovernmental relations.

This essay first appeared as Martha Derthick and John J. Dinan, "Progressivism and Fderalism," in Sidney M. Milkis and Jerome M. Mileur, eds., *Progressivism and the New Democracy* (University of Massachusetts Press, 1999), pp. 81–102.

There was nothing comparable, say, to passage of the Morrill Act of 1862, which overturned an earlier veto by President Buchanan and established categorical grants-in-aid to the states, or to the rise of federal mandates in the 1960s and 1970s.[2] Several new grant-in-aid programs were enacted, including a very important one for highway construction in 1916, but there was nothing comparable to the Great Society explosion of shared programs.

Nevertheless, the period was of utmost importance to the evolution of federalism. Progressive political thought laid an indispensable foundation for the transformations in policy and institutions that were to come later in the twentieth century.

Before the Progressive Era, federalism in the United States was conceived of as a constitutional doctrine that prescribed separate sovereignties. The Civil War and the amendments that followed had decisively shifted the terms of nation-state relations to the nation's advantage, but federalism was still understood as a precept of constitutional law, to be interpreted and applied by the Supreme Court.

In a celebrated aphorism, the Court rendered the essence of its understanding in *Texas* v. *White* (1869), saying that the Constitution had created "an indestructible Union, composed of indestructible States."[3] States could not destroy the nation by seceding, but neither could the nation abolish states. When the Civil War presented an opportunity to abolish some, the opportunity was not used. Nonetheless, the relation between the two levels of government was still understood to be largely conflictual. The task of the Court was to define and enforce the boundaries between nation and states.

The Progressive Era advanced a new way of thinking about federalism, grounded less in constitutional law than in conceptions of community and political ideology. It taught that Americans were one people who would improve themselves individually and socially by cooperating in pursuit of shared social ideals. Cooperation among governments in the federal system was one of many forms of cooperation that were advocated. This shift, with its emphasis on construction of a national community, could easily have denied the importance of federalism altogether, but we will argue that that was not the case. The Progressive attack was qualified.[4]

The Attack

Progressive Era political thought assaulted the conventional conception of federalism in three main ways. First, it both challenged the Constitution as a governing instrument and propounded radically new ways of interpreting it that would have virtually abolished any limitation on the powers of the federal government. Second, by propounding an explanation of the causes of centralization that blamed the victim—the states—it justified and facilitated further centralization. Third, it began constructing a social and philosophical conception of federalism as a substitute for the legalistic one that had dominated American political thought.

Constitutional Doctrine

The principal barrier to the expansion of federal power was the Constitution, and in particular the prevailing Supreme Court interpretation of it. The Progressives tried to overcome this obstacle in a variety of ways.

Their first strategy was to devalue both the federal judiciary as an institution and judicial review as an instrument of government. A series of Supreme Court decisions that overturned regulation of interstate commerce in the last decade of the nineteenth century and labor laws in the first two decades of the twentieth century led a number of scholars to reexamine the origin of judicial review and to cast doubt on its legitimacy.[5] J. Allen Smith, among others, contended that judicial review was illegitimate because it was neither specified in the Constitution nor intended by its drafters.[6] Others followed Charles Beard in concluding that the delegates to the Constitutional Convention did expect that courts would exercise judicial review, but that they had done so for illegitimate reasons, to better secure their property.[7]

Several institutional reforms were proposed to restrain the federal courts, although none was ultimately enacted. Bills backed by Progressives were introduced in Congress to curtail the courts' jurisdiction and to require a supermajority or a unanimous vote before the Supreme Court could invalidate legislation.[8] Some Progressives were also attracted to Theodore Roosevelt's proposed recall of judicial decisions or Robert La Follette's motion to permit Congress to reenact statutes that the Court declared unconstitutional.[9]

Amendment was another avenue through which Progressives sought to overcome the prevailing constitutional interpretation. But as Judge Charles Amidon argued in 1906, "the vast enlargement of our country has made the method of amendment provided by the fathers far more difficult than they contemplated at the time," and in fact, "there is a very general understanding that formal amendment is impossible."[10] Although Amidon's estimate of the difficulty of amendment proved to be overstated, as four amendments were adopted between 1913 and 1920, proposed amendments to permit federal regulation of child labor, minimum wages, and a number of other subjects were all defeated. In any event, constitutional amendment was viewed as "not suitable to bring about those slight but steady modifications of fundamental law which adapt it to the progressive law of the nation. It is far too violent a remedy for that purpose. The Constitution has been and ought to be accommodated to the ever-changing conditions of society by a process as gradual as the changes themselves."[11]

Accordingly, the most prominent Progressive strategy was to challenge the existing understanding of constitutionalism and to put forth a new interpretation of the constitutional balance of powers between the state and federal governments. Until the late nineteenth century, political scientists, historians, and statesmen had been prone to venerate the Constitution. It was viewed as the product of a unique set of circumstances and the embodiment of enduring institutions and principles. This understanding was challenged on several fronts in the Progressive Era. Political scientists began to suggest that the Constitution was no longer an accurate guide to understanding the operation of American governing institutions. In 1885, Woodrow Wilson offered an alternative to the "literary theory" of the Constitution and criticized those who engaged in "an undiscriminating and almost blind worship" of its principles, while in 1906 Albert Bushnell Hart opened his American government textbook by proclaiming the necessity of studying "the actual workings of government: the text of constitutions and of statutes is only the enveloping husk; the real kernel is that personal interest which vitalizes government."[12]

These initial doubts soon turned into a full-blown critique of constitutionalism. J. Allen Smith offered the clearest statement of this view, when he argued that a democratic age required a new understanding of the purpose of a constitution. "A constitution can not be regarded as a check upon the people themselves," he argued. It is properly viewed as "the means of securing the supremacy of public opinion and not an instrument for thwarting it," and therefore "must yield readily to changes in public opinion."[13]

Judge Amidon held to a more moderate view of constitutionalism, but one that differed from the conventional understanding nonetheless. He believed that "the Constitution performs its chief service when it holds the nation back from hasty and passionate action, and compels it to investigate, consider and weigh until it is made sure that the proposed action does not embody the passion of the hour, but the settled purpose of the years."

But "a changeless constitution becomes the protector not only of vested rights but of vested wrongs."[14]

The Progressives were particularly troubled by what Frank Goodnow described as the tendency "to emphasize the rights of the states rather than the powers of the federal government" and to adopt "an extremely individualistic conception of the powers of government," which "resulted in a constitutional tradition which is apt not to accord to the federal government powers it unquestionably ought to have the constitutional right to exercise."[15] In light of the economic changes that had taken place since the founding as well as the experience of other countries that had drafted constitutions in the course of the nineteenth century, Goodnow concluded:

> We are justified, therefore, in assuming that, if the American people were called upon at the present time, to frame a scheme of federal government, they would adopt one which departed in a number of respects from the one under which we now live, and which would resemble that of Germany or of Canada in that it would make provision for greater ease of constitutional amendment and for securing to the national government greater powers than are believed by many to be accorded to the government of the United States under the present constitution.[16]

The Progressives challenged the well-established convention that the federal government was one of enumerated powers. A series of Supreme Court decisions had relied upon this doctrine to permit federal regulation of interstate commerce in prostitution, lottery tickets, and adulterated food and drugs but to limit the ability of the federal government to regulate monopolies and prohibit child labor. A central aim of the Progressive movement, which was expressed most clearly by President Theodore Roosevelt in a speech in 1906, was to introduce a more expansive understanding of national power, particularly with respect to the regulation of interstate commerce. Condemning the Supreme Court's construction of the powers of the national government as too narrow, he called for a return to Founder James Wilson's view. Roosevelt attributed to Wilson the doctrine "that an inherent power rested in the nation, outside of the enumerated powers conferred upon it by the Constitution, in all cases where the object involved was beyond the power of the several states and was a power ordinarily exercised by sovereign nations." He was in particular drawn to Wilson's belief that "whenever the states cannot act, because the need to be met is not one of merely a single locality, then the national government, representing all the people, should have complete power to act." Under a "wise and farseeing interpretation of the interstate commerce clause," Roosevelt concluded, "the national government should have complete power to deal with all of this wealth which in any way goes into the commerce between the States."[17]

The Progressives also challenged limitations on federal power that were grounded in conventional understandings of dual sovereignty and the due process clause. The prevailing judicial conception was that federal power was limited not only by the specific enumeration of powers in Article I of the Constitution but also by the reservation of certain powers to the states in the Tenth Amendment and limitations on federal power in the Fifth Amendment. The Progressives argued that the concept of dual sovereignty was outdated. Goodnow complained that it "laid emphasis on preserving for all time the same degree of state sovereignty and independence as was recognized to exist in the latter part of the eighteenth century."[18] But it was evident, as constitutional scholar John Jameson argued, that, in the aftermath of the Civil War and in view of the increasing scope of political problems, "no theory of sovereignty but that of the people as a whole is in harmony with the facts of American political life."[19]

Additionally, the Progressives sought to bring a halt to expansive interpretations of the due process clause of the Fifth Amendment that served to limit federal power. In light of the fact that many of the most important questions of government were no longer political in nature, they agreed with Walter Weyl that the conception of individual rights had to be "extended and given a social interpretation" so that it might cease to serve as a barrier to national regulation of the conditions under which men, women, and children labored.[20]

Political Theory

The Progressive Era was a period of centralization in measures of public policy. Critics of centralization, defenders of the established way of thinking, conceived of them as constitutional usurpations, or as the partisan acts of congressional majorities.[21] Progressive thinkers, however, justified them as necessary responses to the default and incapacity of state governments.

The classic statement of this view, widely noticed at the time and cited since, came in a speech late in 1906 by Elihu Root, Theodore Roosevelt's secretary of state, even though Root was identified much more with the conservative than the Progressive wing of the Republican Party. He argued that state lines were being obliterated by three forces: an increase in national sentiment, domestic free trade, and technological changes in transportation and communication. Under the new conditions of economic and social interdependence on a national scale, the states were no longer capable of performing such functions as the regulation of railroad rates, inspection of meat, and guaranteeing the safety of foods and drugs.

The states could be preserved, Root continued, only if they awakened to "their own duties to the country at large." To survive, states must act in the national interest, submerging particular agendas to the greater good:

> If any state maintains laws which promote and foster the enormous overcapitalization of corporations condemned by the people of the country generally; if any state maintains laws designed to make easy the formation of trusts and the creation of monopolies; if any state maintains laws which permit conditions of child labor revolting to the sense of mankind; if any state maintains laws of marriage and divorce so far inconsistent with the general standard of the nation as violently to derange the domestic relations, which the majority of the states desire to preserve, that state is promoting the tendency of the people of the country to seek relief through the national government and to press forward the movement for national control and the extinction of local control. The intervention of the national government in many of the matters which it has recently undertaken would have been wholly unnecessary if the states themselves had been alive to their duty toward the general body of the country.[22]

Root's explanation for centralization was that of a statesman—an eminent lawyer, party leader, and public servant. More penetrating theories, cast in terms arguably more devastating to state governments, came from academic sources.

The political scientist Henry Jones Ford argued that, quite apart from the inadequate scope of their individual jurisdictions, states as governments were flawed structurally. They were pre-modern democracies in decay, the symptoms of which were "the historic perversions of democracy—namely, oligarchy and ochlocracy." Formed in the eighteenth century, when it was believed that government power should be diffused, they lacked "appropriate organs of authority." Therefore power flowed to the government that *did* have an appropriate authority—namely, the federal government, "the sole, competent organ of sovereignty in this country," at the pinnacle of which was a powerful, responsible unitary executive. Ford simultaneously condemned the state governments and celebrated the emergence of the active presidency. His condemnation of the states was savage:

> Our state politics exhibit the characteristic phenomena which occur with monotonous regularity in all ages, as republican forms of polity degenerate. They are all there—the growth of plutocratic privilege, the violence of demagogues, the infirmity of legislation, the decay of justice, the substitution of private vengeance for judicial process, the increase of crime and disorder, and the growth of associations formed for self-help in the redress of grievances, and resorting to night-riding, torture, and assassination in furtherance of their purpose.[23]

Still a different academic theory was advanced by the economist Simon N. Patten, who located the cause of the decay of state and local governments in processes of development. Patten noted with dismay that state and local offices had "lost their former independent position" and had come to be valued "largely for the places they furnish for partisans of national politics." State and local officials—even the least of them, such as constables—were chosen not because they advanced individual policies, or exhibited any special fitness for office, but because they had served a national party. State and local governments had been reduced to a "mere nominal existence."

This decay had occurred, Patten argued, because as the population spread across the continent and new state and local governments were formed, they had ceased to have the character of communities, defined by shared interests. The original colonies along the Atlantic seaboard and their towns had arisen "naturally," held together by common bonds of religion or national origin of the settlers. "Each town in this region became a centre of a group of families having common aims and interests which bound them together in a real unit." As development proceeded west of the Alleghenies, however, units of local government were formed arbitrarily, suiting the convenience of surveyors. States similarly were formed without regard to commonality of interest or the logic of geography and climate. Patten cited north-south divisions in Ohio, Indiana and Illinois, marked by differing climates, crops, and currents of migration. Political communities so haphazardly and illogically constituted were certain to lack vitality, he argued, and farther west, this problem was compounded by the extreme size of the states and corresponding thinness of population.[24]

The view that defects of the states were the cause of centralization took hold widely, as is suggested by its appearance in 1925 in a Memorial Day speech by President Calvin Coolidge at Arlington National Cemetery. Unlike Root, Coolidge spoke as an ardent defender of individualism and local self-government, which he judged to be crucial to both the preservation of American liberty and Western civilization. He deplored the tendency toward centralization in the federal system, but also found the source of it in the default of the states: "Without doubt, the reason for increasing demands on the Federal government is that the states have not discharged their full duties."[25]

Progressive Era defenders of state sovereignty did their best to meet this challenge by fashioning uniform state laws, an effort that originated in the late nineteenth century in the New York state legislature and the American Bar Association and was supported financially by some of the states and state bar associations as well as the national association. This was the constitutional conservatives' strategy of constructive response to the demands of the time.[26]

The Great Community

The formation of American nationhood and nationality had been under way for a long time before the Progressives arrived on the scene. They did not invent national consciousness, but they sought to alter its content. They spoke of a national "community," having in mind that the nation should have purposes both moral and public that all of its members shared. This conception—indeed, this political ideology—had implications for government that of course went well beyond the institutions of federalism. To illustrate what it meant specifically for federalism, we draw on the work of Mary Parker Follett, who was one of the few Progressive authors to employ the term in a self-conscious way. Follett's work, *The New State*, contains a revealing chapter on "Political Pluralism and the True Federal State," though it needs to be read in conjunction with a chapter entitled "From Contract to Community," which, drawing on Roscoe Pound, develops a concept of law as the product and instrument of community life.

Follett rejects individualism, contract theory, divided sovereignty, and divided powers or interests. She objects to the concept of balanced powers because to be balanced powers must first be divided, and "there are no absolute divisions in a true federal union." She argues for a state that is unifying, inclusive, dynamic, and internally cooperative. It embraces all groups—and it is only through group life that individual fulfillment and democracy are realized. It embraces new groups as they emerge.

Thus the true federal state is "the unifying state." "Only in the unifying state do we get the full advantage of diversity where it is gathered up into significance and pointed action. . . . Any whole is always the element of a larger whole. . . . Democracy depends on the blending, not the balancing, of interests and thoughts and wills."

As this language suggests, the work is more than a little mystical and does not often address directly the subject of relations between levels of government in a federal system, however federalism is defined. Where it does, it endorses the growing practice of federal grants-in-aid as an instance of "true federal" (that is, cooperative) action. Using the example of grants for vocational education, Follett says that the federal government does not impose something from without; states must take responsibility and determine how their own needs can best be satisfied. "The experience of one state joins with the experience of other states to form a collective experience."[27] Attitudes toward grants-in-aid differentiated Progressives, who favored them, from defenders of the old order of dual sovereignty, who did not.

The Reprieve

This attack on federalism was indubitably powerful. It underpinned or complemented centralizing changes in public policy of the Progressive Era as well as its far-reaching successors in the New Deal and the Great Society. At the same time, it is important to note the several ways in which the attack was qualified. Though powerful, it was not total. The Progressives did not mount a frontal attack on the constitutional principle. To attack federalism fundamentally would have required an assault on the form of the Senate, which was the principal federal feature remaining in the Constitution after the framing convention of 1787.

The logical next step for Progressivism following adoption of the Seventeenth Amendment in 1913 would have been to attack equal representation of the states in the Senate. While the literature of the period occasionally advances this proposal, as in, for example, J. Allen Smith's *The Spirit of American Government*, it did not become a Progressive cause.[28] Woodrow Wilson, who may or may not be regarded as an authentic voice of Progressivism, celebrated the Senate as the embodiment of regional representation, which he argued was necessary "in a country physically as various as ours and therefore certain to exhibit a very great variety of social and economic and even political conditions."[29]

More appealing to Progressives was a proposal to make constitutional amendment easier by substituting popular ratification of amendments for ratification by three-fourths of the state legislatures. Herbert Croly took up this cause in his second book, *Progressive Democracy*, and Wisconsin's great Progressive leader, Robert M. La Follette, sponsored it in the Senate. But this was less an attack on federalism than on judicial supremacy. By making the Constitution easier to amend, Progressives hoped to reduce the need and the scope for judicial discretion. "The guardianship of the robe," Croly explained, "was based in practice upon the extreme difficulty of amending the Constitution." Ending that guardianship was a Progressive priority of utmost importance.[30]

If Progressives had attached greater importance to constitutional forms, they might have devoted more effort to changing them. What mattered for the archnationalist Croly, and for Progressives generally, was not the specific allocation of power among governments, but the fidelity of all governments to the common purpose. Croly distinguished between centralization, for which he claimed no presumption, and nationalization, which he declared to be "an essentially formative and enlightening transformation" in which the "political, economic and social organization or policy" of a people was coordinated with "their actual needs and their moral and political ideals."[31] Follett would have eschewed the term *nationalization* in favor of "true federalism," but they were alike in stressing the overriding importance of shared social ideals.

Particularly in framing an agenda of institutional reform, Progressive Era political thought treated all levels of government as important and distinct. To people bent on political change, the states had an exceptional attractiveness because of the flexibility of their constitutions. This was true whether the change was sought in policy or institutions. Benjamin DeWitt, who was both chronicler and a voice of the Progressive movement, wrote of the states that "because they are not so strictly limited by their constitutions, because they can more easily amend their constitutions when they are limited, because of the liberal interpretation of the so-called police power, states are able to grapple with modern social and economic problems much more effectively than the federal government can."[32]

In *The Promise of American Life*, Croly dismissed most constitutional reform at the federal level as a waste of time but then wrote a lengthy chapter on reform of the state governments, arguing for greater concentration of power and responsibility. He had very benign, positive expectations of the role that state governments so reformed might play. He saw them—and could be cited more convincingly than Brandeis on this point—as places of experiment. As such, they would be far superior to the federal government:

> Obviously a state government is a much better political agency for the making of . . . experiments than is a government whose errors would affect the population of the whole country. No better machinery for the accomplishment of a progressive programme of social reform could be [devised] than a collection of governments endowed with the powers of an American state. . . . Such a system would be flexible; it would provoke emulation; it would encourage initiative; and it would take advantage of local ebullitions of courage and insight and any peculiarly happy local collection of circumstances.

He went on to suggest that governors, endowed with greater powers so that they would be the real political leaders of their states, should meet periodically "for the purpose of comparing notes obtained under widely different conditions and as the result of different legislative experiments."[33] Late in 1907, President Roosevelt invited all of the governors to convene at the White House in 1908 to discuss conservation, a meeting that laid the foundation for subsequent governors' conferences.[34]

In regard to municipal governments, Progressives likewise expressed disappointment with experience of the past but held out high hopes for the future. Much of the energy of Progressivism went into the reform of municipal governments. Croly wrote of this movement in 1909 with great optimism: "In all probability, the American city will become in the near future the most fruitful field for economically and socially constructive experimentation." Like Progressives generally, he endorsed home rule. In exclusively local matters, cities should be able to govern themselves without interference from the states.[35]

Perhaps most important, Progressives exhibited no profound or consistent bias against small-scale polities per se. Simon Patten's plan for reversing the decay of state and local governments was to have smaller units of greater homogeneity. Progressives as a group made no important contribution to that strand of American political thought running from James Madison in *Federalist* No. 10 to Grant McConnell in *Private Power and American Democracy*, which has held that small-scale democracy is inherently defective, more prone to tyranny than the large scale and less able to protect diffuse, intangible, "public" interests.[36] On the contrary, the communitarians among them, such as Follett, Dewey, and Josiah Royce, rested their theories explicitly on respect for small-scale societies, leaving an important legacy in defense of the local.[37]

Follett constructed her ideal democracy on the foundations of neighborhood association. So did Dewey, who declared that "democracy must begin at home, and its home is the neighborly community. . . . Unless local communal life can be restored, the public cannot adequately resolve its most urgent problem: to find and identify itself."[38] But it was Royce who advanced the most compelling and elaborated case for what he chose to call "provincialism." He defined a province as any part of a national domain that had a consciousness of its own unity, was proud of its own ideals and customs, and possessed a sense of its distinction. Provincialism was the tendency of a province to possess its own customs and ideals; the totality of the customs and ideals themselves; and the love and pride that led the inhabitants of a province to cherish these traditions, beliefs, and aspirations.

He then argued that a "wholesome provincialism" is "the absolute necessity for our welfare" because it is a bulwark safeguarding individuality against mob spirit and the homogenizing, leveling tendencies of modern life that breed mediocrity. "Keep the province awake," he counseled, "that the nation may be saved from the disastrous hypnotic slumber so characteristic of excited masses of mankind." Individuals and provinces should both learn freely from abroad, but then insist on their interpretation of the common good.[39] Royce spoke as Tocqueville, but in a native tongue—that of a Californian who became a professor of philosophy at Harvard and who all but apologized to his listeners and readers for having left his province. His continuing fidelity to it is manifest in his history of California, written after the move to Cambridge: a "labor of love" in which he undertook to comprehend "the process whereby a new and great community first came to a true consciousness of itself."[40]

While Progressives wanted to construct a great national community, it was not part of their project to deny claims of community, or yet of greatness, elsewhere. Without using the term, they embraced the spirit of Madison's compound republic.

Conclusion

Progressive Era thought on the subject of federalism is of enduring interest both for the effects that it had and for those that it did not seek. It marks a critical stage in the transition from compact-based, conflictual federalism to what Samuel Beer has called "national federalism," rooted in a conception of popular sovereignty and presuming cooperation rather than conflict in intergovernmental relations. The passing of "dual federalism," which Edward S. Corwin announced in a classic article in 1950 and seemed to locate in the New Deal, is more properly traceable to intellectual developments of the Progressive Era.[41] It also helped lay the basis for a more elastic, forgiving constitutional law and for putting to rest the doctrine that the federal government was a government of limited powers.

Nonetheless, it did not root federalism out of the constitutional framework or even try very hard to do so. By accepting a federal system of distinct and constitutionally protected governments and by failing to conceive of egalitarian measures of public policy, at least implicitly (though in some cases explicitly), it accepted spatially defined political societies within the larger society that differed from one another. The attack on federalism, though powerful, was arguably halfhearted. Why?

Federalism as a constitutional principle may have been too deeply embedded to attack. Yet Progressives did not shrink from proposing constitutional amendments, nor from making the Constitution easier to amend.

Unlike modern liberals, who disdain federalism because they associate it with racism, Progressives were insensitive to issues of race or pessimistic about the ability of the national government to deal with them. Some of them appear to have believed in the superiority of the Anglo-Saxon race, as they would have called it. Others may have harbored the illusion that the Civil War had disposed of racial questions. Thus James A. Garfield could say in 1869, in a speech that foreshadowed Progressivism, "Now that the great question of slavery is removed from the arena of American politics, the next great question to be confronted will be that of the corporations and their relation to the interests of the people."[42] Later, having witnessed the end of Reconstruction, others tended to dismiss the federal government as ineffectual in respect to civil rights for Negroes. Henry Jones Ford wrote that "federal authority showed itself signally incompetent in dealing with the race problem."[43]

Progressives may also have been insufficiently radical to attack the income inequalities that modern liberals decry and more loosely associate with federalism. Croly inveighs against inequalities in wealth only to recommend a graduated inheritance tax, doubtless anticlimatic to a modern liberal reader.

Our view is that modern liberals can take the positions they do, including recommendations for interlocal and interstate redistribution of wealth, because the Progressives laid foundations for them. Progressives took the first giant steps toward destroying laissez-faire and constructing the welfare state. For their modern heirs to object that they failed to take steps even more gigantic ignores the way democracy works, which is for the most part gradually, by discussion, except in times of crisis.

We believe that they were halfhearted because they were reluctant to mount a full-scale attack on localism and regionalism in American public life. Many of them valued what would be destroyed in such an attack. Even in their most radical measure of constitutional change—the proposal for a popular vote on constitutional amendments—they preserved an element of regionalism. They did not call for a national referendum on amendments, but referenda within the states, with a requirement that protected regional interests by making approval depend on a majority of the people in a majority of the states.

In the tension between nation and locality, they sought, for the most part, a middle way, be it balance or blend. Whether it should be a balance, which presumed a large measure of autonomy for all communities, or a blend, which threatened to submerge if not extinguish the local, they never agreed. There was no single Progressive Era prescription for community or federalism; one is hard put to reconcile the views of Patten and Follett.

Their legacy is an engagement with the dilemma of scale in a democracy, a dilemma that contemporary political science has failed to treat with the seriousness it deserves. To a student of federalism and of American political institutions generally, the Progressive Era is of interest because its political thinkers grappled with the central question of the American political experiment: whether it is possible to realize self-government on a grand scale.

This was the question that had pitted Federalists against Anti-Federalists at the framing. One could argue that early experience vindicated the Anti-Federalists' claims. They had said that the heterogeneity of the large nation would cause instability. "Instability" is a mild term for the cataclysm of the Civil War, but the Civil War, ending in Union victory, only imparted new drama to the experiment, which then entered a different phase. So decentralized was the pre–Civil War United States that it had not seriously tested the Anti-Federalist claim that democracies must be small. This was a nation of isolated, self-governing hamlets, the little rural republics immortalized by Tocqueville. Not until the nation developed more fully would it become necessary to confront the question of whether development was compatible with democracy.

That task awaited the Progressives soon after the turn of the century, in a nation now populous, continental, industrializing, urbanizing, increasingly interdependent, stratified, and strained by industrial conflict—in short, "modern."

What they said about federalism constituted one important component of their response. United in a desire to strengthen the national character of American democracy, they were also concerned, though in different ways and to varying degrees, with preserving the virtues of decentralization and provincialism. Their work may or may not seem satisfying at the end of the twentieth century, but its impact is such that it requires the attention of anyone who wishes to understand the evolution of America's federal institutions. Moreover, its intellectual ambition, depth, and seriousness were such that it deserves to be studied, along with contemporaneous rejoinders, by anyone who would prescribe a direction for federalism today.

We began by suggesting that what Progressives said about federalism was of greater long-run significance than any deliberate reform of the institution that they undertook. However, one ought not to overlook the consequences for federalism of the institutional changes that they fashioned with other ends primarily in view. As institutional reformers, they sought above all to perfect democracy by eliciting the purest possible expression of the public will. This had consequences for federalism, whether intended or not.

Most political scientists today would probably agree that the Progressive assault on organized political parties weakened a critical underpinning of the decentralized constitutional form.[44] They would probably also agree that the development of the rhetorical and plebiscitary presidency, speaking directly to and for the people, as fashioned by Theodore Roosevelt and Woodrow Wilson, was a critical step toward a perceived union of democracy and nationality, the particular project of Roosevelt and Croly, whose work remains for many students the quintessence of Progressive Era political thought.[45] Scholars would probably concur that the Progressives' expansion of the civil service at the federal and municipal levels and their promotion generally of professional expertise in government became a force for centralization as professional leaders found positions in large-scale governments.[46]

Perhaps most intriguing and debatable in its implications for federalism was the promotion of direct democracy at the state level. If some Progressives sought to fashion a union of democracy and nationality, some also elected to make use of the smaller-scale polities to institutionalize popular sovereignty, bypassing representative institutions altogether. Roosevelt stood with accustomed vigor for both causes. Arguably, in their political practices as distinct from their elaborated thoughts, Progressives collectively managed to deny that there was any dilemma of scale. Democracy could be realized, and realized in something that aspired to pure form, on any scale.

The ever trenchant Henry Jones Ford argued that the movement for direct democracy arose in response to the corruption of state legislatures: "The American people despise legislatures, not because they are averse to representative government, but because legislatures are in fact despicable." The initiative and referendum were ways of bypassing them and rendering them irrelevant. By providing an alternative and at least superficially superior method of obtaining the popular will, measures of direct democracy served to further discredit state legislatures and diminish them by comparison with Congress, although the Oregon-based sponsors of this movement, according to Ford, thought of their measures as temporary, to be abandoned except for emergency use once the probity of legislatures was secured through reform.[47]

Yet the changes endured and even flourished in some places, and the existence of direct democracy in the state governments, but not in the federal government, was to mean that public opinion would be expressed most directly and explicitly at the subnational level, thereby increasing the capacity of the states to be in the vanguard of policy development and to serve as laboratories of policy experimentation. To be sure, the states were already serving as policy initiators even before the Progressive Era, by virtue of their numbers, their diversity, and a historically privileged constitutional position. The direct democratic reforms that were enacted in the first two decades of the twentieth century had the effect of increasing their ability to do so.

Thus, in the last quarter of the twentieth century, a number of significant political movements have originated in initiative and referendum campaigns at the state level. The tax-limitation movement of the late 1970s and 1980s, which won its first major victory with the passage of Proposition 13 in California in 1978, is the leading example, but one could also point to the contemporary movement for limiting legislative terms, which enjoyed its initial success through the initiative process in Oklahoma in 1990, as well as the movement to require color-blind procedures in college admissions and government contracting, which gained significant momentum after a successful initiative campaign in California in 1996. Direct democratic institutions have also served as the vehicle through which states have experimented with revised public policies in the areas of bilingual education, immigration, and assisted suicide. In this regard, it is noteworthy that California, which has done more than any other state (and possibly more even than any other political actor) to set the national agenda in recent years, is also the most vigorous in its use of direct democracy.

Whether viewed as political thought or as institutional change, Progressivism's legacy remains nationalizing in its central tendency yet ambiguous in its implications for federalism. One might add "appropriately so," given the essential ambiguity of the federal form itself.

9

Roosevelt as Madison: Social Security and American Federalism

American federalism is the result of a calculated ambiguity about how many political communities to be. It began as an effort to be one and many at the same time: neither a nation nor a pure federation, but, in Madison's careful phrase, a "compound" republic, combining qualities of each form.

This ambiguous choice resulted in a government both complicated and changeable. On the whole, change has favored the national government. The dominant tendency in American political development is centralization of the federal system. Nonetheless, there are often ambiguities in the change, just as there was ambiguity in the original. A foremost example is the Social Security Act of 1935, which constructed the statutory framework for American social policy.

The Social Security Act was a landmark of the New Deal. According to Franklin D. Roosevelt's principal collaborator on this legislation, Secretary of Labor Frances Perkins, Roosevelt regarded it as the cornerstone of his administration, and "took greater satisfaction from it than from anything else he achieved on the domestic front."[1]

This essay was written for this volume and has not been published previously.

The act may be used, therefore, to explore Roosevelt's views about federalism. I maintain that he actually had views on the subject and was not merely an improviser. Further, he was sympathetic to the institution and was simultaneously and deliberately both a centralizer and decentralizer. This interpretation is at odds with much recent scholarship on the New Deal, which portrays Roosevelt as a committed centralizer forced to compromise by racist Southerners possessing disproportionate power in Congress.[2]

Framing the Act

On its face, the Social Security Act looked in two directions at once. Only one of its parts—old-age insurance—was independent of the state governments. All of the other titles—old-age assistance, unemployment compensation, aid to dependent children, maternal and child health, public health, and aid to the blind—depended on cooperation with the states. The administration chose to promote federal-state cooperation and preserve a large role for the states. Although there was strong sentiment for a more national approach within the administration, it did not prevail. The administration's leading figures in the field of social policy favored a large role for the states. Crucially, so did the president.

The federalism issue was joined mainly over unemployment compensation. Hard as it is to grasp today, given the program's present size, old-age insurance commanded much less attention. Aid to dependent children, which was the lightning rod of social policy from the mid-1960s to its abolition in 1996, commanded even less. Wilbur Cohen, one of the leading participants in the creation and evolution of the Social Security Act, doubted that Roosevelt even knew in 1935 that aid to dependent children was in the bill.[3]

By contrast, unemployment compensation produced heated debate both as a prelude to the act and throughout its planning. In the early 1930s, legislation to ease the effects of unemployment was under consideration in numerous state governments, New York and Wisconsin foremost among them. Roosevelt as governor of New York and Perkins as his industrial commissioner were leaders in this effort. Roosevelt had called a regional conference of governors on unemployment, which met early in 1931 with representatives of Massachusetts, Rhode Island, Connecticut, New Jersey, Pennsylvania, and Ohio as well as New York. Out of this conference came an Interstate Commission for the Study of Unemployment Insurance, and from it came a proposal for insurance financed by employer contributions. However, the only state actually to enact legislation was Wisconsin in 1932, and it did not implement the law for fear of adverse competitive effects.[4]

Following the presidential election of 1932, leaders of this movement carried their campaign to the national government. The Democratic platform of 1932 called for "unemployment and old-age insurance, under State laws." Perkins was now in Roosevelt's cabinet, and her department drafted an unemployment compensation bill in 1934. She and the president had agreed before she joined the administration to tackle both unemployment and old-age insurance.[5]

Guided by Justice Louis Brandeis—who was playing a vigorous role only slightly behind the scenes—his daughter Elizabeth ("E. B.") Raushenbush, and his son-in-law Paul Raushenbush, an economics instructor at the University of Wisconsin, Perkins's Office of the Solicitor at the Department of Labor produced an unemployment insurance bill consistent with Wisconsin's plan, which the Raushenbushes had been working on at the invitation of Governor Philip La Follette.[6] At Brandeis's suggestion, the bill used a tax offset technique. Congress would impose a tax on employers to finance unemployment compensation, but the tax would be forgiven in states that enacted such a tax themselves. New York's Robert F. Wagner, a pillar of the New Deal, introduced the bill in the Senate, and David Lewis of Maryland introduced it in the House, but Roosevelt chose not to push it. He preferred to wait until after the election of 1934 and then to pursue more comprehensive legislation.[7] In a message to Congress on June 8, 1934, that reviewed the administration's accomplishments and objectives, he affirmed a commitment to unemployment and old-age insurance, based on a "maximum of cooperation between States and the Federal Government."[8]

To plan the more inclusive measure, he created a cabinet-level Committee on Economic Security by executive order in the summer of 1934. Perkins was its chairman. Its executive director was Edwin Witte, who had been one of the framers of Wisconsin's unemployment compensation law, and the head of its technical committee was Arthur J. Altmeyer, also of Wisconsin, who had been head of that state's industrial commission—and thus Perkins's counterpart. Perkins had chosen him to be an assistant secretary of labor in the Roosevelt administration. This put three persons with state-level experience and strong state-level loyalties in crucial roles.

The planning effort also included strong partisans of purely national action. Preeminent among them were Bryce Stewart, who headed the unemployment insurance subcommittee of the technical committee, and Barbara Nachtrieb Armstrong, who with J. Douglas Brown headed the planning of old-age insurance within the technical committee. Both were academics, and Armstrong at least was quite headstrong and disinclined to stay on her own turf. Thomas H. Eliot, who was an assistant solicitor in the Department of Labor and principal drafter of the Social Security bill, or at least the assembler of drafts, recalls her as a "fierce advocate of national action on all fronts."[9]

Roosevelt's preferences emerged in mid-August, before the Committee on Economic Security had had its first meeting. Perkins, Witte, Altmeyer, and Eliot met with the president for nearly an hour. One of them said that some people were suggesting that unemployment insurance should be a national function. According to Eliot's contemporaneous record, Roosevelt responded, "Oh, no, we've got to leave all that we can to the states. All the power shouldn't be in the hands of the federal government. Look—just think what would happen if all the power *was* concentrated here, and *Huey Long* became president!"[10]

This is a remark of some constitutional subtlety and profundity, of a kind that one does not normally associate with U.S. presidents, at least when they are speaking spontaneously rather than in texts prepared with an eye to history's appraisal of their statesmanship. It calls to mind not just the Framers' fundamental argument for federalism—that a division of power between nation and states was desirable per se as a protection for the people—but also a complement to it that was laid out by James Madison in 1791, when he argued that consolidation of power in the national government would unwisely concentrate power in that government's chief executive.[11]

This pronouncement did not settle the matter. When the partisans of a purely national program for unemployment insurance understood that Roosevelt was opposed, they devised an alternative that became known as the "subsidy plan": full federal financing and tight federal controls of a program that the states would administer. Stewart and Armstrong argued for this before the advisory council to the Committee on Economic Security, with inconclusive results.[12]

In the parent committee, there was also continuing disagreement over national versus state control. In her memoirs, Perkins recounts that the committee held four special meetings on this one point between November 15, 1934, and January 1, 1935, and arrived at its recommendation only after an ultimatum that it come to her house during Christmas week and not leave until it reached a decision.[13] It decided on federal-state cooperation, using the tax offset method.

Nor did this settle the question. After the committee reached a decision, Witte had to draft a report and solicit the signatures of committee members, some of whom referred it to subordinates who had not been engaged in the committee's work. Witte encountered opposition particularly in Henry Wallace's Department of Agriculture. Rexford G. Tugwell, the undersecretary, and Jerome Frank, counsel of the Agricultural Adjustment Administration, both stubbornly favored a national system. Although they recognized that the decision had gone the other way, they wanted to influence the language of the committee report so that it did not fully endorse what it was recommending. This too was not the end. Dissenters in the advisory council and staff, including Stewart, submitted a statement of their own to the Senate Finance Committee arguing for the subsidy plan.[14] This attempt to undermine the parent committee had no effect on Congress.

In the other parts of the bill, the federalism issue was much less contentious. In regard to old-age insurance, even those, such as Perkins, who might have preferred intergovernmental cooperation yielded to an argument of administrative necessity. Actuaries who were giving technical advice to the Committee on Economic Security were unanimous in recommending a national program. The mobility of the labor force would make accounting and cost projections on a state-by-state basis impossible. Perkins's biographer says, "Like everyone else Perkins was soon convinced intellectually of the necessity of a federal [national] system, but emotionally the decision went against the grain. Throughout the fall she muttered to herself about it."[15]

Grants-in-aid to the states, which were used in the public assistance titles and also for public health and maternal and child health, did not stir major controversy, although Harry Hopkins, head of the Federal Emergency Relief Administration (FERA), an adviser to Roosevelt within the White House, and an active member of the Committee on Economic Security, opposed means-tested programs in principle.

Old-age assistance and aid to dependent children presumed means tests. Hopkins favored one comprehensive national program that would not distinguish "poor relief" from "insurance" and would give payments as a right. Any citizen, on proof of unemployment, old age, or ill health, regardless of need, could receive payments from the government, financed out of general revenues. Perkins remarks wryly in her memoirs that this was "a pretty extreme point of view for a country which had not had a social insurance system or a relief program before."[16] Perkins and Hopkins argued their rival positions to the president, who sided with Perkins. Roosevelt consistently preferred "insurance" financed with "contributions" from employees or employers over the "dole," income support financed from general revenues. He wanted workers to have a stake in the fiscal condition of the government. And he also wanted to bind future politicians to the payment of benefits to which contributors had secured a right through payment of earmarked taxes. Again, Roosevelt appears as a constitutional philosopher, reflecting on the mutual obligation of citizens and their government, as well as an astute political strategist.[17]

Despite defeat on this crucial issue, Hopkins remained a very engaged member of the Committee on Economic Security, and his agency sought to influence the bill at the congressional stage. Eliot wrote to his parents: "I . . . have to waste hours with the megalomaniacs of the F.E.R.A. who want to change the bill and give Hopkins complete power to toss millions around for old-age pensions just as he sees fit." In Eliot's eyes, Hopkins was Huey Long, even if unelected.[18]

Constitutionality

To present-day analysts of policymaking, it is hard to grasp how thoroughly preoccupied social policy planners of this time were with the Supreme Court and how little, relatively, with Congress. Congress might have loomed as a large obstacle had not the Court loomed as an even larger one. "The problems of constitutional law seemed almost insuperable," Perkins recalled in 1946.[19] Each title, each technique, was scrutinized for its prospects of being validated by the Supreme Court.

Roosevelt himself was the first of this New Deal group to try to cozy up to the justices and get the Court's cooperation. As a first step toward getting along with the Court, he had suggested a consultative relationship to Chief Justice Charles Evans Hughes. He wanted to discuss his legislative plans with the chief justice to get the Court's reaction before acting. Hughes had not accepted this suggestion in a friendly spirit and had let the president know that a strict separation between the branches was appropriate.[20]

Perhaps so, but strict separation does not describe what was going on during planning for the Social Security bill. There is the well-known story of Frances Perkins, at tea with Mrs. Harlan Fiske Stone, receiving sotto voce advice from her hostess's husband, Justice Stone: "The taxing power of the Federal Government, my dear; the taxing power is sufficient for everything you need and want."[21] Perkins thereafter insisted within the committee on the taxing power as the basis for the unemployment and old-age insurance programs.

There was the ardent, indiscreet intercession of Justice Brandeis in regard to unemployment compensation. The tax offset technique had a large advantage in that Brandeis had recommended it. During the summer of 1933, the two Raushenbushes visited Brandeis in Washington, and he urged them to study the Court's decision in *Florida* v. *Mellon* in 1926.[22]

Congress had enacted a federal estate tax but allowed the taxpayer to off-set, against the federal tax, most of whatever was owed in state inheritance taxes. Florida brought suit, arguing that this offset provision was unconstitutionally coercing the states to enact inheritance taxes. The Supreme Court unanimously rejected Florida's claim and upheld the statute. Justice Brandeis urged his daughter and son-in-law to consider how this precedent might be used to construct unemployment insurance. In the fall of 1933 he wrote them a letter further explaining the relevance of *Florida* v. *Mellon*, and on New Year's Day in 1934, when Elizabeth Raushenbush was again in Washington to see her parents, she had an opportunity to explain the idea at a dinner party that included Senator Wagner and Secretary Perkins. Perkins transmitted the idea to the Labor Department's solicitor, Charles Wyzanski, and he to Eliot, who began drafting.[23] Thus did the tax offset technique get off to an early and highly advantageous start.[24]

Grants-in-aid to the states likewise had an advantage, resting on the Supreme Court's decision in *Massachusetts* v. *Mellon* in 1923. A unanimous Court had turned aside Massachusetts' challenge to the Sheppard-Towner Act, which gave conditional grants to the states for maternal and infant health. Massachusetts claimed that the law induced states to yield sovereign rights reserved to them. The Court held that the states' choice to accept the grants was voluntary and that there was no deprivation of a right that fell within judicial cognizance.[25]

It might be supposed that the subsidy plan for unemployment compensation would have been constitutionally safe, inasmuch as the subsidy was a grant. But it would have been an unprecedented grant in that it did not presume any state matching funds and it would have been financed with an earmarked payroll tax. Also, it would have come with a large measure of federal control. Thus it could easily have been interpreted as a regulatory scheme invading the reserved rights of the states.[26]

Given the precedents of *Florida* v. *Mellon* and *Massachusetts* v. *Mellon*, the titles relying on intergovernmental cooperation seemed unproblematic from the standpoint of constitutional law. "But what in the world," Eliot wondered, "could be devised to carry out the president's wish for a contributory old age insurance program that would pass judicial muster?"[27] Anxiety increased in May 1935 when the Supreme Court invalidated the Railroad Retirement Act. The decision came a few days after the Senate Finance Committee began executive sessions on the Social Security bill. *Business Week* reported that it proved that the Court "would smash any social security legislation that may be passed by Congress."[28] Because Justice Owen Roberts was in the majority in this case, there were fears within the administration that he had permanently joined the conservatives, giving them a majority. This anxiety would not be alleviated until 1937, when the old-age insurance titles of the Social Security Act were upheld 7-2 in *Helvering* v. *Davis*. Ironically, the decision was closer (5-4) in the case (*Steward Machine Co.* v. *Davis*) that dealt with the unemployment compensation title.[29]

Congress

Fifty years after the event, at an academic conference, Wilbur Cohen argued that President Roosevelt could have abolished the states in 1935:

> Perhaps with a little exaggeration, I think Franklin Roosevelt in 1934–35 could have wiped out the states in the United States if he hadn't taken the position he did. The governors that live today don't realize that in 1932–33 the states and the counties were bankrupt sovereignties. Franklin D. Roosevelt could have nationalized the banks in 1933, he could have eliminated the states, he could have nationalized unemployment insurance, and welfare and everything else. I think it would have been accepted because people were homeless, the equivalent of thirty million people unemployed today were without work then.[30]

There is more than a little exaggeration here. The Constitution stands in the way of eliminating the states, and so does Congress, which eventually did exert influence on the states' behalf in the course of fashioning the Social Security Act.

As the time approached for submitting a bill to Congress, administration planners grew more sensitive to its likely response. As work on unemployment insurance came down to the wire and the Committee on

Economic Security grappled with the federalism question, it received warning signals. Perkins recalled: "There was grave doubt, our latest interviews with members of Congress had shown, that Congress would pass a law for a purely federal system. State jealousies and aspirations were involved."[31]

In regard to the grant-in-aid programs, the administration had abundant reason to expect a favorable response at least to old-age assistance. There was tremendous political pressure to provide relief to the indigent elderly, and Congress had already gone far toward responding. The House had passed a bill that gave grants to the states for old-age pensions, and a Senate committee had reported it favorably. It was the one part of the Social Security bill that Congress was sure to like, and for that reason was made title 1.

The politics of maternal and child health was more problematic, inasmuch as Congress had let the Sheppard-Towner Act lapse in 1929 because of the opposition of the American Medical Association (AMA). The politics of aid to dependent children was unknown, as Congress had taken no prior action. As it turned out, maternal and child health fared better in Congress in 1935, because the AMA had ceased its opposition. As Cohen explained it, the AMA was so much against health insurance in 1935 that it had to figure out something to be for, and that turned out to be infant and maternal health, financed through grants to the states.[32] The Sheppard-Towner Act was revived and expanded.

Old-age assistance and aid to dependent children passed, but only after Congress eased the conditions that administration planners had proposed to attach to the grants. The key issue was whether to require the state governments to pay individual recipients of public assistance "a reasonable subsistence compatible with decency and health." Led by members from Virginia—Harry F. Byrd in the Senate and Howard W. Smith in the House—Congress objected to that language, which would have opened the door to federal determination of the size of payments. It was dropped. Instead, the purpose of the public assistance titles was framed in terms that left discretion with the states: "for the purpose of enabling each State to furnish financial assistance, as far as practicable under the conditions in such State." Also, the committee reports were cast in such a way as to safeguard the states' discretion in regard to need and size of payments.[33]

In regard to administration, Congress removed a provision that would have required the state governments to establish a merit system for selecting employees who were engaged in the aided functions: old-age assistance, aid to dependent children, maternal and child health. "No damned social workers are going to come into my State to tell our people whom they shall hire," in the words of Representative Fred M. Vinson of Kentucky, an influential member of the Ways and Means Committee.[34]

Congress thus reinforced the decentralizing tendencies that were dominant within the administration. It endorsed federal-state cooperation, and in the public assistance titles it set terms that were advantageous to the states. It also added a public assistance title, grants-in-aid for the blind.

In the unemployment compensation title, as with public assistance, Congress made changes that enlarged the discretion of the states. Senator Robert M. La Follette of Wisconsin offered the key amendment, which provided that each state could have the type of unemployment insurance system it desired.[35] Eliot, reflecting on Congress's preference for protecting the states' discretion, was "glad that I'd so vehemently opposed the subsidy plan [for unemployment compensation]." He had done so because he had feared that the Court would strike it down, but "now I came to feel that its safe passage through Congress would have been problematical at best."[36]

The Merits of Intergovernmental Cooperation

Wilbur Cohen came nearer the mark when he said of Roosevelt and his state-oriented subordinates and allies—Perkins, Altmeyer, Witte, the Raushenbushes—that they defended "the federal-state system," that "they really saved the federal-state system from virtual extinction."[37] It was not that they prevented abolition of the states, which was not constitutionally feasible, but that they built on and substantially enlarged the practice of federal-state cooperation, which had foundations in grant programs of the late nineteenth and early twentieth century and in the philosophy of progressivism.

Trying to capture the spirit that animated Perkins and her state-oriented collaborators—including, possibly, himself—Cohen said that they were motivated "by a social consciousness of preserving the community. . . . Frances Perkins and Arthur Altmeyer and Edwin Witte . . . products of the La Follette-Progressive period . . . were trying to preserve what was good in our social relationships." They were "infused with a sense of trying to keep the body politic, the social fabric, the community solidarity together."[38] Implicit in this statement is the Progressive view that the social fabric was complex and that community existed at different levels of government and on different scales. The essence of governance was cooperation in pursuit of shared social ideals.

Perkins's preference for cooperation with the states rested on a combination of sentiment and experience. "She was always, in everything, 'a states-righter,'" her biographer says. "She had worked in a state government for twelve years, had seen it operate successfully a system of accident insurance (workmen's compensation) and believed in keeping the administration of such programs close to the people." In this, she was to be contrasted with Harry Hopkins, who, "with less experience of state government and as administrator of federal relief in constant battle with several of the states, strongly favored a [national] system."[39]

Perkins's own recollection of her early experience in public life may give more insight:

I only knew the state. I was much more aware of New York and of belonging to it than I was of belonging to the U.S.A., which perhaps is wrong and unpatriotic, but I honestly believe that's how people develop. You become responsible for a small area you can see. You gradually know the rest.[40]

Roosevelt's commitment to intergovernmental cooperation may conceivably have owed something to a rewarding experience as chief executive of New York. He moved quickly from under the shadow of his predecessor, Al Smith, to take command of the executive branch. This was in contrast with the earlier experience of his cousin Theodore, who throughout his term had to contest with Boss Platt (Thomas Collier Platt, who controlled the New York State Republican Party) for control of the government. When the Depression struck, FDR was the first governor to call for state aid for relief, and the New York Temporary Emergency Relief Administration, under Harry Hopkins, was the first state relief agency to take action.[41]

Roosevelt took seriously the argument that states had value as laboratories, which Arthur Altmeyer thought he had derived from Lord Bryce's *The American Commonwealth*. According to Altmeyer, Roosevelt knew Bryce personally and had been deeply impressed by the book. When Frances Perkins came back from California to warn that Upton Sinclair might be elected governor in 1934 on the strength of his EPIC (End Poverty in California) program, which she judged fanatical and dangerous, Roosevelt brushed the news off:

Perhaps they'll get EPIC in California. What difference, I ask you, would that make in Dutchess County, New York, or Lincoln County, Maine? The beauty of our federal-state system is that the people can experiment. If it has fatal consequences in one place, it has little effect upon the rest of the country. If a new, apparently fanatical, program works well, it will be copied. If it doesn't you won't hear of it again.[42]

Significantly, however, Roosevelt's respect for federalism was grounded as well in experience of national politics. The depression era gave rise to demagogues, not just Huey Long, but also Francis Townsend, leader of a movement that sought to cure the depression by having the government guarantee monthly payments of at least $200 to every person over sixty on the condition that the money be promptly spent. Roosevelt as president and later Altmeyer as his administrator of Social Security feared such movements as a threat to the fiscal responsibility of the federal government. As counterweapons, they valued both the contributory principle of social insurance, which taught that citizens earned a right to benefits through work and payment of payroll taxes, and federalism, which diffused the cost of public programs and also relieved the pressure on elected politicians to give away the treasury.[43]

In this respect too, Roosevelt was Madisonian. He saw federalism as a complement to separation of powers within the national government, containing the power of the presidency if it fell into dangerous hands, and also as a way of containing the power of a mass electorate, such as Huey Long's constituents. When liberals in his administration wanted to increase the federal share of public assistance payments, he sharply resisted: "Not one nickel more, not one solitary nickel. Once you get off the 50-50 matching basis, the sky's the limit, and before you know it, we'll be paying the whole bill."[44] He did not want to pay the whole bill or come under political pressure to do so.

Altmeyer adduced still other arguments for relying on federal-state cooperation. In respect to unemployment compensation, he argued political necessity. There was no consensus about the form that unemployment compensation should take. In addition to the federalism question, numerous others had caused intense controversy: the amount and duration of benefits, whether protection should extend to seasonal unemployment and partial unemployment, whether there should be employee and government contributions in addition to those of the employer, whether employer taxes should be pooled or remain individualized, and whether to use experience rating. Should individual firms or industries pay more if they had poor records of maintaining employment?

In Altmeyer's view, these questions were not ripe for resolution. Under either a straight federal system or even the proposed subsidy system, there would have to be national rules in the absence of the necessary experience and agreement. Besides, the administrative problems in setting up a nationwide system appeared "staggering."[45]

The New Deal figure most intellectually engaged in federalism was Justice Brandeis, whom the archnationalist Tugwell, from his base in the Department of Agriculture, suspected of having undue influence on Roosevelt. Brandeis's philosophy was a species of Anti-Federalism updated for the twentieth century. He favored public undertakings on a small scale because this kept matters within the reach of ordinary individuals. He had written to Felix Frankfurter in 1921 that "men must be induced to set to work to do those things public which are within their immediate grasp and within their capabilities of performance. In that way possibly they may also be taught to love their community enough to make it livable."[46]

To young New Dealers, Brandeis counseled work in state and local governments rather than Washington. When his son-in-law declined a job with the Social Security Board to stay in Madison and remain in charge of Wisconsin's unemployment program, Brandeis was pleased because the "important" work was in the states.[47] "His ideal," law professor Edmond Cahn declared in 1956, "is a society throbbing with novelty, improvisation, creative invention—a society in which, at any given moment, there are countless experiments under way to discover better and still better methods, not only to produce and sell goods but—what is more important—to adjust and harmonize human relations."[48]

Similarly, Frankfurter testified,

> Mr. Justice Brandeis' regard for the States is no mere lip service. He is greatly tolerant of their powers because he believes intensely in the opportunities which they afford for decentralization. And he believes in decentralization not because of any persisting habit of political allegiance or through loyalty to an anachronistic theory of states' rights. His views are founded on deep convictions regarding the manageable size for the effective conduct of human affairs and the most favorable conditions for the exercise of wise judgment.[49]

One month after the Supreme Court struck down the National Industrial Recovery Act in *Schechter Poultry Corp.* v. *United States*, Brandeis gave a confidential interview to two journalists at his summer home in Chatham, Massachusetts, citing the day of decision as "'the most important day in the history of the Court and the most beneficent,'" because it had "'compelled a return to human limitations.'"[50]

Weighing the Balance

From the perspective of today, the Social Security Act appears much more nationalizing than it did at enactment. Primarily this is because not all of its titles were equal. With backing from the Social Security Board (later, Administration), whose leaders preferred contributory insurance to means-tested assistance, and who eventually were joined in that preference by congressional leaders and organized labor, title 2 grew into today's gargantuan program of retirement, survivors, and disability insurance. Over time, means-tested programs declined in relative importance.

Likewise from the perspective of today, it is hard to credit Tugwell's fear that Roosevelt was unduly influenced by Justice Brandeis. Although Roosevelt declined to choose overtly between Brandeis and the rival advisors, such as Hopkins and Tugwell, who favored a large and powerful national government, the sum total of his deeds over the course of his four terms was far more nationalizing than not. He invited citizens to look to government as they had not done before, to the national government more than state and local governments, and to the executive branch—president and agencies—more than to parties or legislature. To be sure, he thought that the national bureaucracy should be decentralized. He had the notion that the administrators of social insurance would inhabit post offices, and citizens would visit them as they visited the local grocery store or bank. In conversation, he would use the hypothetical case of his farm manager, Mose Smith.[51]

Despite this rhetorical concession to local sentiment, it strains credulity to portray Roosevelt as Brandeisian in practice. He had too much relish for the use of power on a large scale, and he worked assiduously to fashion new instruments to that end. It is fair to locate him, as I have tried to do here, in the protean tradition of Madison—Madison, that is, more than the rigidly nationalistic Hamilton—because of the way in which he applied a constitutional intuition and judgment based on experience.

Again from the perspective of today, one can see that the Social Security Act became an occasion for the Supreme Court to execute its famous switch and begin withdrawing objections to social and economic legislation. Along with *West Coast Hotel* v. *Parrish* and *NLRB* v. *Jones and Laughlin Steel Corp.*, decisions on the Social Security Act in 1937 heralded the change.[52] The decision in *Steward Machine Co.* v. *Davis*, on the unemployment compensation title, was particularly significant for federalism. Justice Cardozo's opinion for the Court held that the excise tax imposed by the statute did not coerce the states in violation of the Tenth Amendment or call for a surrender by the states of powers essential to their "quasi-sovereign" existence. The opinion sided with the supporters of the statute, who argued that "its operation is not constraint, but the creation of a larger freedom, the states and the nation joining in a cooperative endeavor to avert a common evil."[53] Thus the New Deal put into large-scale practice, and ultimately sanctioned with a new constitutional law and no small rhetorical sleight of hand, the Progressive commitment to cooperation among governments to combat common evils. Such cooperation was not just permissible. It was good.

Wilbur Cohen had a point in arguing that the Social Security Act propped up the state governments. By requiring them to contribute matching funds for public assistance, submit state plans, and be responsible for administering those plans, whether directly or through supervision of local governments, it drew them into a major public function that previously they had left almost exclusively to local governments and private charities.

In 1932 the states spent only $74 million of their own funds directly for welfare, a sum surpassed both by local governments' spending for that function ($370 million) and by the states' own spending for other functions: education, highways, health, hospitals, and natural resources. Twenty years later, state direct spending for welfare had passed local direct spending ($1.410 billion to $1.378 billion), had passed spending for health, hospitals, and natural resources, and was roughly even with spending for education. It lagged behind only spending for highways.

Until Social Security Act amendments in 1972 federalized aid to the aged, blind, and disabled with the Supplemental Security Income (SSI) program, states retained primary responsibility for means-tested assistance to those three categories of the poor. And even then it proved politically impossible to federalize Aid to Families with Dependent Children, although beginning in the mid-1960s, as that program grew and ignited controversy, it became an object of expanding federal supervision, both legislative and judicial. In 1996 it was abolished in favor of Temporary Assistance for Needy Families (TANF), a measure that was nominally decentralizing but nonetheless expressed an altered national policy preference in favor of work and responsibility over a right to income support. Medicaid has developed as a major shared program, building on the New Deal foundation of sharing for means-tested programs, and unemployment compensation remains shared.

One could debate for all of the shared programs just where prevailing influence lies, but the fact that this question is debatable—that scholars who gather at conferences still argue about it—is testimony to the original ambiguity, whether by "original" one means 1789 or 1935.

10

Crossing Thresholds:
Federalism in the 1960s

Compounded as it is of contrasting forms, the purely national and the purely federal, federalism in the United States is inherently unstable.[1] The division of power and prerogative between nation and states constantly changes, tending normally to become more national. Sometimes change occurs more swiftly and penetrates more deeply than others, and that was the case in the 1960s. One after another, constitutional thresholds were crossed. By the mid-1970s, American federalism had become something very different from what it had been fifteen years before. Place had lost much of its importance in the American polity. Autonomous individuals as political actors had gained at the expense of place-based communities. So had groups identified by such rival attributes as race or gender.

The Prior Condition

The original constitutional design, with Civil War amendments, made the states vulnerable to subordination. The national government emerged supreme from the work of constructive revision undertaken in Philadel-

This essay first appeared as "Crossing Thresholds: Federalism in the 1960s," *Journal of Policy History*, vol. 8 (1996), pp. 64–80.

phia in 1787, as the supremacy clause above all attests. Eight decades later, national supremacy was very much enhanced by the language of the Fourteenth Amendment. But the federal system is shaped as much by use and wont as by constitutional language, and use and wont favored the states in many ways for a very long time.

No doubt, *Brown* v. *Board of Education* in 1954, the imposition of force in Little Rock in 1957, and the Supreme Court's ringing assertion of its own supremacy in *Cooper* v. *Aaron* in 1958 were heralds of what would come.[2] Also in the mid-1950s, authorization of the interstate highway system took the national government's involvement in public works to a new extreme. Yet when Eisenhower left office at the end of the decade, federalism had merely been challenged, not transformed. An array of constitutional customs that protected the states was largely intact.

One such custom was leaving to the states decisions about the most basic forms and procedures of representative government: the definition of legislative districts and determination of voter qualifications. The Fifteenth Amendment (1870) had prohibited denial of the right to vote on the basis of race or "previous condition of servitude," and the Nineteenth Amendment (1920) had prohibited denial of that right on account of sex. *Smith* v. *Allwright* (1944) had outlawed the white primary. But in *Colegrove* v. *Green* (1946), the Supreme Court had declined to enter the "political thicket" of reapportionment, and the Fifteenth Amendment had not been enforced in the twentieth century.[3]

The precept that the national government had limited powers still contained life. Not much life, perhaps, because it had begun to give way as soon as the Constitution of 1787 was put into practice. Yet there remained at least two major domestic functions, schools and police, both of them crucial to defining and enforcing local mores, that the national government had barely touched. Neither local police departments nor elementary and secondary schools received grants-in-aid, except for the "impact aid" that went to schools near military bases and grants to improve the teaching of mathematics, science, and foreign languages under the National Defense Education Act of 1958. Those who argued for enlarging the domestic functions of the national government still had to bear a burden of proof and be ready to quell fears of federal control.

The South possessed disproportionate influence in the Democratic Party and in Congress, which it used to safeguard regional exceptionalism in the name of states' rights. While the South could not win the Democratic presidential nomination, it could influence the composition of that ticket.

While it could not command the congressional majorities necessary to enact law, it could, with the instruments of minority power—committee chairmanships, manipulation of the rules, the filibuster—veto laws, although once again there was a herald in the 1950s of impending change. A civil rights act had passed Congress in 1957, significant more for the fact of its passage than for what it contained.

The *Civil Rights Cases* of 1883 were still good law, with their holding that Congress could not prohibit private acts of discrimination because to do so would invade a domain reserved to the state governments. Likewise still valid was Chief Justice Roger B. Taney's holding in *Kentucky* v. *Dennison* (1861) that "the Federal Government, under the Constitution, has no power to impose on a State officer, as such, any duty whatever, and compel him to perform it." Henry M. Hart, Harvard's authority on constitutional law, wrote in 1954 that "Taney's statement can stand today, if we except from it certain primary duties of state judges and occasional remedial duties of other state officers."[4] Mandates—that is, affirmative commands upon the states from Congress or the courts—were as yet undeveloped, if not actually unknown.

The national government was spending large amounts for grants-in-aid to state governments for highways and public assistance. The conditions that accompanied these grants had had significant effects on the composition and structure of state and local governments. Merit system requirements had been instrumental in extending civil service coverage; under the national government's prodding, patronage had yielded more rapidly to professionalism. Also, requirements for the development of state plans and statewide uniformity had very much strengthened state governments vis-à-vis local ones in respect to the aided functions. Grant conditions had not, however, been designed to recast local social structures or alter the relations between citizens and local governments. In public assistance, which was the biggest single program of grants-in-aid before the interstate highway act took effect, individuals' eligibility remained largely under state and local control, and with it the potential remained for using eligibility to enforce locally sanctioned norms of behavior. Moreover, grant conditions were hard to enforce. The only weapon available to the national government was to withhold funds, which was self-defeating. Hence grants were not in general an instrument with which national policy could be used to challenge local mores.[5]

For the most part, state and local officials went about their routine business with little awareness of national government supervision. While aided functions received some scrutiny for limited, mainly administrative purposes, even they remained fundamentally subject to the state governments' discretion. There was no elaborated body of constitutional law in respect to the conduct of local police. Still less did any such law constrain school-teachers or welfare workers. Without a thought to the Constitution or laws of the United States, school principals could expel unruly students and send boys' athletic teams onto grassy fields and hardwood courts while girls were confined to flouncing on the sidelines as cheerleaders. There was no comprehensive, generalized system of national scrutiny of state and local government conduct.

This would change in the 1960s.

The Changes

For the most part, the changes that transformed federalism were expressed in congressional acts and Supreme Court decisions. Only one constitutional amendment bearing on federalism—abolition of the poll tax—was adopted in the 1960s. Because most of them defy simple categorization, I will list chronologically the most important things that Congress and the Court did. Ordinarily, they involved some combination of the following types of action: they expanded the definition of constitutional rights; they enlarged the jurisdiction staked out by Congress under Article I of the Constitution; they revised the infrastructure of citizen participation to make it more inclusive and egalitarian; or they increased the leverage of the national government and the depth of its intervention in programs shared with subnational governments.

—In 1961 the Supreme Court decided *Monroe* v. *Pape*, which broadened interpretation of section 1983 of title 42 of the U.S. Code.[6] Enacted in 1871, this law made federal judicial remedies available to anyone who was deprived of a U.S. constitutional or statutory right by a person acting "under color of any statute, ordinance, regulation, custom, or usage, of any State."

Although not a dead letter, section 1983 had been used infrequently until the 1960s. Then two things happened. First, judicial interpretation and legislative enactment together began broadening the domain of nationally defined rights, and hence the potential reach of section 1983. Second, the Court in *Monroe* enabled plaintiffs to seek damages in a federal court as a first resort—a front-line remedy—rather than as a backstop to be used only after state-level remedies had been exhausted. *Monroe* also made clear that the law provided protection against actions by state officials even when there had been no showing that their actions were encouraged in any way by state law or policy.[7] In 1961, the year of the *Monroe* decision, fewer than 300 suits were brought in federal courts under civil rights acts. A quarter century later, in 1986, more than 40,000 such suits were brought, chiefly under section 1983. About half of these were prisoner petitions, filed by individuals incarcerated in state and local jails. The rest covered the full range of state and local government activity.[8]

Litigation in federal courts might be used by private citizens against government agencies, such as detainees against the police, public housing tenants against official landlords, or the mentally ill against mental health institutions. Public school students proved to be prolific litigators, with challenges to dress codes, expulsions, attendance assignments, curriculum materials, corporal punishment, personal searches, limits on expression in student newspapers, restrictions applying to marriage or pregnancy, and access to programs of special education. But section 1983 suits might also be used by public employees against their employers, as in the case of schoolteachers who challenged loss of employment or alleged restrictions on speech and association.[9]

Cases might be addressed to individual conduct only, resembling conventional tort actions against state and local officials. Or they could be fashioned to address systemic problems, challenging whole regimes of law enforcement, imprisonment, education, or mental health administration. As the rights revolution advanced, federal judicial supervision began to extend, through the instrument of section 1983, to everything that state and local governments did.

—In 1962, with *Baker* v. *Carr,* and 1964, with *Reynolds* v. *Sims* and a set of companion cases on state legislatures, the Supreme Court plunged into the political thicket of reapportionment, accepted jurisdiction of the question, and laid down a rule. The equal protection clause of the Fourteenth Amendment required states to draw districts in both houses of their legislatures so as to achieve equality of population because individual citizens possessed a right to an equally weighted vote. Place in the form of political subdivisions, which had frequently been represented as such in the upper houses of state legislatures, might be taken into account, but even "a clearly rational state policy" recognizing this factor would be unconstitutional if "population is submerged as the controlling consideration."[10]

The dogmatism of the new rule was evident especially in the case of *Lucas* v. *Forty-Fourth General Assembly.* The formula that was struck down in Colorado had based apportionment of the lower house strictly on population and deviated only modestly from that principle in the upper house. It had been approved in a referendum by voters in all counties of the state, who had simultaneously rejected an alternative plan that would have based districts in both houses on population only. Chief Justice Warren dismissed the Colorado plan with the argument that "a citizen's constitutional rights can hardly be infringed simply because a majority of the people choose that [they] be."[11]

In the wake of these decisions state legislatures were reapportioned throughout the country; also the new nationally prescribed rule was applied to representative districts within local units of government. State and local governments and, not incidentally, state and local electorates were stripped of much of their discretion in the critical matter (in a democracy) of defining the meaning of representation. Moreover, the constitutional ground that the Court chose for its decision—the equal protection clause of the Fourteenth Amendment—was one inherently inimical to federalism. As Robert Bork has argued, the Court could have honored majority rule and federalism simultaneously had it been willing to employ instead the constitutional clause that guarantees each state a republican form of government (Article IV, section 4).[12]

—In 1964 Congress enacted the Economic Opportunity Act, title 2 of which authorized funds for community action programs, through which localities were supposed to mount innovative, coordinated efforts to combat poverty. Programs could be sponsored by private nonprofit agencies, in which case grants would bypass local governments. Regardless of who administered them, the programs had to be "developed, conducted, and administered with the maximum feasible participation of the residents and areas and members of the groups served." As administered by the Office of Economic Opportunity, this program deliberately sought to organize the poor and engage them in self-serving political activity even if this fostered conflict with city governments. Mayors protested, and President Johnson, who had backed the program, retreated. The effort did not last long, but it remains emblematic of national officials' urge in the 1960s to change the relation between local governments and the citizenry, especially poor citizens.[13] Also at this time, Congress attached citizen participation requirements to various grants for welfare and urban development. This was a new type of grant-in-aid condition, contrasting with the earlier emphasis on promoting efficiency and professionalization of administration.

—In 1964 Congress passed the most far-reaching civil rights act since Reconstruction. For the first time, the Senate defeated a southern filibuster over civil rights. The act contained new provisions to secure voting rights for African Americans; guaranteed access to public accommodations such as hotels, motels, restaurants, and amusement places; authorized the Department of Justice to sue to desegregate public facilities, including schools; extended the life of the Civil Rights Commission for four years and enlarged its powers; and required most companies and labor unions to grant equal employment opportunity. With respect to federalism, the most important part was title 6, which prohibited racial discrimination in the administration of federal grants-in-aid. Although little debated by comparison with the public accommodations or equal employment sections, it ultimately had perhaps the most sweeping effects. "Within a year after President Johnson signed the Civil Rights Act," Gary Orfield has written, "unknown bureaucrats were drawing on the authority granted by Title VI to administer a major social revolution in thousands of southern school districts."[14]

—In 1965 Congress enacted the first program of general aid to elementary and secondary education, a measure that it had debated off and on without result since the end of World War II. Distribution of funds was weighted to benefit districts with a high incidence of poverty, of which there were many in the South.

—Also in 1965, Congress extended the Medical Assistance for the Aged program, which it had enacted in 1960, to cover children, the blind, and the disabled. Now called Medicaid, this was a program of grants-in-aid to state governments to provide medical care to indigent persons. The enactment of 1965 changed the character of the national authorization by requiring the states to provide certain services. Previously, the national government had helped to pay for state programs of medical and hospital care. Now it became much more prescriptive, introducing a distinction between services that were mandatory and those that were permitted. Eventually, in the 1980s, the enlargement of Medicaid's mandatory coverage became one of the strategies that Congress, led by the highly entrepreneurial Representative Henry Waxman of California, employed to broaden public provision of health care.

—In 1965 Congress enacted the Water Quality Act, which directed each state to set water quality standards for interstate waters within the state and to adopt a plan for implementing and enforcing the standards. If a state failed to establish and enforce standards that were approved by the

U.S. Secretary of Health, Education, and Welfare, then the secretary could propose national standards that would take effect after a stipulated waiting period.

—Likewise in 1965, Congress enacted bold new guarantees of voting rights for African Americans in the South. The most sweeping voting rights bill in ninety years suspended the use of literacy tests or similar qualifying devices and authorized the U.S. attorney general to appoint national examiners to order registration in certain southern states and counties.

The statute also required national approval ("preclearance") of all changes in the method of voting in covered jurisdictions: those identified as having a record of minority disfranchisement by an arguably questionable formula. The impact of this provision very much increased after 1969, when the Supreme Court in *Allen* v. *State Board of Elections* interpreted a voting change to include the redrawing of district lines, the institution of at-large elections or multimember districts, the relocation of a polling place, and urban annexations of adjacent suburban or rural areas.[15] Between 1965 and 1991, the Department of Justice reviewed 188,048 such changes and objected to more than 2,000 of them.[16] The voting rights revolution thus extended the reapportionment revolution. Together they turned the national government into the supervisor of a wide array of electoral arrangements that the customs of federalism had once committed to state and local discretion.

—In 1966 the Supreme Court decided *Miranda* v. *Arizona*, which held that no statement made by a person in custody of the police could be used in court unless the suspect had been offered the assistance of a lawyer.[17] *Miranda* was the climax of an effort to extend constitutional supervision over the conduct of local police. Beginning in 1961 with *Mapp* v. *Ohio*, which dealt with search and seizure, the Court repeatedly refined the due process requirement of the Fourteenth Amendment, which until then had been held to mean only that states must observe "fundamental fairness" in criminal matters. The Court changed the due process requirement to demand absolute compliance by state and local police with key provisions of the Bill of Rights. In an effort to make criminal law more egalitarian, the Court reinterpreted some of the major provisions of the Bill of Rights, with emphasis on the privilege against self-incrimination and the right to counsel. From 1961 with *Mapp* to Earl Warren's departure as chief justice in 1969, the Court handed down more than 200 opinions on criminal issues, spinning a web of constitutional restriction around local police and prosecutors.[18]

—In 1968 Congress passed the Omnibus Crime Control and Safe Streets Act, the most ambitious anticrime legislation it had ever produced. Among other things, the law authorized grants via the state governments to upgrade state and local police forces and law enforcement methods. Widely adjudged a failure, the grant program was slashed in the wave of budget cutting with which the 1980s began. Yet it remains a symbol of nationalization. The police, like schools, had long been insulated from national intervention. For both police and schools, insulation ended in the 1960s.[19]

—Early in 1968 Congress enacted a law that prohibited discrimination in the sale or rental of housing with the sole exception of privately owned housing being sold or rented without the services of a real estate agent or broker. Some months thereafter, the Supreme Court handed down its decision in *Jones* v. *Alfred H. Mayer Co.*, which, contrary to the *Civil Rights Cases* of 1883, established Congress's power under the Thirteenth Amendment to prohibit private racial discrimination.[20]

—Also in 1968, the Supreme Court decided *Green* v. *County School Board of New Kent County*, which insisted upon the disestablishment of dual school systems, white and black. The case arose out of a freedom-of-choice plan in Virginia, under which white and black students were ostensibly free to choose which of two schools they wished to attend, but which produced virtually no integration in three years. In effect, the Court now decreed integration. Fourteen years after *Brown*, it demanded a plan that would "promise realistically to convert promptly to a system without a 'white' school and a 'Negro' school, but just schools." Within three years, the case would lead to *Swann* v. *Charlotte-Mecklenburg Board of Education*, which endorsed busing.[21]

—Between 1968 and 1972, the Supreme Court reversed a long-standing presumption of state control over eligibility standards for Aid to Families with Dependent Children (AFDC). Before 1968, state control over benefit levels and eligibility standards was the norm, and national regulation the exception. Then, in a series of cases known as the *King-Townsend-Carleson* trilogy, the Court made states' restrictions on eligibility invalid unless they were explicitly authorized by Congress. This interpretation threw nearly all state eligibility rules into doubt. Before 1968, the Supreme Court had never decided a case dealing with AFDC, for which the federal government began giving the states grants in 1935. Between 1968 and 1975 it decided eighteen such cases, some constitutional in nature, others "merely" statutory, as were *King*, *Townsend*, and *Carleson*.[22]

This list of Court decisions and congressional enactments is by no means exhaustive. There were other civil rights laws and other civil rights decisions. There were other important nationalizing measures in the field of environmental protection. And there were dozens, if not hundreds, of new grant-in-aid programs. Indeed, students of federalism often remember the 1960s as above all a time in which categorical grants-in-aid exploded. More appropriately, the decade should be remembered as a time in which the mores of federalism underwent a massive change. The national government moved freshly and boldly into the critically important domains of civil rights, schools, police, and legislative districting. It very much enlarged its place in the domain of welfare. It sought to impart equality to African Americans and political efficacy to the poor. With goals so ambitious across so broad a front, it groped for more effective instruments of influence vis-à-vis state and local governments. And it found them.

Federalism Afterward

What Congress and the Court did in the 1960s amounted to more than the sum of the parts. In a way unprecedented for domestic purposes, national programs, institutions, and techniques of influence came together to enlarge national power at state and local governments' expense. Federalism as a constitutional principle was sharply devalued. Long-established understandings of what was proper and permissible were cast aside.

A synergy of national actions in support of social reconstruction developed at this time, evident above all in regard to southern school desegregation. National judicial action by itself had not sufficed. As of 1964 only Texas and Tennessee, the two southern states with the lowest percentage of black enrollment, had more than 2 percent of their African American students in integrated schools. But after Congress acted to prohibit discrimination in the use of national funds and the executive branch developed a means of enforcement, change came much faster. These instruments, in turn, would have been far less useful had Congress not enacted a general program of education aid.

In developing guidelines for school desegregation, executive officials in the Office of Education depended heavily on courts. They drew on case law, because administrative standards that were actually judicial standards were sure to withstand attacks in court. The executive's guidelines generalized and implemented decisions that the courts acting alone lacked power to enforce. Then, as the bureaucracy consolidated judicial gains, the judges were free to break new ground—and they did so even as political support appeared to weaken. With *Green* v. *County School Board of New Kent County,* "the courts again emerged at the forefront of the battle."[23]

The reconstruction of southern schools took place within a context of the reconstruction of southern politics, itself part of the transformation of federalism. First legislative reapportionment and then, more dramatically, the Voting Rights Act increased the power of African Americans as voters. Change on one institutional front impelled change on others.

Such changes could take place only because federalism had ceased to be valued as it once was. While that may seem mere tautology, it could have been the case that changes in the mores of federalism occurred as incidental and cumulative by-products of efforts to reform race relations, education, police, or welfare. That was by no means entirely so.

Consider the testimony of John Marshall Harlan, a justice of the Supreme Court who often hesitated to join the majority in its threshold crossings. Speaking off the bench in 1969 in a tribute to the memory of Justice Robert H. Jackson, Harlan reflected on the Court's enlargement of the Fourteenth Amendment as a prescriptive device:

> The most wide-ranging impacts have been in the fields of criminal law and of state legislative apportionment, and I do not think that it can be said that the end is yet in sight. . . . The important thing, I think, is not so much whether the particular changes themselves are good or bad as it is the fundamental shift such changes evince in the current approach to federal-state relationships. This shift must be recognized as involving something more than mere differences among judges as to where the line should be drawn between state and federal authority in particular cases arising under the Fourteenth Amendment. It reflects, I believe, at bottom a distrust in the capabilities of the federal system to meet the needs of American society in these fast-moving times, and a readiness on the part of the federal judiciary to spearhead reform without circumspect regard for constitutional limitations upon the manner of its accomplishment. To those who see our free society as dependent primarily upon a broadening of the constitutional protections afforded to the individual, these developments are no doubt considered to be healthy. To those who regard the federal system itself as one of the mainsprings of our political liberties, this increasing erosion of state authority cannot but be viewed with apprehension.[24]

The tenacity and violence of southern resistance to changes in race relations gave federalism a very bad name. Repeatedly, extreme acts of resistance elicited a national response. When a system of decentralized power was seen to produce flagrant violations of fairness (now literally seen on national television), the system itself was discredited.

Further evidence that the momentum of policy change did not alone drive institutional change is the fact that policy change was eventually slowed or reversed on several fronts while subordination of the states continued to advance. School desegregation stalled in the 1970s as it moved north. Congress signaled disapproval of the due process revolution in criminal justice with attempts to qualify *Miranda*, while Richard Nixon won election at the end of the decade partly by campaigning against a court that was "soft on crime." After Nixon made several appointments, the Court began to qualify its positions on welfare rights, criminal justice, and even apportionment.

Once again, the history of school desegregation is pivotal, and it illustrates the point. School desegregation elicited extreme and unprecedented exercises of national power in the late 1960s and early 1970s as district judges sought to fashion decrees for particular school districts. Desegregation by decree, Archibald Cox observed in 1975, required courts to formulate "controversial programs of affirmative action requiring detailed administration for protracted periods under constant judicial supervision." In major metropolitan areas the busing decrees had "all the qualities of social legislation: they pertain to the future; they are mandatory; they govern millions of people; they reorder people's lives in ways that benefit some and disappoint others in order to achieve social objectives."[25]

So unpopular was busing by decree that it reached its limits swiftly; in *Milliken* v. *Bradley*, the Court in 1974 declined to endorse interdistrict, metropolitan area–wide busing.[26] *Milliken* v. *Bradley* is no doubt a case in which the Court deferred to the traditions of federalism, yet the instrument itself—the affirmative judicial decree—once deployed did not disappear. In the 1970s federal judges repeatedly ordered state and local governments to do quite specific things in regard to prisons, mental hospitals, police behavior, and much else. A whole new perception of the state governments as subordinates of the national government, properly subject to command, had taken root, laying the basis for the regulation that spread like kudzu through the garden of American federalism in the 1970s.

In a major study issued in 1984, the Advisory Commission on Intergovernmental Relations (ACIR) reported that "over the past two decades . . .—and since 1969 in particular—there has been a dramatic shift in the way in which the federal government deals with states and localities. . . . Federal policymakers . . . turned increasingly to new, more intrusive, and more compulsory *regulatory* programs to work their will."[27] In retrospect, the 1960s appear as a necessary prelude to the 1970s, or the latter as an inevitable sequel to the former.

Increasingly through the 1970s, states became the proximate targets of regulation, subject to what the ACIR called "direct orders." They came to be regulated just as private entities are. Thus, for example, in 1972 the Equal Employment Opportunity Act prohibited job discrimination by state and local governments on the basis of race, color, religion, sex, and national origin, extending to them prohibitions that in 1964 had been imposed on private employers. In 1974, the Age Discrimination in Employment Act prohibited discrimination on the basis of age in state and local government employment.

In addition to regulating state and local governments directly, the national government increasingly made them agents of its purposes through aggressive use of grant-in-aid conditions and partial preemptions. The ACIR gave the name "cross-cutting requirements" to conditions that applied across the board to federal grant programs. The Office of Management and Budget had taken an inventory of such conditions in 1980, finding that there were fifty-nine of them, of which two-thirds had been imposed since 1969. In particular, title 6 of the Civil Rights Act of 1964 had been a precedent-setter, the granddaddy of cross-cutting requirements. Having barred racial discrimination in federally aided programs, Congress had proceeded similarly to protect the disabled, the elderly, and, in education programs, women.

"Partial preemption" was the ACIR's name for a technique that in 1965 had made a benign initial appearance in the Water Quality Act. In the Clean Air Act Amendments of 1970, it appeared in a more stringent, less qualified form. Each state was commanded to prepare a plan ("each State shall . . .") for implementing, maintaining, and enforcing national ambient air quality standards. The law prescribed the contents of such a plan and provided that the administrator of the Environmental Protection Agency should create an implementation plan for a state if the state failed to do so itself or failed to secure the administrator's approval for its submission.

Such use of the states to enforce national standards became an increasingly common technique in national regulatory programs, and it was upheld by the Supreme Court in *Hodel* v. *Virginia Surface Mining and Reclamation Association* in 1981.[28] States had to adopt national standards as their own, although they were sometimes permitted to adopt more exacting standards than those of the national government. If they declined to accept national standards or fell short in implementation, at least in theory the national government would take over the function, displacing them.

What the 1960s had begun, the 1970s made routine and pervasive. It remained for the 1980s to give a name—"mandates"—to the new custom, which was by then well established.[29]

The change in American federalism that took place in the 1960s was more profound than any that occurred in the New Deal. During the New Deal, Congress had laid claim to much broader powers of spending and economic regulation, and the Supreme Court, after initial opposition, came to sanction this departure. In *U.S.* v. *Darby*, which in 1941 upheld the Fair Labor Standards Act, the Court dismissed claims of state prerogative with the pronouncement that the Tenth Amendment was "but a truism."[30]

The New Deal was notable as well for various decisions in which the Supreme Court repudiated the long-standing postulate that the states were separate, equal, and sovereign governments and as such were entitled to a wide range of immunities. This was one of the key postulates of what constitutional scholar Edward S. Corwin called "dual federalism," and by 1950 Corwin had pronounced the doctrine of dual federalism dead.[31]

Still, it was one thing for the national government to make radically broadened claims of authority to regulate commerce, and another to make rules applying to the state governments' own conduct. That, the New Deal refrained from doing. The old-age insurance provisions of the Social Security Act did not cover state and local employees because in 1935 no one thought that Congress could impose a payroll tax on state and local governments. The Fair Labor Standards Act did not apply to state and local governments as employers because in 1938 no one thought that it was constitutionally appropriate to regulate them. Not until 1966 did Congress begin to extend the law to cover state and local employees.

It was one thing to regulate relations between capital and labor, as Congress boldly did during the New Deal, arguably at the states' expense, and quite another to alter the social structures of local communities or regulate relations between citizens and state and local governments, as Congress and the Court undertook to do in the 1960s. It was one thing to cease viewing the state governments as separate, sovereign, and equal, and another to view them as dependent, subordinate, and inferior.

The transformation in American federalism that took place in the 1960s is often interpreted as Justice Harlan interpreted it in his tribute to Justice Jackson. Federalism, embodying a calculated distribution of power between nation and states, was sacrificed for the sake of constitutionally guaranteed individual rights. In a clash between individual rights and a set of institutions that dispersed government power, rights won.

Another way of looking at the matter, perhaps more consonant with the outcomes that are perceptible today, is that one type of group—the place-based group that federalism had honored—yielded to groups otherwise defined, as by race, age, disability, or orientation to an issue or cause. Historically, the place-based community, often defined as a unit of government, had played a preeminent part in American politics and governance, most particularly and fundamentally in the design of representative arrangements. The institutions of federalism had protected the place of place in the American political system. In modern society, the territorial community is exposed to many technological, sociological, and economic insults. As the institutions of federalism weakened, the territorial community lost governmental protection, and this contributed to diminishing its importance relative to all the other types of groups that form and make claims to political favor.

The erosion of federalism per se was not unique to the 1960s. Centralization of governmental power within the American federal system has been a secular trend of long standing, and Americans' attachment to place has always been ambiguous. Perhaps nothing has been as inimical to the decentralized institutions of federalism as total war, which invigorates the nation and uproots the populace, as in the 1860s and 1940s.

What was distinctive about the 1960s was that, for the first time in a century, changing federalism became an end in itself, consciously pursued by numerous holders of national power who were trying to reconstruct American society and politics. It was not just an incidental by-product of war or modernization.[32] With a view invariably to southern racism, which tainted states and localities as a class, Supreme Court majorities repeatedly rendered decisions that were more than indifferent to federalism; they were inimical. And when the Court's actions were complemented by the aggressively liberal, nationalizing presidency of the Texan Lyndon Johnson and the Congress of his Great Society, in which northern liberals successfully challenged southern conservatives' control of the Democratic Party in the Senate, the result was a profound and permanent change in the relations among governments in the federal system.

11

Half-Full or Half-Empty?

In the summer of 1999, the *Wall Street Journal* noted that some taxpayers had been claiming that they did not have to pay federal income taxes because they were residents of a state, not the United States. At about the same time, the *New York Times* carried a story describing the plan of Vice President Albert Gore, then the leading candidate for the Democratic presidential nomination in 2000, to have detailed positions on a very wide range of issues. He had begun with education, a function that not so long ago was considered a preserve of state and local governments, and had made such proposals as preschool for all children, a ban on gang-style clothing, teacher testing, parent-teacher meetings at the start of the year in which the participants would sign a strict discipline code, and "character education" courses in the schools.[1]

As these contrasting conceptions of American federalism suggest, it is a highly protean form, subject to constant reinterpretation. It is long on change and confusion and very low on fixed, generally accepted principles. In the event, a tax court judge imposed fines on the citizens who made their radical claim about not being citizens of the United States. Gore did not get the chance to put his plans to a test, but the *Times* reporter in 1999 noted that it was perhaps unrealistic of a presidential candidate to speak of such positions as "requirements" that a president would impose.

This essay was first published as "American Federalism: Half-Full or Half-Empty?" in *Brookings Review*, vol. 18 (Winter 2000), pp. 24–27.

As the twentieth century ends, it is often suggested in public commentary that this is a time of decentralization in the federal system. This view derives mainly from passage of a welfare reform act in 1996 that officeholders and analysts alike interpreted as radically devolutionary and from a series of Supreme Court decisions that have sought to rehabilitate the states in constitutional doctrine.

I will argue that matters are more complicated. Change is occurring. It perpetually occurs in American federalism, though the scope and pace vary from one era to another. It is not unusual for the change to go in contrary directions—centralizing and decentralizing—at once. American federalism was born in ambiguity, it institutionalizes ambiguity in our form of government, and changes in it tend to be ambiguous too.

To sort out what is happening, I will distinguish among three spheres of activity: constitutional interpretation by the Supreme Court; electoral politics; and the everyday work of government as manifested in policies and programs.

The Supreme Court

A narrow majority of the Rehnquist court, led by the chief justice, attaches importance to the preservation of federalism, and this has led to a series of daring and controversial decisions that purport to limit the powers of Congress or secure constitutional prerogatives of the states.

One leading case is *Printz* v. *U.S.* (1997), in which the Court invalidated a provision of the Brady Handgun Violence Prevention Act that required local law enforcement officers to conduct background checks on all gun purchasers. The Court found that the provision impermissibly violated the Tenth Amendment by commandeering the state governments to carry out a federal law. An earlier opinion, *New York* v. *U.S.* (1992), had begun to lay the ground for the anticommandeering principle. Another leading case is *U.S.* v. *Lopez* (1995), in which the Court held that Congress had exceeded its commerce clause power by prohibiting guns in school zones. Still other decisions signaled a retreat from federal judicial supervision of school desegregation, prison administration, and the judgments of state courts. Another line of cases has secured the state governments' immunity from certain classes of private suits under federal law.[2]

Some analysts profess to see a revolutionary development here, but qualifications are in order. The Court decides many cases in which it does not give primacy to federalism, as for example a 7-2 decision in 1999 in which it ruled that state welfare programs may not restrict new residents to the welfare benefits that they would have received in their states of previous residence. This struck down a California law and by implication a provision of federal law that had authorized it.[3] Moreover, the majority that has decided the leading federalism cases is narrow (often 5-4) and tenuous, inasmuch as it includes some of the oldest members of the Court. The decisions have not exactly been hailed by legal scholars, even some who might be thought sympathetic. Charles Fried of the Harvard Law School, a former solicitor general in the Reagan administration, denounced the June 1999 series of decisions on immunity from suits as "truly bizarre" and "absurd."[4]

If this is a revolution, it is one that may not last.

Electoral Politics

Speaker Thomas P. O'Neill's famous aphorism that "all politics is local" applied very well to virtually all structural aspects of electoral politics for a very long time. Determination of electoral districts and voter qualifications, mobilization of voters, and campaign finance were governed mainly by state laws and customs and were locally rooted well into the twentieth century. That has ceased to be true, as a result of twentieth-century constitutional amendments extending the electorate and federal statutes and judicial decisions governing apportionment and voting rights. Federal supervision now extends even to such matters as ward-based versus at-large elections in local governments. Also, changes in technology and social and economic structures mean that candidates for congressional seats or even lesser offices do not depend exclusively on funds raised from within local constituencies. They may get help from party committees and interest groups organized on a national scale.

That nationalization of electoral practices proceeds apace at the century's end is shown by the Motor Voter Act of 1993, which requires states to provide all eligible citizens the opportunity to register to vote when they apply for or renew a driver's license. It also requires states to allow mail-in registration and to provide registration forms at agencies that supply public assistance, such as welfare checks or help for the disabled. The costs are to be borne by the states.[5]

Nevertheless, one hesitates to insist that our electoral processes are being comprehensively nationalized at a time when, in regard to nominations for the presidency, governors seem to have gained an advantage. Of the four last presidents in the twentieth century, three were governors immediately preceding their election, and in the run-up to the 2000 election, a governor, George W. Bush of Texas, secured a large and early advantage over other Republican candidates. He did so partly because other Republican governors backed him. There were thirty-two such governors after the election of 1998, and Michigan's John Engler took the lead in soliciting their support for Bush.[6] A presidential nomination originating in the action of elected officials of state governments takes one back in time all the way to 1824, when several state legislatures put forth candidates.

Policies and Programs

Here it is necessary to be selective, because there are so many policies and programs. I will concentrate on three that traditionally have been quite decentralized: welfare, schools, and criminal justice. For decades, they constituted the bedrock of local government activity.

The welfare reform legislation of 1996 (the Personal Responsibility and Work Opportunity Reconcilation Act) is everyone's leading example of decentralization in action. The law converted what had been an open-ended matching grant, with federal funds tied to the number of cases, to a fixed-sum ("block") grant, and it explicitly ended individuals' entitlements to welfare. States gained freedom to design their own programs, a change that had already been largely effectuated by White House decisions during the Reagan, Bush, and Clinton administrations to grant waivers of certain federal requirements to individual states.[7] The decentralization of program authority in this case was an important change in intergovernmental relations. Still, its significance should be put in perspective with the following facts.

Whatever may have happened with welfare in 1996, the function of income support, which is the core function of the modern welfare state, has been largely federalized in the United States in the six decades since 1935.[8] Social Security, Supplemental Security Income, and food stamps accounted for $431 billion in federal spending in 1998, compared with $22 billion for welfare, now known as Temporary Assistance for Needy Families (TANF). This is not to mention the role played by the earned-income tax credit, a use of federal tax laws for income support that weighs in at a volume comparable to that for welfare.

Welfare could be decentralized in 1996 in large part because, unlike support for the aged and the disabled, it had never been effectively centralized. The main change that occurred in 1996 was a policy change at the national

level strongly in favor of discouraging dependency and certain behavior—
especially out-of-wedlock pregnancies and fathers' abandonment of their
children—that had come to be associated with it. Some stringent federal
requirements on the states designed to effectuate this policy change, such
as time limits for receipt of welfare, were incorporated in the law.
Surprisingly, a liberal president and conservative members of the new
Republican majority in Congress coalesced in support of legislation, but
the national-level coalition was so frail and incomplete that it became necessary to lodge discretion in the states to achieve a result.

That is one of the political functions that American federalism has
always performed: in the absence of agreement at the national level, discretion can be left to the states. Historically, this has been done through
inaction by Congress. Matters were left with the states, which had initial
jurisdiction. What was new in 1996 was that so much centralization in Aid
to Families with Dependent Children (AFDC) had occurred in the generation since the mid-1960s that giving discretion to the states required an
affirmative act. It required giving back some portion of what had been
taken away, as much by federal courts as by Congress.[9] "No more individual entitlement," the most arresting phrase in the act, was directed at alter-
ing relations between Congress and the federal judiciary. I would argue that
the law had at least as much significance for what it said about interbranch
relations at the federal level as about relations among governments in the
federal system.

Elementary and secondary education, far from being off limits to
national politicians as a local matter, has risen to the top of presidents' and
presidential candidates' rhetorical agendas and is the subject of partisan
debate in Congress. It took a year to reauthorize the Elementary and
Secondary Education Act in 1993–94. The resulting law consumed fourteen titles and 1,200 pages, covering subjects as wide-ranging as academic
standards, racial desegregation, language assessments, migrant education,
teacher training, math and science equipment, libraries, hate-crime prevention, vouchers, school prayer, sex education, gay rights, gun control, the
handicapped, English as a second language, telecommunications, pornog-
raphy, single-sex schools, national tests, home schooling, drugs, smoking—
and more. As an example of the level of detail, consider the provisions
regarding gun possession. Any state receiving federal funds had to have a
policy requiring that any student who brought a gun to school would be
expelled for at least a year. Local officials could, however, modify this
requirement on a case-by-case basis. School districts also had to refer such

students to local law enforcement officials. Developmentally disabled students were subject to this rule for expulsion, except that if school officials established that the behavior of such students was related to their disability, the offender could be placed in an alternative educational setting for up to forty-five days instead of being expelled.[10]

In 1999, when the act was again up for reauthorization, Congress by wide margins enacted "Ed-Flex," the Education Flexibility Partnership Demonstration Act, which authorized the secretary of education to implement a nationwide program under which state educational agencies could apply for waivers of federal rules in some programs, though not in all. To be eligible for Ed-Flex, states had to develop educational content and performance standards and procedures for holding districts and schools accountable for meeting educational goals.[11] One could point to this law, of course, as an example of decentralization; members of Congress naturally did so. But in education as in welfare, the subject of waivers would never even have arisen had not a vast body of law and regulation developed from which relief was to be sought.

In criminal justice, it remains true that most police and prosecutors are state and local officials. Ninety-five percent of prosecutions are handled by state and local governments. Yet federal criminal law has grown explosively as Congress has taken stands against such offenses as carjacking and church burning, disrupting a rodeo, and damaging a livestock facility. As Senator Joseph Biden of Delaware, a veteran member of the Judiciary Committee, has put it, "We federalize everything that walks, talks and moves." A task force report of the American Bar Association published early in 1999 documented and decried this development, but is unlikely to stop, let alone reverse, it.[12]

In addition, there is a fourth and more elusive category of activity that I will call the "mores" of intergovernmental relations. In everyday affairs, how do citizens and officials think and talk about governments in the federal system? Without having any evidence to support my point, I would argue that citizens and journalists routinely refer to "the government" as if there were only one: the Big One. That this is a country of many governments, though a patent fact, is nonetheless a fact that it takes a pedant or a lawyer to insist on.

Moreover, we are now accustomed routinely to reading that Washington is giving orders to the states, or at least exhorting them to act in regard to one or another matter in which they have been found deficient. Here are some sample headlines from end-of-the-century stories in the *New York Times*, stories that would appear very odd to a student of American government who had gone to sleep in, say, 1955 and just awakened: "Clinton to Require State Efforts to Cut Drug Use in Prisons," "White House Plans Medicaid Coverage of Viagra by States," and "Clinton to Chide States for Failing to Cover Children."[13] None of this is necessarily to say that the states promptly act upon orders or admonitions from Washington, only that Washington is accustomed to giving them, without pausing to question the appropriateness of doing so.

This leads to a final subject: an executive order on federalism that the Clinton administration issued, suspended when state officials angrily protested both its contents and the fact that they were not consulted about it, and then issued in much revised form following consultation. The offending order, issued in May 1998, contained a set of criteria for policymaking by federal agencies that were broad and inclusive enough invariably to justify federal government action:

> (1) When the matter to be addressed by federal action occurs interstate as opposed to being contained within one State's boundaries. (2) When the source of the matter to be addressed occurs in a State different from the State (or States) where a significant amount of the harm occurs. (3) When there is a need for uniform national standards. (4) When decentralization increases the costs of government thus imposing additional burdens on the taxpayer. (5) When States have not adequately protected individual rights and liberties. (6) When States would be reluctant to impose necessary regulations because of fears that regulated business activity will relocate to other States.[14]

Only the most restrained and unimaginative federal administrator could not have put this list to use.

The executive order that replaced this one, issued following consultation with state officials, was completely different. The section on policymaking criteria called for "strict adherence to constitutional principles," avoiding limits on policymaking discretion of the states except with constitutional and statutory authority, granting "maximum administrative discretion" to the states, encouraging states to "develop their own policies to achieve program objectives," where possible deferring to the states to "establish standards," consulting with appropriate state and local officials "as to the need for national standards," and consulting with them in the development of national standards when such were found to be necessary.[15]

It is hard to imagine a more complete about-face. It is also hard to know how to interpret the event. One can cite the original order as evidence of the imperious attitudes that high federal officials actually bring to intergovernmental relations, or one can cite the revision as evidence of the continuing power of the states. In studying American federalism, the analyst is forever asking whether the glass is half empty or half full. That is the appropriate question as the century turns, and the answers are to be found more in the day-to-day operations of intergovernmental relations than in either Supreme Court decisions or executive orders.

Arguably, it is perverse to hail devolution as a *revival* of American federalism when the very idea—with its intimations that the federal government is handing power back to the states—signifies a change in modes of thought about federalism, and in conceptions of the sources of government authority, that is fundamentally inimical to the states.

In American constitutional theory, the federal government possesses no powers that it can give to the states. The powers of all governments, federal and state, come from the people, and are prescribed in written constitutions that originate with them. The federal government began as a government of limited and enumerated powers. As the Tenth Amendment says, the powers not granted to it were reserved to the states and to the people. Thus, when the Supreme Court, in its historic and freshly reasserted role as arbiter of the federal system, makes a decision of constitutional law that is favorable to the states, it is not "devolving" power. It is rendering a judgment that the people's supreme law requires a certain allocation of power and functions between the federal government and the states. Such judgments are of course debatable, the more so today because the Court for several decades eschewed a conscious defense of federalism. But the shock with which such decisions have been received among many students of constitutional law suggests the extent to which federalism has lost legitimacy over time. The widespread perception, indicated by the choice of *devolution* to describe the phenomenon, is that a centralized system is being dismantled rather than that a complex compound is being preserved.

Insofar as devolution refers to reduction of the many grant-in-aid conditions that have come to restrict state governments as the price of receiving federal financial assistance (as in welfare reform), one must recall that the precondition of decentralization is centralization. The states originally conducted most domestic functions without federal aid or encumbrance.

Only over time, and mostly since the mid-1960s, did Congress and the federal courts impose pervasive restrictions. One should recall as well that the very act of decentralizing welfare in 1996 entailed a vigorous exercise of national power and produced a national law of a length and complexity that would have been unimaginable before the 1960s.

Notes

Introduction

1. *The Papers of James Madison*, vol. 9 (University of Chicago Press, 1975), p. 369.

2. Ibid., p. 299.

3. Walter Berns, "The Meaning of the Tenth Amendment," in Robert A. Goldwin, ed., *A Nation of States* (Rand-McNally, 1963), pp. 126–48; and Herbert J. Storing, "The Constitution and the Bill of Rights," in M. Judd Harmon, ed., *Essays on the Constitution of the United States* (Port Washington, N.Y.: Kennikat Press, 1978), pp. 32–48.

4. For analyses of the Court's recent work in regard to federalism, see John J. Dinan, "The Rehnquist Court's Federalism Decisions in Perspective," *Journal of Law and Politics*, vol. 15 (Spring 1999), pp. 127–94; Timothy J. Conlan and Francois Vergniolle de Chantal, "The Rehnquist Court and Contemporary American Federalism," forthcoming, *Political Science Quarterly* (Summer 2001); and Frank Goodman, ed., *The Supreme Court's Federalism: Real or Imagined?*, Annals of the American Academy of Political and Social Science, vol. 574 (March 2001).

5. "Stunning" was used by Vicki Jackson, associate dean and professor at the Georgetown University Law School, in a seminar presentation, "Federalism and the Supreme Court," at the National Academy of Public Administration in Washington, February 21, 2001. Jeffrey Rosen of the George Washington University Law School writes in a portrait of Justice Sandra Day O'Connor that she is the leader of the "federalism revolution that may be the Rehnquist court's most distinctive legacy, returning power from Washington to the states." "A Majority of One," *New York Times Magazine*, June 3, 2001, p. 34. See also Steven G. Calabresi, "Federalism and the Rehnquist Court: A Normative Defense," in Goodman, ed., *The Supreme Court's Federalism*, p. 25, for testimony to the "revolutionary importance" of the recent decisions.

6. See, for example, Linda Greenhouse, "The High Court's Target: Congress," *New*

York Times, February 25, 2001, p. WK3, in which she writes: "More clearly than any precedent on which it built, the decision [in *Board of Trustees of the University of Alabama* v. *Garrett,* dealing with discrimination suits under the Americans With Disabilities Act] revealed the Supreme Court's real concern with the way power is allocated in the American political system to be less the balance between the federal government and the states than that between the Supreme Court and Congress."

Chapter One

1. Martin Diamond, "The Ends of Federalism," in William A. Schambra, ed., *As Far as Republican Principles Will Admit: Essays by Martin Diamond* (Washington: American Enterprise Institute, 1992), p. 145.

2. Alexis de Tocqueville, *Democracy in America,* ed. J. P. Mayer (Anchor Books, 1969); and David M. Potter, "Social Cohesion and the Crisis of Law," in Lawrence M. Friedman and Harry N. Scheiber, eds., *American Law and the Constitutional Order: Historical Perspectives* (Harvard University Press, 1978), pp. 420–34.

3. William Riker, "The Senate and American Federalism," *American Political Science Review,* vol. 49 (June 1955), pp. 452–69.

4. On the elaboration of state constitutions as "the people's law," see Herbert Croly, *Progressive Democracy* (Macmillan, 1914), chap. 12, esp. p. 260.

5. William Seal Carpenter and Paul Tutt Stafford, *State and Local Government in the United States* (F. S. Crofts, 1936), pp. 41–43.

6. Woodrow Wilson, *The State,* rev. ed. (D. C. Heath, 1898), pp. 501, 506. Generally on the restriction of the powers of state legislatures, see Arthur N. Holcombe, *State Government in the United States* (Macmillan, 1926), chap. 5; and Howard Lee McBain, *The Law and Practice of Municipal Home Rule* (Columbia University Press, 1916).

7. *American Almanac and Treasury of Facts, Statistical, Financial, and Political, for the Year 1886* (American News Company, 1886), p. 305.

8. Holcombe, *State Government,* pp. 133–34. See also Alfred Zantzinger Reed, *The Territorial Basis of Government under the State Constitutions* (Columbia University, Studies in History, Economics and Public Law, 1911), vol. 40, no. 3, pp. 54–56.

9. For contemporary observations on the significance of this fact, see Gregory R. Weiher, *The Fractured Metropolis: Political Fragmentation and Metropolitan Segregation* (State University of New York Press, 1991); Jon C. Teaford, *City and Suburb: The Political Fragmentation of Metropolitan America, 1850–1970* (Johns Hopkins University Press, 1979); Gary J. Miller, *Cities by Contract: The Politics of Incorporation* (MIT Press, 1981); and Arthur B. Gunlicks, ed., *Local Government Reform and Reorganization* (Port Washington, N.Y.: Kennikat Press, 1981).

10. James A. Schellenberg, *Conflict between Communities: American County Seat Wars* (New York: Paragon House, 1987).

11. Jon C. Teaford, *The Municipal Revolution in America* (University of Chicago Press, 1975), esp. chap. 5.

12. Charles S. Sydnor, *The Development of Southern Sectionalism, 1819–1848* (Louisiana State University Press, 1948), chap. 12; and Fletcher M. Green, *Constitutional Development in the South Atlantic States, 1776–1860* (University of North Carolina Press, 1930; Norton, 1966).

13. Reed, *Territorial Basis of Government*, p. 237.

14. John A. Fairlie, *The Centralization of Administration in New York State* (Columbia University Press, 1989; New York: AMS Press, 1969), p. 186.

15. Holcombe, *State Government*, p. 134.

16. David J. Rothman, *The Discovery of the Asylum: Social Order and Disorder in the New Republic* (Little, Brown, 1971).

17. Michael W. Kirst, *Who Controls Our Schools? American Values in Conflict* (Stanford Alumni Association, 1984), p. 27.

18. In a monograph on political development in New York between 1800 and 1860, L. Ray Gunn writes that beginning about 1840, public involvement in the economy began to contract. Mercantilist regulations disappeared from the statute books. Gunn also documents the shift of power from state to local governing institutions, arguing that delegation of authority to local governments invigorated them, county boards of supervisors especially. L. Ray Gunn, *The Decline of Authority: Public Economic Policy and Political Development in New York State, 1800–1860* (Cornell University Press, 1988), pp. 1, 199–200.

19. *Town Officer: Or, Laws of Massachusetts Relative to the Duties of Municipal Officers*, 2d ed. (Worcester, Mass.: Dorr and Howland, 1829), pp. 177–85.

20. This development is documented in a series of studies done at Columbia University at the turn of the century: Fairlie, *Centralization of Administration*; Robert H. Whitten, *Public Administration in Massachusetts: The Relation of Central to Local Activity* (1898); Samuel P. Orth, *The Centralization of Administration in Ohio* (1903); Harold Martin Bowman, *The Administration of Iowa: A Study in Centralization* (1903); and William A. Rawles, *Centralizing Tendencies in the Administration of Indiana* (1903). All appeared in the series *Studies in History, Economics and Public Law*, edited by the political science faculty at Columbia, and were reprinted by AMS Press (New York) in 1968 and 1969.

21. Cited in Martha Derthick, *The Influence of Federal Grants: Public Assistance in Massachusetts* (Harvard University Press, 1970), p. 20.

22. Philip H. Burch Jr., *Highway Revenue and Expenditure Policy in the United States* (Rutgers University Press, 1962), p. 213.

23. Jane Perry Clark, *The Rise of A New Federalism* (Columbia University Press, 1938), pp. 193, 203.

24. Burch, *Highway Revenue*, p. 81.

25. *Social Security in America* (Washington: Social Security Board, 1937), chaps. 8, 13, 14, 19.

26. Derthick, *Influence of Federal Grants*, pp. 72–73.

27. For a detailed account of the federal effort in one state's welfare program, see ibid., esp. chaps. 5, 7. For a summary of the federal impact on state and local personnel systems generally, see Albert H. Aronson, "State and Local Personnel Administration," in U.S. Civil Service Commission, *Biography of an Ideal: A History of the Federal Civil Service* (Washington: n.d. [1973?]), pp. 127–59. When the Social Security Act was passed, only nine states had civil service systems. Federal requirements and advice contributed to their extension within and among the states. *Oklahoma v. Civil Service Commission* appears at 330 U. S. 127 (1947).

28. For example, Philip Selznick, *TVA and the Grass Roots: A Study in the Sociology of Formal Organizations* (Harper and Row, 1966).

29. 338 U.S. 25 (1949); 268 U.S. 652 (1925).

30. *Mr. Justice Jackson: Four Lectures in His Honor* (Columbia University Press, 1969), p. 60.

31. Robert Bork, *The Tempting of America: The Political Seduction of the Law* (Free Press, 1990), p. 84. On Warren's estimate of the importance of reapportionment, see Archibald Cox, *The Court and the Constitution* (Houghton Mifflin, 1987), p. 290.

32. 369 U.S. 186, 301 (1962).

33. 377 U.S. 533 (1964); 377 U.S. 713 (1964).

34. This argument is made by Bork, *Tempting of America*, pp. 85–86.

35. The phrase was used by Justices Clark and Stewart in dissent in the *Lucas* (Colorado) case, objecting to the majority's "uncritical, simplistic, and heavy-handed application of sixth-grade arithmetic."

36. 384 U.S. 436 (1966). David Fellman, "The Nationalization of American Civil Liberties," in M. Judd Harmon, ed., *Essays on the Constitution of the United States* (Port Washington, N.Y.: Kennikat Press, 1978), p. 56; and Archibald Cox, *The Warren Court: Constitutional Decision as an Instrument of Reform* (Harvard University Press, 1968), p. 84.

37. On the uses of section 1983, see Paul M. Bator, "Some Thoughts on Applied Federalism," *Harvard Journal of Law and Public Policy*, vol. 6 (1982), pp. 51–59; Daan Braveman, *Protecting Constitutional Freedoms: A Role for the Federal Courts* (Westport, Conn.: Greenwood Press, 1989); and "Section 1983 and Federalism," *Harvard Law Review*, vol. 90 (1977), p. 1133. *Monroe v. Pape* is at 365 U. S. 167 (1960).

38. 347 U. S. 483 (1954); 349 U. S. 294 (1955).

39. 402 U. S. 1 (1971).

40. Arthur S. Hayes, "As Others Scale Back on School Integration, Charlotte Presses On," *Wall Street Journal*, May 8, 1991, p. A1; and Davison M. Douglas, *Reading, Writing, and Race: The Desegregation of the Charlotte Schools* (University of North Carolina Press, 1995).

41. J. Anthony Lukas, *Common Ground* (Vintage Books, 1986); and Ronald P. Formisano, *Boston against Busing: Race, Class and Ethnicity in the 1960s and 1970s* (University of North Carolina Press, 1991). For a comprehensive and critical account of the effort at school desegregation, see David J. Armor, *Forced Justice: School Desegregation and the Law* (Oxford University Press, 1995).

42. Gary Orfield, *Public School Desegregation in the United States, 1968–1980* (Washington: Joint Center for Political Studies, 1983).

43. For an excellent account, see Gary Orfield, *The Reconstruction of Southern Education: The Schools and the 1964 Civil Rights Act* (Wiley-Interscience, 1969).

44. Lukas, *Common Ground*.

45. Drew S. Days III, "Section 5 and the Role of the Justice Department," and Timothy G. O'Rourke, "The 1982 Amendments and the Voting Rights Paradox," in Bernard Grofman and Chandler Davidson, eds., *Controversies in Minority Voting: The Voting Rights Act in Perspective* (Brookings, 1992), pp. 53–54, 86–87.

46. O'Rourke, "1982 Amendments," pp. 88–89; and Laughlin McDonald, "The 1982 Amendments of Section 2 and Minority Representation," in Grofman and Davidson, *Controversies in Minority Voting*, pp. 66–74.

47. On Rehnquist's commitment to federalism, see Sue Davis, *Justice Rehnquist and the Constitution* (Princeton University Press, 1989).

48. 410 U. S. 315 (1973); 462 U. S. 835 (1983).

49. 411 U.S. 1, 42, 44, 58 (1973).

50. 418 U. S. 717, 741–42, 743–44 (1974). For a scholarly account of the Detroit case, see Eleanor P. Wolf, *Trial and Error: The Detroit School Desegregation Case* (Wayne State University Press, 1981).

51. 422 U.S. 90, 500, 508 n. 18 (1975). Gerald Gunther, ed., *Constitutional Law*, 11th ed. (Westbury, N.Y.: Foundation Press, 1985), pp. 1559–64.

52. Kenneth K. Wong, "State Reform in Education Finance: Territorial and Social Strategies," *Publius: The Journal of Federalism*, vol. 21 (Summer 1991), p. 125, contains a summary of action up to that point. For an analysis of the litigation strategies employed, see William E. Thro, "Judicial Analysis during the Third Wave of School Finance Litigation: The Massachusetts Decision as a Model," *Boston College Law Review*, vol. 35 (May 1994), pp. 597–617.

53. Peter J. Galie, "Social Services and Egalitarian Activism," in Stanley H. Friedelbaum, ed., *Human Rights in the States: New Directions in Constitutional Policymaking* (Westport, Conn.: Greenwood Press, 1988), pp. 108–09. The initial decision came in 1977. In a subsequent case (*Fernley v. Board of Supervisors*, 1985), the court struck down an exclusionary ordinance with a finding that any ordinance that totally excludes a legitimate use will be regarded with "circumspection, and therefore, must bear a substantial relationship to a stated public purpose."

54. Ibid., pp. 109–10. See also Richard F. Babcock and Charles L. Siemon, *The Zoning Game Revisited* (Cambridge, Mass.: Lincoln Institute of Land Policy, 1985), pp. 207–33, for a case study, "*Mount Laurel II*: Apres Nous le Deluge."

55. Armor, *Forced Justice*, pp. 3, 60–61, 83; Elizabeth P. McCaughey, "Can Courts Order School Integration across Town Lines?" *Wall Street Journal*, October 28, 1992, p. A19; and "Hartford Court Bars Imbalance in the Schools," *New York Times*, July 10, 1996, pp. A1, B6.

56. See, among many sources, G. Alan Tarr and Mary Cornelia Aldis Porter, *State Supreme Courts in State and Nation* (Yale University Press, 1988); and Advisory Commission on Intergovernmental Relations, *State Constitutional Law: Cases and Materials* (Washington, 1988).

57. Kenneth K. Wong, "Fiscal Support for Education in American States: The 'Parity-to-Dominance' View Examined," *American Journal of Education*, vol. 97 (August 1989), pp. 329–57.

58. Hugh Davis Graham, *The Uncertain Triumph: Federal Education Policy in the Kennedy and Johnson Years* (University of North Carolina Press, 1984), pp. 153–55. I am indebted to Andrew Busch for calling my attention to this point.

59. Kirst, *Who Controls Our Schools?* pp. 98–99.

60. Ibid., pp. 11–12, 38.

61. See also John Kincaid, "Is Education Too Intergovernmental?" *Intergovernmental Perspective* (Winter 1992), pp. 28–34.

62. Mitchell Pacelle, "Not in Your Backyard, Say Community Panels in Suburban Enclaves," *Wall Street Journal*, September 21, 1994; Stephen E. Barton and Carol J. Silverman, eds., *Common Interest Communities: Private Governments and the Public Interest* (Berkeley: Institute of Governmental Studies, 1994); Evan McKenzie, *Privatopia: Homeowner Associations and the Rise of Residential Private Government* (Yale University

Press, 1994); and Robert Jay Dilger, *Neighborhood Politics: Residential Community Associations in American Governance* (New York University Press, 1993).

63. Advisory Commission on Regulatory Barriers to Affordable Housing, *"Not In My Back Yard": Removing Barriers to Affordable Housing* (Washington, 1991); and Michael H. Schill, "The Federal Role in Reducing Regulatory Barriers to Affordable Housing in the Suburbs," *Journal of Law and Politics*, vol. 8 (Summer 1992), pp. 703–30; for a scholarly critique of exclusionary practices, see Michael N. Danielson, *The Politics of Exclusion* (Columbia University Press, 1976).

64. 495 U.S. 33 (1990).

65. For recent empirical attempts by social scientists to come to grips with the contemporary value and meaning of small-scale communities, see, for example, Jane J. Mansbridge, *Beyond Adversary Democracy* (University of Chicago Press, 1983); and Harold A. McDougall, *Black Baltimore: A New Theory of Community* (Temple University Press, 1993).

66. Diamond, "The Ends of Federalism," p. 156.

67. Richard S. Vacca and H. C. Hudgins Jr., *Liability of School Officials and Administrators for Civil Rights Torts* (Charlottesville: Michie Co., 1982), pp. 117–30. This source explains (p. 117) that "over the years the notion of people expressing themselves (speaking out) through their mode of dress and attire (including hair style) has developed . . . into an acceptable concept of constitutional law."

Chapter Two

1. Advisory Commission on Intergovernmental Relations, *Regulatory Federalism: Policy, Process, Impact and Reform* (Report A-95, February 1984). See also the essays in Jerome J. Hanus, ed., *The Nationalization of State Government* (Lexington, Mass.: D. C. Heath, 1981).

2. 469 U. S. 528 (1985).

3. 485 U. S. 505 (1988).

4. Executive Order 12612, *Federal Register* 52, no. 210 (October 26, 1987), pp. 41685–88.

5. Timothy Conlan, *From New Federalism to Devolution: Twenty-Five Years of Intergovernmental Reform* (Brookings, 1998), pp. 191–211.

6. Richard P. Nathan, "Federalism—the Great 'Composition,'" in Anthony King, ed., *The New American Political System*, 2d version (Washington: American Enterprise Institute, 1990), pp. 231–61; and Morton Keller, "State Power Needn't Be Resurrected Because It Never Died," in Laurence J. O'Toole Jr., ed., *American Intergovernmental Relations*, 3d ed. (Washington: CQ Press, 2000), pp. 351–60.

7. *The Federalist Papers* (New York: New American Library, Mentor ed., 1961), pp. 245–46.

8. 347 U.S. 488 (1954); 369 U.S. 186 (1962). On state-sponsored attempts to overturn *Brown* v. *Board of Education* and *Baker* v. *Carr* through constitutional amendment, see Russell L. Caplan, *Constitutional Brinksmanship: Amending the Constitution by National Convention* (Oxford University Press, 1988), pp. 70–76.

9. The classic statement of this view, applied to grant-in-aid programs, is Phillip Monypenny, "Federal Grants-in-Aid to State Governments: A Political Analysis," in O'Toole, ed., *American Intergovernmental Relations*, pp. 211–16.

10. Edward S. Corwin, "The Passing of Dual Federalism," in Alpheus T. Mason and Gerald Garvey, eds., *American Constitutional History: Essays by Edward S. Corwin* (Harper and Row, 1964), pp. 145–64.

11. *Federalist Papers*, p. 380.

12. Adrienne Koch, intro., *Notes of Debates in the Federal Convention of 1787 Reported by James Madison* (Ohio University Press, 1966), p. 165.

13. *Federalist Papers*, p. 177.

Chapter Three

1. Transcript of First Planning Meeting, "Furthering Public Understanding of Social Insurance in a Federal System," National Academy of Social Insurance, January 29, 1993, p. 12.

2. *The Federalist Papers* (New York: New American Library, Mentor ed., 1961), p. 296.

3. Woodrow Wilson, *The State*, rev. ed. (D. C. Heath, 1898), p. 523.

4. Edward S. Corwin,"The Passing of Dual Federalism," in Alpheus T. Mason and Gerald Garvey, eds., *American Constitutional History: Essays by Edward S. Corwin* (Harper and Row, 1964), pp. 145–64.

5. 247 U. S. 251 (1918), in Alpheus T. Mason and William M. Beaney, eds., *American Constitutional Law* (Prentice-Hall, 1959), p. 280.

6. Henry M. Hart Jr., "The Relations between State and Federal Law," in Arthur W. Macmahon, ed., *Federalism: Mature and Emergent* (Doubleday, 1955), p. 194.

7. *Puerto Rico* v. *Branstad*, 483 U. S. 219 (1987).

8. *Federalist Papers*, p. 298.

9. William H. Riker, "The Senate and American Federalism," *American Political Science Review*, vol. 49 (June 1955), pp. 452–69.

10. Late in 1993, Indiana was flirting with an attempt to surrender to the federal government authority to regulate landfills and control water pollution. See *Governing*, vol. 7 (November 1993), p. 70.

11. *The President's Health Security Plan: The Complete Draft and Final Reports of the White House Domestic Policy Council*, pp. 52–59, in *The President's Health Security Plan* (Times Books, 1993).

12. For an extended analysis of the rise of mandates and the failure of state governments to resist them, see Paul Posner, *The Politics of Unfunded Mandates: Whither Federalism?* (Georgetown University Press, 1998).

13. For a review and analysis of the various measures that state governments employ in trying to protect their interests vis-à-vis the federal government, see John J. Dinan, "State Government Influence in the National Policy Process: Lessons from the 104th Congress," *Publius: The Journal of Federalism*, vol. 27 (Spring 1997), pp. 129-42. On passage of mandate reform, see David R. Beam and Timothy J. Conlan, "The 1995

Unfunded Mandates Reform Act: The Politics of Federal Mandating Meets the Politics of Reform," *Public Budgeting and Financial Management*, vol. 7 (Fall 1995), pp. 355–85.

14. *Wall Street Journal*, December 21, 1993, p. A14; and *Washington Post*, January 29, 1994, p. A8.

15. For a suggestive academic analysis of the federal-state difference from the field of criminal justice, see Robert M. Cover and T. Alexander Aleinikoff, "Dialectical Federalism: Habeas Corpus and the Court," *Yale Law Journal*, vol. 86 (1976–77), p. 1035. Cover and Aleinikoff identify two opposing tendencies in constitutional interpretation: the "utopian," which they associate with federal courts, and the "pragmatic," which they identify with state courts.

16. For a catalog of environmental mandates, see *Governing*, vol. 7 (March 1994), pp. 73–86.

Chapter Four

1. Herbert Wechsler, "The Political Safeguards of Federalism: The Role of the States in the Composition and Selection of the National Government," in Arthur W. Macmahon, ed., *Federalism: Mature and Emergent* (Doubleday, 1955), pp. 97–114 ; and Jesse H. Choper, *Judicial Review and the National Political Process: A Functional Reconsideration of the Role of the Supreme Court* (University of Chicago Press, 1980).

2. *Maryland* v. *Wirtz*, 392 U. S. 183 (1968).

3. 426 U. S. 833, 852 (1976).

4. For a painstaking, erudite argument that Congress has yielded to "judicial monopoly" in the determination of constitutional questions, see Donald G. Morgan, *Congress and the Constitution: A Study of Responsibility* (Harvard University Press, 1966).

5. *Congressional Record*, vol. 119, 93 Cong. 1 sess. (1973), p. 37718.

6. In the remaining two states, only one senator voted—one in favor of national regulation, the other against it. Choper, *Judicial Review*, pp. 182-83.

7. 469 U. S. 528, 552 (1985).

8. Choper, *Judicial Review*, pp. 201–03.

9. 469 U. S. 528, 588.

10. Ibid., 556.

11. *Letters and Other Writings of James Madison*, vol. 3, Congress ed. (New York: R. Worthington, 1884), p. 625. The *Garcia* majority quotes Madison selectively in support of its view that adequate restraints on the power of Congress inhere in the composition of the federal government and do not depend on judicial interpretion. See 469 U. S. 528, 551–52. But there is abundant evidence in Madison's writing that he expected the Supreme Court to settle federalism controversies. The most important and accessible statement is in *Federalist* No. 39; see *The Federalist Papers* (New York: New American Library, Mentor ed., 1961), pp. 245–46.

12. Walter Berns, "The Meaning of the Tenth Amendment," in Robert A. Goldwin, ed., *A Nation of States* (Rand McNally, 1963), p. 132.

13. Edward S. Corwin, "The Passing of Dual Federalism," in Alpheus T. Mason and Gerald Garvey, eds., *American Constitutional History: Essays by Edward S. Corwin*

(Harper and Row, 1964), pp. 145–64; and David Fellman, "The Nationalization of American Civil Liberties," in M. Judd Harmon, ed., *Essays on the Constitution of the United States* (Port Washington, N.Y.: Kennikat Press, 1978), pp. 49–60.

14. Choper, *Judicial Review*, pp. 179–80.

15. Denis P. Doyle and Terry W. Hartle, *Washington Post*, September 5, 1985. See also their *Excellence in Education: The States Take Charge* (Washington: American Enterprise Institute for Public Policy Research, 1985).

16. T. R. Reid, "Montana Implements Policy of 'Unisex' Insurance," *Washington Post*, October 1, 1985.

17. Dennis Kneale, "Buyer Beware: Software Plagued by Poor Quality and Poor Service," *Wall Street Journal*, October 2, 1985.

18. Larry Green, "States Exchanging Wild Animals," *Washington Post*, December 28, 1985.

19. Andrea Bonnicksen and Edward Brazil, "The Policy of Alternative Conception: Looking to the States," prepared for delivery at the 1985 annual meeting of the American Political Science Association.

20. Jay Mathews, "California Work-for-Welfare Plan Viewed as Model," *Washington Post*, September 24, 1985. In 1981 and 1982 the Reagan administration sought to require, as a condition of grants-in-aid under Aid to Families with Dependent Children, that the states establish work programs for recipients. Congress made such programs optional for the states and spelled out several alternative approaches from among which they might choose. States responded with a flurry of initiatives. Julie Kosterlitz, "Liberals and Conservatives Share Goals, Differ on Details of Work for Welfare," *National Journal*, October 26, 1985, pp. 2418–22.

21. William K. Muir Jr., *Legislature: California's School for Politics* (University of Chicago Press, 1982), p. 14.

22. Charles E. Lindblom, *Politics and Markets* (Basic Books, 1977).

23. 84 Stat. 1676 (1970). See the discussion in Mel Dubnick and Alan Gitelson, "Nationalizing State Politics," in Jerome J. Hanus, ed., *The Nationalization of State Government* (D. C. Heath, 1981), pp. 56–59.

24. Gerald E. Frug, "The Judicial Power of the Purse," *University of Pennsylvania Law Review*, vol. 126 (April 1978), pp. 715–94.

25. *Brown* v. *Environmental Protection Agency*, 521 F. 2d 827, 831 (1975).

26. Ibid., 837ff.; and *District of Columbia* v. *Train*, 521 F. 2d 971, 992-94 (1975). However, only the most extreme and unprecedented intrusions on the states, which these EPA regulations represented, have failed to win judicial assent. Grant-in-aid conditions have invariably been upheld, for courts invariably find that Congress is pursuing a valid national purpose and that the states are not subject to coercion (inasmuch as they have the option of declining the grant).

27. See Robert F. Nagel, "Federalism as a Fundamental Value: National League of Cities in Perspective," *Supreme Court Review* (1981), pp. 81–109, for a sympathetic interpretation of the Court's decision in 1976 and an argument that jurists and scholars have been far less creative in defense of "structural values" (the principles that allocate decisionmaking responsibility among governmental units) than of individual rights.

Chapter Five

1. Alfred M. Skolnik and Sophie R. Dales, "Social Welfare Expenditures, 1972–73," *Social Security Bulletin*, vol. 37 (January 1974), pp. 3–18, 43. The trend toward increased social welfare spending has persisted. In 1995, 67.5 percent of all government outlays (federal, state, and local) went for social welfare. Per capita spending for social welfare stood at $5,622, compared with $3,788 in 1980 (measured in 1995 dollars). Bureau of the Census, *Statistical Abstract of the United States, 1999*, 119th ed. (Department of Commerce, 1999), p. 386, tables 607, 608.

2. At the end of the century, far from growing fast, the food stamp program was shrinking, both because of a strong economy and changes in law that discouraged access. From 27.5 million participants in 1994, it fell to 18.2 million in 1999. See Parke Wilde and others, *The Decline in Food Stamp Program Participation in the 1990's* (U.S. Department of Agriculture, Economic Research Service, Food and Rural Economics Division, Food Assistance and Nutrition Research Report 7, June 2000); and *Review of the Operations of the Food Stamp Program*, Hearing before the Subcommittee on Department Operations, Oversight, Nutrition, and Forestry of the House Agriculture Committee, 106 Cong. 1 sess. (Government Printing Office, 1999).

3. *1973 Annual Report of the Board of Trustees of the Federal Old-Age and Survivors Insurance and Disability Insurance Trust Funds*, H. Doc. 91-130, 93 Cong. 1 sess. (GPO, 1973), pp. 31–32; and *Committee Staff Report on the Disability Insurance Program*, House Committee on Ways and Means, 93 Cong. 2 sess. (July 1974). Disability insurance expenditures have continued to grow erratically. They doubled between 1975 and 1981, from $8.5 billion to $17.2 billion. They then leveled off in the early 1980s, only to resume a steep climb in the 1990s, when they went from $24.8 billion to $51.4 billion. Social Security Administration, Office of Reseach, Evaluation, and Statistics, *Annual Statistical Supplement, 2000, to the Social Security Bulletin*, p. 137, table 4.A2. In general, the sudden, unpredicted increases are most likely to be explained by changes in the economy, changes in the governing statute, or changes in the way that courts and administrative agencies interpret the statute.

4. In 1980 the Department of Health, Education and Welfare was renamed the Department of Health and Human Services as a result of the creation of a separate Department of Education during the administration of President Jimmy Carter.

5. But federal law and regulations may define areas of discretion for the states. When TANF replaced AFDC, the states' discretion in regard to food stamps broadened. Robert Greenstein, a former food stamp administrator, testified as follows in 1999: "The 1996 welfare law and subsequent . . . guidance have substantially increased the range of options available to states in the Food Stamp Program. States now can adopt, without waivers, many policies that had previously either been permissible only with a waiver or flatly prohibited. States can impose deeper and longer penalties for failure to comply with work requirements, can penalize households for failure to cooperate with child support enforcement or for falling into arrears in child support payments, can sanction adults for non-compliance with *any* behavioral requirements in their TANF-funded programs, and can reduce the food stamps of an entire household up to 25 percent based on a failure by any member of that household to comply with any TANF behav-

ioral requirement. States now can require applicants for food stamps to engage in work or training activities before it is determined whether they qualify for food stamps. In addition, the welfare law eliminated numerous limitations on the kinds of work activities states may require of food stamp households. The 1996 law also removed mandates for states to conduct telephone interviews for disabled persons and families in isolated rural communities that lack transportation to the food stamp office, to obtain approval for application forms that did not follow [a] national model, and to review their office hours to ensure access for the working poor." These changes, though per se decentralizing, nonetheless illustrate the extraordinary detail that federal prescription has attained in income support programs that are administered by the states. *Review of the Operations of the Food Stamp Program*, p. 93.

6. As of 2000, fifteen states and the District of Columbia have contracts with the SSA to administer state supplements. Since fiscal year 1994 the federal government has charged a fee for this service. *2000 Green Book: Background Material and Data on Programs within the Jurisdiction of the Committee on Ways and Means*, Committee Print, House Committee on Ways and Means, 106 Cong. 2 sess. (GPO, 2000), pp. 233-35.

7. The Personal Responsibility and Work Opportunities Reconcilation Act of 1996, which created TANF, is a very long and complicated law, containing a paradoxical mixture of federal prohibitions, permissions, and monetary incentives addressed to the states.

8. For a comprehensive reference, see *Studies in Public Welfare*, Paper No. 2: *Handbook of Public Income Transfer Programs*, a staff study prepared for the use of the Subcommittee on Fiscal Policy of the Joint Economic Committee, 92 Cong. 2 sess. (GPO, 1972).

9. See, for example, Paul Pierson, "The Creeping Nationalization of Income Transfers in the United States, 1935–94," in Stephan Leibfried and Paul Pierson, eds., *European Social Policy: Between Fragmentation and Integration* (Brookings, 1995), pp. 301–28.

10. In 2000 the federal standard was $512 a month for an individual and $769 for a couple. *2000 Green Book*, p. 228.

11. *Studies in Public Welfare*, Paper No. 10: *The New Supplemental Security Income Program—Impact on Current Benefits and Unresolved Issues*, Joint Economic Committee, 93 Cong. 1 sess. (GPO, 1973); and *Future Directions in Social Security*, Hearings before the Senate Special Committee on Aging, 93 Cong. 2 sess. (GPO, 1974), pt. 7. The administrative problems of SSI are treated in detail in Martha Derthick, *Agency under Stress: The Social Security Administration in American Government* (Brookings, 1990).

12. In 1995 it was $25.3 billion. Bureau of the Census, *Statistical Abstract of the United States, 1999*, p. 387, table 609.

13. On the role of the federal courts in supervising AFDC eligibility, see Martha F. Davis, *Brutal Need: Lawyers and the Welfare Rights Movement, 1960–1973* (Yale University Press, 1993); and R. Shep Melnick, *Between the Lines: Interpreting Welfare Rights* (Brookings, 1994), pt. 2.

14. Under TANF in 1998, the average monthly payment for a family ranged from $314 in Indiana to $1,244 in Wisconsin.

15. Robert Stevens and Rosemary Stevens, *Welfare Medicine in America: A Case Study of Medicaid* (Free Press, 1974). For more recent data, see *Medicaid Source Book: Background Data and Analysis*, Committee Print, Subcommittee on Health and the Environment of the House Committee on Energy and Commerce, 103 Cong. 1 sess. (GPO, 1993).

16. The following description is drawn from Donald E. Rigby, "State Supplementation under Federal SSI Program," *Social Security Bulletin*, vol. 37 (November 1974), pp. 21–28.

17. Mandatory supplementation became less important as time passed and affected recipients died. As of December 1999, approximately 1,800 recipients, or fewer than 0.02 percent of all recipients, were receiving mandatory supplements. All but six states currently provide optional supplements. As of December 1999, 2,441,482 beneficiaries, or 37 percent of the total, were receiving an optional state supplement. *2000 Green Book*, pp. 233, 235. See also Social Security Administration, Office of Research, Evaluation, and Statistics, *State Assistance Programs for SSI Recipients*, SSA Pub. 13-11975 (January 2000).

18. And they persist today. In Maryland, for example, the combined total of the federal payment and the state supplement may reach $1,178 a month for persons in certain group living facilities, because Maryland grants as much as $666 a month as a supplement. In another state (Oregon), the supplement is $2 a month for an individual needing little supervision and care. *2000 Green Book*, pp. 234–39.

19. *Report on Nutrition and Special Groups*, pt. 1: *Food Stamps*, prepared by the Staff of the Senate Select Committee on Nutrition and Human Needs, 94 Cong. 1 sess. (GPO, 1975); and Gary W. Bickel, "Participation Rates in the Food Stamp Program: Estimated Levels for 1974, by State," app. B to pt. 1.

20. When food stamp participation rates dropped in the late 1990s following enactment of welfare reform, the rate of decline varied sharply among states, ranging from 6 percent in Hawaii to 32 percent in Wisconsin. "Food Stamp Program: Various Factors Have Led to Declining Participation" (Letter Report, 07/02/1999, GAO/RCED-99-185) (www.gao.gov [April 2, 2001]).

21. Martha Derthick, *Uncontrollable Spending for Social Services Grants* (Brookings, 1975).

22. Expenditures for this purpose have not risen significantly because they have been capped by law. Currently the cap is $2.38 billion a year, although in some years it has been as high as $2.8 billion. *2000 Green Book*, pp. 633-34.

23. Nor, I would add, did the enactment of TANF, although it was widely interpreted as a decentralizing measure. In some respects it was; in others, not. In this instance, the program that was decentralized had never been fully centralized, and the discretion that was returned to the states only serves to illustrate how much had been taken away previously by the proliferation of grant-in-aid conditions and regulations.

Chapter Six

1. Paul E. Peterson, *City Limits* (University of Chicago Press, 1981); Paul E. Peterson, Barry G. Rabe, and Kenneth K. Wong, *When Federalism Works* (Brookings, 1986); Grant McConnell, *Private Power and American Democracy* (Knopf, 1966), chap.

4; and Robert A. Dahl and Edward R. Tufte, *Size and Democracy* (Stanford University Press, 1973).

2. *The Federalist Papers* (New York: New American Library, Mentor ed., 1961), p. 323.

3. Ibid., pp. 180–81.

4. 501 U.S. 452 (1991).

5. "The Status of Federalism in America," A Report of the Working Group on Federalism of the Domestic Policy Council (November 1986); Executive Order 12612, *Federal Register* 52, no. 210 (October 26, 1987), p. 41685; and U.S. Advisory Commission on Intergovernmental Relations, *Federal Regulation of State and Local Governments: The Mixed Record of the 1980s.* Report A-126 (July 1993), chap. 3.

6. "Consolidation," in Marvin Meyers, ed., *The Mind of the Founder: Sources of the Political Thought of James Madison* (Indianapolis: Bobbs-Merrill, 1973), pp. 237–39.

7. On courts as umpires, see, for example, Richard E. Johnston, *The Effect of Judicial Review on Federal-State Relations in Australia, Canada, and the United States* (Louisiana State University Press, 1969); Edward McWhinney, *Comparative Federalism: States' Rights and National Power*, 2d ed. (University of Toronto Press, 1965), chap. 3; and Paul A. Freund, *The Supreme Court of the United States: Its Business, Purposes, and Performance* (Cleveland: World Publishing, 1961), chap. 4.

8. Innumerable sources might be cited. For a succinct and insightful analysis of the Supreme Court's activism—its sources and objects—see Lawrence Baum, "Supreme Court Activism and the Constitution," in Peter F. Nardulli, ed., *The Constitution and American Political Development* (University of Illinois Press, 1992), chap. 6.

9. Adrienne Koch, *Jefferson and Madison: The Great Collaboration* (Knopf, 1950), chap. 7; and Herman V. Ames, ed., *State Documents on Federal Relations: The States and the United States* (New York: Da Capo Press, 1970), pp. 15–26.

10. Richard Hofstadter, *The Idea of a Party System: The Rise of Legitimate Opposition in the United States, 1780–1840* (University of California Press, 1970).

11. William H. Riker, "The Senate and American Federalism," *American Political Science Review*, vol. 49 (June 1955), pp. 452–69.

12. See Laurence J. O'Toole Jr., ed., *American Intergovernmental Relations*, 2d ed. (Washington: Congressional Quarterly, 1993), p. 16. Two experts on federalism whom I consulted, David Beam and David Walker, associated the term with the report of the Kestnbaum Commission in 1955, which says: "In the absence of [supervision and review by the state governor and legislature], there is a tendency for groups of professional administrators in a single, specialized field, working at National, State, and local levels, to become a more or less independent government of their own, organized vertically and substantially independent of other State agencies." Commission on Intergovernmental Relations, *A Report to the President for Transmittal to the Congress* (Washington, June 1955), p. 44.

13. John J. DiIulio Jr., *Governing Prisons: A Comparative Study of Correctional Management* (Free Press, 1987), chap. 5.

14. Frank R. Kemerer, *William Wayne Justice: A Judicial Autobiography* (University of Texas Press, 1991), p. 359.

15. J. Anthony Lukas, *Common Ground* (Random House, 1985); Stephen Wermiel, "Can a Federal Judge Raise Property Taxes? One in Missouri Did," *Wall Street Journal*, October 2, 1989, p. 1; in the Mobile case, federal district and appellate courts invalidated

a three-member city commission as a form of general-purpose local government because it diluted black voting strength, but were reversed by the Supreme Court on the ground that no purposeful discrimination had been established (*Mobile* v. *Bolden*, 446 U.S. 55 [1980]).

16. Kemerer, *William Wayne Justice*, p. 368.

17. "Consolidation," p. 238.

18. David O. Sears and Jack Citrin, *Tax Revolt: Something for Nothing in California* (Harvard University Press, 1985); and Terry Schwadron, ed., *California and the American Tax Revolt* (University of California Press, 1984).

19. See, for example, Aaron Wildavsky, "Birthday Cake Federalism," in Robert B. Hawkins, ed., *American Federalism: New Challenges for the 1980s* (New Brunswick, N. J.: Transaction Books, 1982), pp. 181–91.

Chapter Seven

1. The full text of the settlement may be found on the website of the National Association of Attorneys General (www.naag.org); a summary may be found on the website of the National Conference of State Legislatures (www.ncsl.org).

2. On cigarettes as a cause of death, see *Morbidity and Mortality Weekly Report*, vol. 46 (May 23, 1997), pp. 444–51. For a critique, see Robert Levy and Rosalind Marimont, "Lies, Damned Lies, and 400,000 Smoking-Related Deaths," *Regulation*, vol. 21 (Fall 1998), pp. 24–29.

3. Some of the leading critiques are Thomas C. O'Brien, "Constitutional and Antitrust Violations of the Multistate Tobacco Settlement," Cato Institute Policy Analysis 371, May 18, 2000; Thomas C. O'Brien and Robert A. Levy, "A Tobacco Cartel Is Born, Paid for by Smokers," *Wall Street Journal*, May 1, 2000, p. A35; Jeremy Bulow and Paul Klemperer, "The Tobacco Deal," *Brookings Papers on Economic Activity, Microeconomics, 1998*, pp. 323–94; Michael I. Krauss, *Fire and Smoke* (Oakland, Calif.: The Independent Institute, 2000); and *Regulation by Litigation: The New Wave of Government-Sponsored Litigation* (New York: The Manhattan Institute, 1999 [?]).

4. The Centers for Disease Control and Prevention (CDC) periodically publishes data on tobacco use and control by states. The latest such source is U.S. Department of Health and Human Services, CDC, *State Tobacco Control Highlights, 1999* (CDC Publication 099-5621).

5. Information about the attorneys general may be found on the NAAG website and in Cornell W. Clayton, "Law, Politics, and the New Federalism: State Attorneys General as National Policymakers," *Review of Politics*, vol. 56 (Summer 1994), pp. 525–53.

6. *State of Florida* v. *Exxon Corporation*, 526 F. 2d 266 (1976), pp. 268–69, as cited in Clayton, "Law, Politics, and the New Federalism," p. 528.

7. The event spawned an outpouring of excellent books by journalists: Peter Pringle, *Cornered: Big Tobacco at the Bar of Justice* (Holt, 1998); Carrick Mollenkamp and others, *The People vs. Big Tobacco* (Princeton: Bloomberg Press, 1998); Michael Orey, *Assuming the Risk* (Little, Brown, 1999); and Dan Zegart, *Civil Warriors* (Delacorte Press, 2000). My understanding of tobacco politics rests heavily on all of these sources.

8. Pringle, *Cornered*, pp. 217-18; and Orey, *Assuming the Risk*, p. 341.

9. Pryor's statements may be found on his website (www.ago.state.al.us).

10. Humphrey's position is detailed in Deborah Caulfield Rybak and David Phelps, *Smoked: The Inside Story of the Minnesota Tobacco Trial* (Minneapolis: MSP Books, 1998). On Harshbarger, see Frank Phillips, "Bay State Drops Out of Tobacco Pact Talks; Harshbarger Eyes Mass. Settlement," *Boston Globe*, August 30, 1998, p. A1.

11. The details of the Mississippi case are in Orey, *Assuming the Risk*, pt. 3.

12. Junda Woo, "Tobacco Firms Face Greater Health Liability—Florida Bill Seeks to Recover State's Cost of Treating Smoking-Related Illnesses," *Wall Street Journal*, May 3, 1994, p. A3; Larry Rohter, "Florida Prepares New Basis to Sue Tobacco Industry," *New York Times*, May 27, 1994, p. A1; *Agency for Health Care Administration et al. v. Associated Industries of Florida, Inc.*, Supreme Court of Florida, 678 So. 2d 1239, decided June 27, 1996; and Robert A. Levy, "Tobacco Medicaid Litigation: Snuffing Out the Rule of Law," Cato Institute Policy Analysis 275, June 20, 1997, pp. 7–8.

13. Rohter, "Florida Prepares New Basis."

14. "Judge Dismisses Indiana's Tobacco Suit," *Los Angeles Times*, July 25, 1998, p. D2; and "Indiana Judge Dismisses State's Tobacco Lawsuit," *Wall Street Journal*, July 27, 1998, p. B2.

15. *Regulation by Litigation*, p. 29.

16. *The Federalist Papers* (New York: New American Library, Mentor ed., 1961), p. 323.

17. *Regulation by Litigation*, p. 64.

18. *Federalist Papers*, p. 294.

19. Everett Carll Ladd, "The Tobacco Bill and American Public Opinion," *Public Perspective* (August–September 1998), pp. 6, 16.

20. Ibid., p. 19.

21. Lydia Saad, "A Half-Century of Polling on Tobacco: Most Don't Like Smoking But Tolerate It," *Public Perspective* (August–September 1998), pp. 1–2.

22. Peter H. Stone, "GOP Mulls Stubbing Out an Old Ally," *National Journal*, vol. 30 (April 25, 1998), p. 924. The poll was by Yankelovich Partners Inc. for CNN-Time Magazine.

23. "Poll Readings," *National Journal*, vol. 30 (May 16, 1998), p. 1116.

24. Peter D. Jacobson and Jeffrey Wasserman, *Tobacco Control Laws: Implementation and Enforcement* (Santa Monica, Calif.: Rand Corporation, 1997), p. xvii.

25. Cited in U.S. Department of Health, Education, and Welfare, *Smoking and Health: A Report of the Surgeon General* (Government Printing Office, 1979), p. iii.

26. The best sources on the history of government policies are A. Lee Fritschler and James M. Hoefler, *Smoking and Politics: Policy Making and the Federal Bureaucracy*, 5th ed. (Prentice-Hall, 1996); and Richard Kluger, *Ashes to Ashes* (Random House, Vintage Books, 1997).

27. For accounts of grassroots activity, see Kluger, *Ashes to Ashes;* and Stanton A. Glantz and Edith D. Balbach, *Tobacco War: Inside the California Battles* (University of California Press, 2000).

28. David Rohde, "Lawyers Complain City Crackdown Expanded to Subway Smoking," *New York Times*, June 11, 2000, p. 35.

29. *Morbidity and Mortality Weekly Report*, vol. 44 (November 3, 1995), pp. 1–15.

30. *Morbidity and Mortality Weekly Report*, vol. 48 (November 5, 1999), pp. 986–93.

31. Jacobson and Wasserman, *Tobacco Control Laws*, pp. 62–63; the data on numbers of state laws are from *Morbidity and Mortality Weekly Report*, November 3, 1995.

32. Barry Meier, "States and Cities Impose New Laws on Young Smokers," *New York Times*, December 7, 1997, p. A1.

33. Daynard's arguments may be found in several venues. See Richard Daynard, "Tobacco Liability Litigation as a Cancer Control Strategy," *Journal of the National Cancer Institute*, vol. 80 (March 1988), pp. 9–13; and Daynard, "Catastrophe Theory and Tobacco Litigation," *Tobacco Control*, vol. 3 (Spring 1994), pp. 59–64.

34. Saad, "A Half-Century of Polling."

Chapter Eight

1. William H. Riker, "The Senate and American Federalism," *American Political Science Review*, vol. 49 (June 1955), pp. 452–69.

2. On uniform state laws as a Progressive reform, see William Graebner, "Federalism in the Progressive Era: A Structural Interpretation of Reform," *Journal of American History*, vol. 64 (September 1977), pp. 331–57. On the governors' conference, see Glenn E. Brooks, *When Governors Convene* (Johns Hopkins University Press, 1961).

3. 47 U.S. 700 (1869).

4. For a contrary interpretation, arguing the wholehearted commitment of Progressives to "the national idea," see Michael S. Joyce and William A. Schambra, "A New Civic Life," in Peter L. Berger and Richard John Neuhaus, eds., *To Empower People: From State to Civil Society* (Washington: AEI Press, 1996), pp. 11–29.

5. The decisions that generated the most hostile reactions were *United States v. E. C. Knight Co.*, 156 U.S. 1 (1895), which limited Congress's ability to restrain monopolistic trade practices; the *First Employers' Liability Cases*, 207 U.S. 463 (1908), which overturned a federal statute that required railroads to assume liability for workplace injuries; *Adair v. United States*, 208 U.S. 161 (1908), which overturned a statute that sought to prohibit companies that were engaged in interstate commerce from making use of yellow-dog contracts, which required workers to give up their right to join labor unions; and *Hammer v. Dagenhart*, 247 U.S. 251 (1918), and *Bailey v. Drexel Furniture Co.*, 259 U.S. 20 (1920), which prevented Congress from regulating child labor, either by prohibiting interstate commerce in goods that were made by children or by imposing a tax on such products. For an overview of the various Progressive responses to these decisions, see William G. Ross, *A Muted Fury: Populists, Progressives, and Labor Unions Confront the Courts, 1890–1937* (Princeton University Press, 1994), p. 20.

6. J. Allen Smith, *The Spirit of American Government* (Macmillan, 1907), p. 90. See also Louis Boudin, "Government by Judiciary," *Political Science Quarterly*, vol. 26 (June 1911), p. 238.

7. Charles Beard, *An Economic Interpretation of the Constitution of the United States* (Macmillan, 1913), p. 163.

8. Ross, *Muted Fury*, pp. 57–59.

9. Ibid., pp. 145, 194.

10. Charles Amidon, "The Nation and the Constitution," address delivered before the American Bar Association in 1907, in Lamar T. Beman, ed., *Selected Articles on States' Rights* (New York: H. W. Wilson, 1926), pp. 129, 130. Beman's compilation of

Progressive Era sources on federalism has been invaluable to us, as subsequent citations will show. Amidon was a federal judge in North Dakota.

11. Ibid., p. 130.

12. Woodrow Wilson, *Congressional Government* (Houghton Mifflin, 1885), pp. 10–12, 4; and Albert B. Hart, quoted in Herman Belz, "The Constitution in the Gilded Age: The Beginnings of Constitutional Realism in American Scholarship," *American Journal of Legal History*, vol. 13, no. 2 (1969), pp. 118, 123.

13. Smith, *Spirit of American Government*, p. 40.

14. Amidon, "The Nation and the Constitution," p. 128.

15. Frank Goodnow, *Social Reform and the Constitution* (Macmillan, 1911), p. 16. Goodnow, a professor at Columbia University, was the first president of the American Political Science Association and arguably the most eminent political scientist of his day. This book grew out of lectures sponsored by the Charity Organization Society of the City of New York and delivered before the New York School of Philanthropy. While Goodnow professed in the preface to take no position on measures of social reform, the book constituted a comprehensive brief for the constitutionality of the agenda of Progressivism. Individual chapters covered the constitutionality of uniform commercial regulation, the power of Congress to charter interstate corporations, the power of Congress over private law, and the constitutionality of political reform, government regulation, and grants-in-aid.

16. Ibid., p. 13.

17. Theodore Roosevelt, "State and Federal Powers," address delivered at Harrisburg, Pennsylvania, October 4, 1906, reprinted in Beman, *Selected Articles*, pp. 152–54.

18. Goodnow, *Social Reform and the Constitution*, p. 9.

19. John A. Jameson, "National Sovereignty," *Political Science Quarterly*, vol. 5 (June 1890), p. 213.

20. Walter Weyl, *The New Democracy* (Macmillan, 1912), p. 161.

21. A powerful rebuttal to the Progressives came from Henry Wade Rogers, dean of the Yale Law School, in "The Constitution and the New Federalism," *North American Review*, vol. 188 (September 1908), pp. 321–35. See also John Sharp Williams, "Federal Usurpations," *Annals of the American Academy of Political and Social Science*, vol. 32 (July 1908), pp. 185–211. Williams was a member of Congress from Mississippi.

22. Reprinted in Beman, *Selected Articles*, pp. 61–68; and in Paul S. Reinsch, *Readings on American Federal Government* (Boston: Ginn, 1909), pp. 731–36. For a discussion of its historical importance, see W. Brooke Graves, *American Intergovernmental Relations: Their Origins, Historical Development, and Current Status* (Scribners, 1964), p. 797.

23. Henry Jones Ford, "The Influence of State Politics in Expanding Federal Power," *Proceedings of the American Political Science Association* (Baltimore: Waverly Press, 1909), pp. 53–63.

24. Simon N. Patten, "The Decay of State and Local Governments," *Annals of the American Academy of Political and Social Science*, vol. 1 (July 1890), p. 26.

25. Calvin Coolidge, "Responsibilities of the States," in Beman, *Selected Articles*, pp. 68–78.

26. "The Effort to Secure Uniform State Laws," excerpted from the report of the forty-seventh annual meeting of the American Bar Association, 1924, in Beman, *Selected Articles*, pp. 81–87. See too Graebner, "Federalism in the Progressive Era."

27. Mary Parker Follett, *The New State: Group Organization the Solution of Popular Government* (New York: Longmans, Green and Co., 1918). Quotations are on pp. 296, 300, 301, 306, 307, 309, but have been rearranged.

28. Smith mentions the possibility in one brief paragraph: *The Spirit of American Government*, p. 339. Progressives may have been discouraged from making any such proposal by the Constitution itself, Article V of which stipulates that no state shall be deprived of equal suffrage in the Senate without its consent.

29. Woodrow Wilson, *Constitutional Government in the United States* (Columbia University Press, 1908), p. 116.

30. Herbert Croly, *Progressive Democracy* (Macmillan, 1914), pp. 231–32.

31. Herbert Croly, *The Promise of American Life* (Bobbs-Merrill, 1965), p. 273. See *Progressive Democracy*, pp. 241-43, in which the same argument appears.

32. Benjamin Parke DeWitt, *The Progressive Movement* (Macmillan, 1915), p. 244.

33. Croly, *Promise of American Life*, p. 347.

34. *Proceedings of a Conference of Governors in the White House, Washington, D.C., May 13–15, 1908* (Government Printing Office, 1909). For an illuminating account of the significance of this conference, which puts it in the context of Progressive policies toward conservation and development, see Michael J. Lacey, "Federalism and National Planning: The Nineteenth-Century Legacy," in Robert Fishman, ed., *The American Planning Tradition: Culture and Policy* (Washington: Woodrow Wilson Center Press, 2000), pp. 89–145.

35. Croly, *Promise of American Life*, p. 349.

36. *The Federalist Papers* (New York: New American Library, Mentor ed., 1961), pp. 77–84; and Grant McConnell, *Private Power and American Democracy* (Knopf, 1966), esp. chap. 4.

37. For illuminating secondary analyses, see Jean B. Quandt, *From the Small Town to the Great Community: The Social Thought of Progressive Intellectuals* (Rutgers University Press, 1970); and David E. Price, "Community and Control: Critical Democratic Theory in the Progressive Period," *American Political Science Review*, vol. 68 (December 1974), pp. 1663–78.

38. John Dewey, *The Public and Its Problems* (Denver: Alan Swallow; copyright 1927 by Mrs. John Dewey), pp. 213, 216.

39. John J. McDermott, ed., *The Basic Writings of Josiah Royce*, vol. 2 (University of Chicago Press, 1969), pp. 1067–88.

40. Josiah Royce, *California* (Houghton Mifflin, 1886), pp. vii–xii.

41. Edward S. Corwin, "The Passing of Dual Federalism," in Alpheus T. Mason and Gerald Garvey, eds., *American Constitutional History: Essays by Edward S. Corwin* (Harper and Row, 1964), pp. 145–64.

42. "Ninth Census: Speech of the Honorable James A. Garfield of Ohio, Delivered in the House of Representatives December 16, 1869," cited in Michael J. Lacey, "The World of the Bureaus: Government and the Positivist Project in the Late Nineteenth Century," in Michael J. Lacey and Mary O. Furner, eds., *The State and Social Investigation in Britain and the United States* (Woodrow Wilson Center Press and Cambridge University Press, 1993), p. 141.

43. Ford, "The Influence of State Politics," p. 62.

44. For a powerful statement, see Sidney M. Milkis, "Localism, Political Parties, and Civic Virtue," in Martha Derthick, ed., *Dilemmas of Scale in America's Federal Democracy* (Cambridge University Press, 1999), pp. 89–124.

45. On the rhetorical presidency, see Jeffrey K. Tulis, *The Rhetorical Presidency* (Princeton University Press, 1987); and Richard J. Ellis, ed., *Speaking to the People: Presidential Rhetoric and Popular Leadership in Historical Perspective* (University of Massachusetts Press, 1998).

46. For a case study that illustrates the point, see Martha Derthick, *The Influence of Federal Grants: Public Assistance in Massachusetts* (Harvard University Press, 1970), chap. 7.

47. Henry Jones Ford, "Direct Legislation and the Recall," *Annals of the American Academy of Political and Social Science*, vol. 43 (1912), pp. 65–77, quotation at 72.

Chapter Nine

1. Frances Perkins, *The Roosevelt I Knew* (Viking Press, 1946), p. 301.

2. This is not, I judge, the standard interpretation. See, for example, the much acclaimed recent book by Robert C. Lieberman, *Shifting the Color Line: Race and the American Welfare State* (Harvard University Press, 1998), where it is said that Roosevelt desired "a unified national administrative welfare state," embodying "a comprehensive and coordinated program of economic security under the close direction of the federal government" (pp. 65, 26). To be sure, between these opening and closing sentences in his chapter on the organization of social policy, Lieberman concedes that Roosevelt favored federal-state cooperation. The confusion, of course, may originate with Lieberman's subject rather than Lieberman. My purpose is to figure out what Roosevelt in fact desired, if that is possible.

3. Gerald D. Nash, Noel H. Pugach, and Richard F. Tomasson, eds., *Social Security: The First Half Century* (University of New Mexico Press, 1988), p. 91.

4. Thomas H. Eliot, *Recollections of the New Deal: When the People Mattered*, (Northeastern University Press, 1992), p. 75.

5. George Martin, *Madam Secretary: Frances Perkins* (Houghton Mifflin, 1976), pp. 239–41. In their meeting, Perkins presented a long agenda for the president's approval.

6. Eliot, *Recollections of the New Deal*, pp. 73–89; and Philippa Strum, *Louis D. Brandeis: Justice for the People* (New York: Schocken Books, 1984), p. 382.

7. Perkins, *Roosevelt I Knew*, pp. 278–79; and Martin, *Madam Secretary*, pp. 341–42.

8. *The Public Papers and Addresses of Franklin D Roosevelt*, vol. 3: *The Advance of Recovery and Reform, 1934* (Random House, 1938), pp. 291–92. He explained that insurance should be national in scope, with the federal government in charge of investing and safeguarding the insurance reserve funds, while the states "should meet at least a large portion of the cost of management." Again in November, when the issue of control over unemployment insurance was coming to a head (see below), he said that the federal government should control and invest unemployment insurance reserves, while the states remained in charge of administering benefits (ibid., pp. 452–53). Unfortunately for anyone trying to discern his intentions for intergovernmental relations,

this formulation is elliptical, in that it fails to address the key question of which governments would make the laws and regulations.

9. Eliot, *Recollections of the New Deal*, p. 96.

10. Ibid., p. 98.

11. Marvin Meyers, ed., *The Mind of the Founder: Sources of the Political Thought of James Madison* (Bobbs-Merrill, 1973), pp. 237–39.

12. Eliot, *Recollections of the New Deal*, pp. 99–100.

13. Perkins, *Roosevelt I Knew*, p. 292. In an address to the advisory council of the Committee on Economic Security on November 14, Roosevelt again affirmed a commitment to a joint federal-state program, and again said that the federal government should manage the insurance reserve funds while the state government should be in charge of administration of benefits, for which they were "the most logical units." He added, "At this stage, while unemployment insurance is still untried in this country and there is such a great diversity of opinion on many details, there is room for some degree of difference in methods, though not in principles. That would be impossible under an exclusively national system." *Public Papers and Addresses*, vol. 3, pp. 452–53.

14. Edwin E. Witte, *The Development of the Social Security Act* (University of Wisconsin Press, 1963), pp. 71–72, 86–87.

15. Martin, *Madam Secretary*, p. 348.

16. Perkins, *Roosevelt I Knew*, p. 284.

17. Ibid.; Martin, *Madam Secretary*, pp. 345–46; and *Public Papers and Addresses*, vol. 3, pp. 452–55.

18. Eliot, *Recollections of the New Deal*, p. 107.

19. Perkins, *Roosevelt I Knew*, p. 286.

20. Joseph Alsop and Turner Catledge, *The 168 Days* (Doubleday, Doran, 1938), p. 16.

21. Perkins, *Roosevelt I Knew*, p. 286.

22. Eliot, *Recollections of the New Deal*, p. 75. The case is at 273 U.S. 12 (1926).

23. Ibid., pp. 74–78.

24. One of Brandeis's biographers, Philippa Strum, says that he personally urged his plan for unemployment compensation on Roosevelt in the fall of 1933, but the evidence she cites does not establish that a meeting took place. It shows only that Roosevelt told Felix Frankfurter of his desire to talk to Brandeis generally about matters potentially to come before the Court, and that Brandeis planned to bring up unemployment legislation if a meeting occurred. Strum, *Louis D. Brandeis*, p. 386. There is evidence elsewhere that Roosevelt and Brandeis talked at length about social insurance just after Roosevelt's message of June 1934 on that subject was completed but before it became public. Max Freedman, annot., *Roosevelt and Frankfurter: Their Correspondence, 1928–1945* (Little, Brown, 1967), p. 224, in a letter from Thomas Corcoran and Benjamin Cohen to Frankfurter.

25. 262 U.S. 447.

26. Arthur J. Altmeyer, *The Formative Years of Social Security* (University of Wisconsin Press), pp. 20–21.

27. Eliot, *Recollections of the New Deal*, p. 96.

28. Cited in William E. Leuchtenburg, *The Supreme Court Reborn: The Constitutional Revolution in the Age of Roosevelt* (Oxford University Press, 1995), p. 89.

29. 301 U.S. 619 (1937); 301 U.S. 518 (1937).

30. Nash and others, *Social Security*, p. 39.

31. Perkins, *Roosevelt I Knew*, p. 292.

32. Nash and others, *Social Security*, p. 93, but see Altmeyer, *Formative Years*, p. 33, for a contrary statement.

33. Gareth Davies and Martha Derthick, "Race and Social Welfare Policy," *Political Science Quarterly*, vol. 112 (Summer 1997), pp. 226ff.

34. Altmeyer, *Formative Years*, p. 36.

35. Ibid., p. 40.

36. Eliot, *Recollections of the New Deal*, p. 111.

37. Nash and others, *Social Security*, p. 88.

38. Ibid., p. 39.

39. Martin, *Madam Secretary*, p. 348.

40. Ibid., p. 164. The original source is Perkins's oral history at the Oral History Research Office of Columbia University.

41. On Franklin Roosevelt as governor, see Arthur M. Schlesinger Jr., *The Crisis of the Old Order* (Houghton Mifflin, 1957), pp. 386–410; and Ted Morgan, *FDR: A Biography* (Simon and Schuster, 1985), pp. 297–334. Theodore Roosevelt's autobiography contains a fascinating account of his relations with Boss Platt during the governorship. Theodore Roosevelt, *An Autobiography* (Macmillan, 1914), pp. 279–322.

42. Perkins, *Roosevelt I Knew*, p. 124.

43. Regarding the support of Sheridan Downey, a liberal Democratic candidate for the Senate in California, for the Townsend plan, Roosevelt said that he was highly skeptical but "there was no question of the state's [California's] right to try it out if he so desired." "Roosevelt Scorns Party Lines in Plea to Elect Liberals," *New York Times*, September 3, 1938, p. 1. (Downey had initially been associated with Upton Sinclair's EPIC movement, but subsequently became a disciple of Townsend.) The *Times* story then recounts, as would Arthur Altmeyer in his memoirs (see above), Roosevelt's recollection of Lord Bryce on the subject of federalism. "In this connection the President recalled having been told by Lord Bryce soon after the turn of the century that in some respects the American form of government was superior to the British. One of these advantages the British statesman said was the right of one or more States to try out a plan which many people might regard as unsound financially. It was all very much like the direct primary system, President Roosevelt observed. First, one or two States tried out the direct primary method and found out it worked, with the result that it was adopted nationally." I am indebted to Sidney Milkis for calling this source to my attention.

44. Altmeyer, *Formative Years*, p. 112.

45. Ibid., pp. 21–22.

46. Strum, *Louis D. Brandeis*, pp. 394–95.

47. Ibid., p. 387.

48. Ervin H. Pollack, ed., *The Brandeis Reader: The Life and Contributions of Mr. Justice Louis D. Brandeis* (New York: Oceana Publications, 1956), p. 28.

49. Ibid., p. 42.

50. Strum, *Louis D. Brandeis*, pp. 391–93.

51. Altmeyer, *Formative Years*, p. 12.

52. Leuchtenberg, *Supreme Court Reborn,* pp. 216–20. The cases are at 300 U.S. 379 (1937) and 301 U.S. 1 (1937).

53. 301 U.S. 548, 587 (1937).

Chapter Ten

1. On the compound character of the American federal system, see *The Federalist Papers* (New York: New American Library, Mentor ed., 1961), no. 39. See also Martin Diamond, "What the Framers Meant by Federalism," in Robert A. Goldwin, ed., *A Nation of States* (Rand-McNally, 1963), pp. 24–41.

2. 347 U.S. 483 (1954); 358 U.S. 1 (1958).

3. 321 U.S. 649 (1944); 328 U.S. 549 (1946).

4. Henry M. Hart Jr., "The Relations between State and Federal Law," in Arthur W. Macmahon, ed., *Federalism: Mature and Emergent* (Doubleday, 1955), p. 194. The cases are at 109 U.S. 3 (1883) and 24 How (65 U.S.) 66 (1861).

5. On the effects of grant-in-aid conditions in the public assistance program, see Martha Derthick, *The Influence of Federal Grants: Public Assistance in Massachusetts* (Harvard University Press, 1970).

6. 365 U.S. 167 (1961).

7. Paul M. Bator, "Some Thoughts on Applied Federalism," *Harvard Journal of Law and Public Policy*, vol. 6 (1982), pp. 51-58; "Section 1983 and Federalism," *Harvard Law Review*, vol. 90 (1977), p. 1133; and Peter W. Low and John Calvin Jeffries Jr., *Civil Rights Actions: Section 1983 and Related Statutes* (Westbury, N.Y.: Foundation Press Inc., 1988), p. 16.

8. Paul M. Bator and others, *Hart and Wechsler's The Federal Courts and the Federal System*, 3d ed. (Westbury, N.Y.: Foundation Press, 1988), pp. 1221–77; and Theodore Eisenberg, *Civil Rights Legislation: Cases and Materials*, 2d ed. (Charlottesville, Va.: Michie Co., 1987), pp. 55-136.

9. The education examples are from H. C. Hudgins Jr. and Richard S. Vacca, *Law and Education: Contemporary Issues and Court Decisions* (Charlottesville, Va.: Michie Co., 1979).

10. 377 U.S. 533 (1964); 369 U.S. 186 (1962).

11. My account of reapportionment is condensed from a secondary source, Gordon E. Baker, *The Reapportionment Revolution: Representation, Political Power, and the Supreme Court* (Random House, 1966). See also Richard C. Cortner, *The Apportionment Cases* (Norton, 1972). The *Lucas* case is at 377 U.S. 713, 736 (1964).

12. Robert H. Bork, *The Tempting of America: The Political Seduction of the Law* (Free Press, 1990), pp. 85–86. Use of the guarantee clause, according to Bork, "would have resulted in an order that a majority of the state's voters be permitted to reapportion their legislature, whether by referendum, convention, or some other mechanism." The court need not have told a state's voters what system of representation they were required to "choose."

13. Two leading sources are Daniel P. Moynihan, *Maximum Feasible Misunderstanding: Community Action in the War on Poverty* (Free Press, 1969); and Peter Marris and Martin Rein, *Dilemmas of Social Reform: Poverty and Community Action in the United States* (Chicago: Aldine, 1973).

14. Gary Orfield, *The Reconstruction of Southern Education: The Schools and the 1964 Civil Rights Act* (Wiley-Interscience, 1969), p. 46. This is much the best source on the origins and impact of title 6.

15. 393 U.S. 544 (1969). I have drawn on the entry, "Vote, Right to," by Abigail M. Thernstrom in Kermit L. Hall and others, *The Oxford Companion to the Supreme Court of the United States* (Oxford University Press, 1992), pp. 899–902.

16. Bernard Grofman and Chandler Davidson, eds., *Controversies in Minority Voting: The Voting Rights Act in Perspective* (Brookings, 1992), pp. 53n, 86–87.

17. 384 U.S. 436 (1966).

18. This summary is taken, sometimes nearly verbatim, from Fred P. Graham, *The Due Process Revolution: The Warren Court's Impact on Criminal Law* (New York: Hayden Book Co., 1970), chaps. 1, 13.

19. On the rise and fall of national aid to the police, see Thomas E. Cronin, Tania Z. Cronin, and Michael E. Milakovich, *U.S. v. Crime in the Streets* (Indiana University Press, 1981).

20. 392 U.S. 409 (1968).

21. 391 U.S. 430 (1968); 402 U.S. 1 (1971).

22. R. Shep Melnick, *Between the Lines: Interpreting Welfare Rights* (Brookings, 1994), pp. 83–84.

23. Orfield, *Reconstruction of Southern Education*, pp. 358–60.

24. *Mr. Justice Jackson: Four Lectures in His Honor* (Columbia University Press, 1969), p. 60.

25. Archibald Cox, *The Role of the Supreme Court in American Government* (Oxford University Press, 1976), p. 77.

26. 418 U.S. 717 (1974).

27. U.S. Advisory Commission on Intergovernmental Relations, *Regulatory Federalism: Policy, Process, Impact, and Reform* (Washington, 1984), p. 1.

28. 452 U.S. 264 (1981).

29. The term seems to have been given currency, if not actually introduced, by New York Mayor Edward I. Koch's article, "The Mandate Millstone," *The Public Interest* (Fall 1980), pp. 42–57.

30. 32 U.S. 100 (1941).

31. Edward S. Corwin, "The Passing of Dual Federalism," in Alpheus T. Mason and Gerald Garvey, eds., *American Constitutional History: Essays by Edward S. Corwin* (Harper and Row, 1964), pp. 145–64. The other postulates of dual federalism were: the national government is one of enumerated powers only; the purposes that it may constitutionally promote are few; and the relation of the two centers of power with each other is one of tension rather than collaboration.

32. On the relation between modernization and centralization, see Samuel H. Beer, "The Modernization of American Federalism," *Publius: The Journal of Federalism*, vol. 3 (Fall 1973), pp. 49–95.

Chapter Eleven

1. *Wall Street Journal*, August 11, 1999, p. A1; and Katharine Q. Seelye, "Gore's Plan for Success in '00: An Array of Solid Positions," *New York Times*, July 29, 1999, pp. A1, A16.

2. 521 U.S. 898 (1997); 505 U.S. 144 (1992); 514 U.S. 549 (1995). For reviews of the Rehnquist court's federalism jurisprudence, set in historical context, see John J. Dinan, "The Rehnquist Court's Federalism Decisions in Perspective," *Journal of Law and Politics*, vol. 15 (Spring 1999), pp. 127–94; and Frank Goodman, ed., *The Supreme Court's Federalism: Real or Imagined? Annals of the American Academy of Political and Social Science*, vol. 574 (March 2001). The Court's decisions on immunity are both contentious and abstruse. For a discussion of the issues, see a symposium in the *Notre Dame Law Review*, vol. 75 (March 2000).

3. Linda Greenhouse, "Newcomers to States Win A Right to Equal Welfare," *New York Times*, May 18, 1999, p. A1. The case was *Saenz* v. *Roe*, 526 U.S. 489 (1999).

4. Charles Fried, "Supreme Court Folly," *New York Times*, July 6, 1999, p. A21.

5. *Congress and the Nation, 1993–1996*, vol. 9 (Washington: Congressional Quarterly, 1998), p. 807.

6. Michael Duffy and Nancy Gibbs, "Who Chose George?" *Time*, June 21, 1999, p. 28.

7. On the origin of waivers, see Steven M. Teles, *Whose Welfare? AFDC and Elite Politics* (University Press of Kansas, 1996).

8. Paul Pierson, "The Creeping Nationalization of Income Transfers in the United States, 1935–94," in Stephan Liebfried and Paul Pierson, eds., *European Social Policy: Between Fragmentation and Integration* (Brookings, 1995), pp. 301–28.

9. R. Shep Melnick, *Between the Lines: Interpreting Welfare Rights* (Brookings, 1994), chap. 5.

10. *Congress and the Nation*, vol. 9, pp. 614–20.

11. Lizette Alvarez, "Both Houses Back Easing of Strings on Aid to Schools," *New York Times*, March 12, 1999, p. A1; and Sue Kirchhoff, "What the Education Flexibility Bill Does," *CQ Weekly Report*, vol. 57 (May 29, 1999), pp. 1296–97.

12. Edwin Meese III, "The Dangerous Federalization of Crime," *Wall Street Journal*, February 22, 1999, p. A19; and Steven A. Holmes, "Lawmakers Are Warned Not to Expand Federal Police Powers," *New York Times*, February 16, 1999, p. A13. The quotation from Biden is in the *Journal*.

13. Christopher S. Wren, "Clinton to Require State Efforts to Cut Drug Use in Prisons," *New York Times*, January 12, 1998, p. A1; Robert Pear, "White House Plans Medicaid Coverage of Viagra by States," *New York Times*, May 28, 1998, p. A1; and Robert Pear, "Clinton to Chide States for Failing to Cover Children," *New York Times*, August 8, 1999, sec. 1, p. 1.

14. "The Federalism Report," vol. 22 (Center for the Study of Federalism, Spring 1998), pp. 5–7.

15. Executive Order 13132, *Federal Register* 64 (August 10, 1999), p. 43255.

Other Work by
Martha Derthick
on Federalism

Books

The National Guard in Politics (Harvard University Press, 1965).

The Influence of Federal Grants: Public Assistance in Massachusetts (Harvard University Press, 1970).

New Towns In-Town: Why A Federal Program Failed (Washington: Urban Institute Press, 1972).

Between State and Nation: Regional Organizations of the United States (Brookings, 1974).

Uncontrollable Spending for Social Services Grants (Brookings, 1975).

Ed., *Dilemmas of Scale in America's Federal Democracy* (Cambridge University Press and Woodrow Wilson Center Press, 1999).

Articles and Essays

"Intergovermental Relations in the 1970s," in Lawrence E. Gelfand and Robert J. Neymeyer, eds., *Changing Patterns in American Federal-State Relations during the 1950's, the 1960's, and the 1970's* (Iowa City: Center for the Study of the Recent History of the United States, 1985).

"American Federalism: Madison's 'Middle Ground' in the 1980s," *Public Administration Review* (January–February 1987).

"The Structural Protections of American Federalism," in Harry N. Scheiber, ed., *North American and Comparative Federalism* (Berkeley: Institute of Governmental Studies Press, 1992).

"Federal Government Mandates," *Brookings Review* (Fall 1992).

"Grant-in-Aid," in Donald C. Bacon, Roger H. Davidson, and Morton Keller, eds., *The Encyclopedia of the United States Congress* (Simon and Schuster, 1995), vol. 2.

"New Players: The Governors and Welfare Reform," *Brookings Review* (Spring 1996).

With Gareth Davies, "Race and Social Welfare Policy: The Social Security Act of 1935," *Political Science Quarterly* (Summer 1997).

"States and the Federal Government," in George T. Kurian, ed., *A Historical Guide to the U.S. Government* (Oxford University Press, 1998).

Index